THE
DELECTABLE
DOLLIES

THE
DELECTABLE
DOLLIES

THE DOLLY SISTERS, ICONS OF THE JAZZ AGE

GARY CHAPMAN

SUTTON PUBLISHING

This book is dedicated to
Andrew Orr with thanks

First published in 2006 by
Sutton Publishing Limited · Phoenix Mill
Thrupp · Stroud · Gloucestershire · GL5 2BU

British Library Cataloguing in Publication Data
A catalogue record for this book is available from the British Library.

ISBN 0-7509-4395-5

Typeset in 11/14pt Garamond.
Typesetting and origination by
Sutton Publishing Limited.
Printed and bound in England by
J.H. Haynes & Co. Ltd, Sparkford.

CONTENTS

AUTHOR'S NOTE

The Christian names of the Dolly Sisters were used in several different forms throughout their career. For ease and convenience I have chosen to name them Rosie and Jenny throughout. Jenny's daughters' names have been standardised as Manzi and Klari. The Dolly Sisters were also collectively referred to as the Dollys, the Dolly's and the Dollies – the latter being used especially when describing their famous musical number 'The Dollies and the Collies' and in the title of their only movie together, *The Million Dollar Dollies*. I have chosen to use 'the Dollies'.

The many press reports of the Dollies list money values in dollars, pounds sterling and French francs. To avoid the confusion of using multiple currencies, I have decided to apply dollars throughout.

For a rough estimate of what these sums would be worth in the early twenty-first century, visit the inflation calculator at www.westegg.com/inflation.

For a quick conversion, note that $1 in the 1920s would be worth over $10 today. Exchange rates fluctuated in the 1920s, but the following formula may be used as a rough guide to equivalents during the period: $5 = £1; $1 = FF25; £1 = FF125. To get some understanding of the sheer size of the sums of money involved, it is worth noting that Rosie's divorce settlement in 1932 was in the region of $2 million, which would be worth over £20 million today. Meanwhile, Jenny's collection of jewels was estimated to be worth over $1 million, which would be worth over $10 million today.

Please visit the website at www.dollysisters.co.uk, which includes a range of illustrations not shown in this book.

It must be admitted that the chief fascination of the twin Dollies lies not so much in the grace of their dancing, nor in the charm of their personalities, nor in the naiveté of this manner, nor yet the quaintness of their accents — sufficient as are all of these — but rather in the amazing duplicity of Nature.

(Margaret Burr, Theatre Magazine, May 1916)

INTRODUCTION

Variously described as the delectable Dollies, the heavenly twins, the tootsie-wootsies of the world, *les grandes amoureuses* or the oomph girls of their day, the Dolly Sisters were legends in their own time on both sides of the Atlantic.[1] They danced their way to fame and fortune on Broadway in the early twentieth century before conquering London and Paris in the twenties, and were certainly the most famous sister act to appear on the stage, paving the way for the many duos and trios that proliferated in their wake. Even the Gabor sisters followed in the Dollies' dainty footsteps.

Born in Hungary in 1892, the sisters moved to America at the age of 12 and began making their living as entertainers in big shows, vaudeville and the movies, including the aptly titled *The Million Dollar Dollies*. They were close friends of the elite of Broadway and Hollywood and became the essential ingredient of any celebrity social gathering. Success on Broadway made them the toast of the town and personalities in their own right, but they were not accepted by American society. And yet, by the 1940s, the society gossip columnist Cholly Knickerbocker would affirm that they had been responsible for enabling American society to accept 'theatrical types'.[2]

It was a different story in Europe, where they believed they were the first stage performers to become accepted socially.[3] Their beauty and effervescent personalities, not to mention their novelty value as identical twins, had initially been their principal assets, but those who got to know them soon realised what genuinely good company they were. And yet, despite their popularity, there were some who felt that their excessive display of jewellery was ostentatious, their compulsive gambling inappropriate and their behaviour vulgar and American to boot.

1

There were also murmurings about how exactly they had acquired their fortunes. Their social success was matched by their professional achievement on the Parisian stage as they starred in a series of extravagant revues, giving Josephine Baker and Mistinguett a run for their money. Earning incredible salaries and the attention of wealthy admirers, the Dollies invested in property and vast collections of jewellery. 'Behung with baubles like a couple of Christmas trees',[4] they became recognised as the most extravagant gamblers in Europe, as they followed the social seasons of Saint-Moritz in January, Cannes in February and March, Paris in June for the horse racing, Deauville in August and Biarritz in September.

What was it that made the Dolly Sisters so popular and living legends? What was their magic? For a start they were unusually beautiful. Their unique 'look' was well defined early in their career. They did not conform to the accepted notion of beauty of the time. They were small and dark with striking almond-shaped eyes and an oriental grace that made them exotic, a feature that they blatantly accentuated with the careful use of make-up, hair styles and costumes. As a result of their 'look' and their thoroughly modern behaviour, they may well have preceded and even influenced the concept of the flapper, and they most definitely had 'it' before Elinor Glyn coined the phrase.

Their dancing delighted audiences and critics alike with the sheer flamboyance of their elaborate and identical costumes and their perfectly matched routines. They also gained a reputation as the daintiest comediennes, with wonderful personalities and an irresistible presence. As the London stage producer C.B. Cochran stated: 'Two more electric personalities it has never been my fate to meet. . . . and any revue benefited enormously by their presence on the stage. . . . On the stage and off the Dolly Sisters were unique.'[5] Most importantly, they were not just sisters but identical twins – one being the mirror image of the other – and this was the real secret of their allure.

Although they were devoted to one another and did everything together in their early years, a degree of tension emerged as they matured and reached adulthood. This could be explained by the fact that, although they were identical in appearance, they were completely different in personality. Generous to a fault, Jenny was more gregarious and out-going, and, since she was the older twin, she became the spokeswoman of the pair and led the way. 'Oh whatever I do Rosie will do,' [6] she once said. Rosie, on the other hand, although impulsive, was more stable and reserved, and, although she deferred to Jenny on many issues, she continually strove for her own independence. It would appear that Jenny relied on Rosie more than Rosie relied on Jenny, and Jenny's dominance became an issue for Rosie. This underlying friction was exacerbated by their rivalry in love and affected their relationship. Eventually it had serious repercussions.

During their Broadway years they claimed that they had married for love and not money, while at the same time they were pampered and spoilt by the millionaire Diamond Jim Brady – one of New York's most colourful characters. When he died, their marriages gradually dissolved, and in 1920 they used their trip to London to distance themselves from and then finally to ditch their first husbands. They clearly had fond memories of Diamond Jim, since millionaires became their game, and they dated the most eligible men in Europe. It was also alleged that they were chased around the Continent by David, Prince of Wales, later Edward VIII.

Their elaborate game of flirtation, falling in love and engagement, marked an unease between the two sisters that increased with the years. Each new love affair ended in abandonment, because marriage effectively meant the end of the Dolly Sisters as a headlining act. The unthinkable finally happened in the spring of 1927, and retirement followed when they were only 35. When Jenny was in the throes of intriguing liaisons with Gordon Selfridge, owner of the London department store, and Jacques Wittouck, a wealthy Belgian businessman, rumours of her impending marriage to Selfridge became more strident. Rosie was betrothed to the French businessman François Dupré but sneaked off and attempted to acquire a fortune by marrying the Canadian multi-millionaire Mortimer Davis Junior, heir to a $150-million estate. Alas, gold was not at the end of the rainbow, and they were swiftly divorced.

Selfridge spent perhaps £2 million on Jenny, helping to finance the renovation of a Parisian townhouse, the purchase and refurbishment of a country chateau in Fontainebleau and the abortive launch of a glamorous couture establishment. Jenny also adopted two orphans and believed that they could become the new Dolly Sisters.

As Rosie found love and happiness with another rich husband – Irving Netcher from Chicago – tragedy struck. In the course of an affair with a somewhat sinister French aviator and film star, Jenny suffered serious injuries in a car accident. Her financial and emotional condition was already poor and the accident accentuated the need for her to sell her jewellery, reputed to be the largest collection in private hands in the world, to help finance extensive surgery. She was never the same again. Moving back to America without her fortune, Jenny married attorney Bernard Vinissky, but, during a trip to Los Angeles in 1941, she committed suicide, confirming the generally held view that Rosie was the lucky one and Jenny the less fortunate.

Over the years many myths have developed about the Dolly Sisters, primarily because neither twin published her life story and the press sensationalised aspects of their lives. The 1945 musical *The Dolly Sisters* did not help, as it was not an accurate representation of their lives, merely a musical loosely based on their career. Some of the myths were reflected by Robert Wennersten, who interviewed Rosie before her death and decided that the Dollies did not live to dance but used their talent as a passport to good times. [7]

Meredith Etherington-Smith, author of a book on the couturier Patou, declared rather caustically that all they did was walk on and off stage in a succession of superbly extravagant clothes and were kept by a series of rich protectors.[8] Yet it was undeniable that they loved their career and loved performing. They clearly had talent, otherwise they would not have been as successful as they were. The fact that rich suitors besieged them with marriage proposals and showered them with gifts was simply a fabulously large bonus. And it has to be remembered that in those days every young actress aspired to marry a millionaire and every young millionaire aspired to marry a gorgeous actress!

Living close to the rhythm of the time, the Dolly Sisters were adept at always being in the right place with the right people, which maximised their success. Their lives mirrored the luxurious existence of high society on both sides of the Atlantic and provide a fascinating glimpse of this privileged world, which was eventually swept away by the Second World War. Although one eventually found happiness, the other found only that her destiny was not the one she had hoped for. Lurking behind their glamorous story of fame, fortune and sisterly devotion is another one of duplicity and tragedy.

One appears as the reflection of the other and just as you could not see a man without his shadow, you could not conceive of how one of the Dolly Sisters could dance and live without the other.

(Jazz, 15 June 1927)

1

THE HEAVENLY TWINS

Shortly after the birth of her delightful identical twins, their mother, Margarethe, instructed the nurse to tie a pink ribbon on the first born, who was named Jenny, and a blue ribbon on the other, who was Rosie. This worked well until the twins were about three months old. One day, while the infants were being bathed, the ribbons became unfastened, and Margarethe almost fainted when she found she was unable to tell them apart. They were alike as two peas in a pod, and neither bore a single distinguishing mark. Margarethe, being devoutly religious, went on her knees and prayed to God to help her. She tied the coloured ribbons on their legs again, trusting to divine guidance that she got it right. But ever after there was some doubt. Which was really which? The distinguishing colours of pink for Jenny and blue for Rosie were used well into adulthood, and the issue of mistaken identities became an integral part of their lives.

The Dolly Sisters were born Yansci and Roszika in Budapest, the capital of Hungary, on 25 October 1892, to Julius Deutsch (born *c.* 1864) and his wife Margarethe Weiss (born *c.* 1874). Both Julius and Margarethe had been brought up with the hope of a brighter future as a result of the formation of the

Austro-Hungarian Empire in 1867, and, until the outbreak of the First World War in 1914, a golden age of progress blossomed in Hungary. Budapest became the focal point for the drift of country people in search of a better life, and during the 1890s it became one of the fastest-growing cities in Europe. Hungarian culture thrived, especially in the theatre and the arts, and rivalled Vienna. Yet the superficial prosperity masked deep domestic problems, with civil unrest, strikes and increased emigration to the New World.

Julius Deutsch had become wealthy as the best-known photographer in Budapest. He became acquainted with Margarethe while photographing her when she was a famous dancer and actress at the Volka Theatre, where she had an eight-year engagement. Rosie remembered that she often heard her father tell the story of how they used to applaud and throw flowers at Margarethe because she was such a great favourite.[1] Yet, despite her success, she gave up her promising career to become a wife and mother. Before the girls were born she cherished the hope that she would be blessed with a son, whom she had already named Yansci, Hungarian for Johnnie. But when her first girl arrived, she decided to retain the name, and so the older of the twins was regarded as 'the man' of the pair, and even as a child Yansci (Jenny) was always the tomboy while Roszika (Rosie) was dreamy and romantic.[2]

At a young age they were introduced to the world of the theatre in a rather extraordinary fashion through their nursemaid, who was in love with a soldier. She was meant to take the girls to the park but instead went to the theatre, where she could hold her sweetheart's hand in the dark, which is how the Dollies saw many now-forgotten stars, although it was the dancers who interested them most. Rosie recalled:

> We watched them, round eyed and as soon as we got home we fell to imitating their postures. Our parents could not imagine where we got such notions. They were rather innocent minded and did not seem to suspect the truth. We, on the other hand, were wise for our ages, and not once did we so much as dream of telling on the nursemaid.[3]

As they grew up, dancing became their first love. They felt it came as naturally to them as breathing, and, as Rosie explained later, with a mother who had been an actress and a dancer they felt they could not escape the influence.[4] Yet this talent was not encouraged by their grandmother, who, when they were about 5 or 6, was filled with grave fears. 'Do make those children put their skirts down and stop hopping madly about . . . they'll be dancers if you're not careful,'[5] she told their mother.

The girls attended school in Budapest for three years and, despite the lack of encouragement, at the age of 8 officially started their dancing career. They decided to put on an original play with dancing at home in their drawing room to an audience of three boys and two girls, who had all paid the entrance fee. Rosie wore an old costume of her mother's of yellow gauze that had to be doubled around her waist and pinned to fit. She matched this with an ill-fitting wig, while Jenny wore boy's clothes. Although their debut went well, their father came in when they were in the middle of the performance, and the audience retired in disorder.[6]

Their father's attitude to the stage ambitions of his gifted daughters was not encouraging. He sent them to a convent school in Berlin for two years, where, among other things, they learned English, German and French. However, if Julius had believed sending them away to school would remove any theatrical inclination, he was mistaken. Although they did not have any actual dance lessons, they simply improvised, always took leading roles in school plays and continued to dance for their own pleasure. At their school in Berlin they tried the splits, practised kicks over their heads and danced in their bare feet. The nuns did not approve of the girls' antics, and they were asked to leave. Thereupon they spent a further year in another school in Vienna.[7]

During one of their trips home, when they were 10, they were taken to see the world-famous dancer Isadora Duncan by their grandmother. Although she clearly had strong views about not encouraging the girls to dance, she was keen to ensure that they were given every opportunity to embrace important cultural experiences. Duncan had revolutionised modern dance by advocating that it should be natural and free. An adventurer, revolutionist, proto-feminist and a rebel against tradition and marriage, for some she was too bohemian and her flimsy stage costumes shocking. Nevertheless, her arrival in Hungary was an event of enormous significance, since she had already made her mark in London, Paris and Vienna.

Duncan arrived in Budapest in mid-March 1902 and rehearsed for a month before opening at the Urania Theatre on 19 April 1902, the first of twenty sold-out performances.[8] She was adored and her performance had a major effect on Jenny and Rosie's determination to become dancers. 'We saw her once. But that was enough. We could think of nothing else.'[9]

That night on their return home the two girls appeared in the living room. Remembering that Isadora danced barefoot in just a flimsy bit of drapery holding a lily in her hand, the girls, barefoot and in their nighties, clutching some cotton flowers from an old hat, gave an imitation of the great dancer with 'weird little gestures' of their own invention. Margarethe approvingly played the piano and smiled encouragingly at their precocity, while Julius applauded with typical paternal pride in his delightful offspring. They proved that they had an astonishing natural grace, but, alas, Grandma grew peevish. 'Those children will never come to any good. They are natural-born actresses,' she said. She did not believe in encouraging such foolishness: it could turn a child's thoughts toward the stage, the last profession in the world for a young woman to consider – it was simply not respectable – even though their mother had been on the stage.[10]

Once put to bed, they could not sleep; they were still entranced by the vision of Isadora. Way past midnight, Margarethe saw a light in their tiny room and heard strange, rhythmic noises. She peered in and saw Jenny sitting up in bed humming a Hungarian dance and waving her hand while Rosie was tripping about the room keeping time to Jenny's humming. They were both scolded and put back to bed, but their excitement could not be constrained.

Subsequently, they danced publicly at benefits for titled people in Budapest and Berlin but never for money.[11] The girls were pretty and had character and were so popular that one of the managers of the Berlin Wintergarten (the premier variety establishment) asked their mother to let him take them and develop their skills; Margarethe refused.[12] Although she was willing to pander to her daughters' desire to dance for themselves or at charity events, Margarethe needed to maintain some dignity and preserve her sense of middle-class respectability.

It was during this period that life for their father began to deteriorate, and, as the result of an undisclosed financial disaster, he lost much of his money. The only explanation was offered by Rosie, who said that 'Father failed in business – art being dull in Budapest'; perhaps Julius found that photography was not as lucrative as it had been in the past and invested his money in a business venture that failed.[13] Like so many others in similar circumstances, he made the decision to go to America.[14] Julius arrived in New York on 8 May 1903 on board the *Graf Waldersee* from the German port of Hamburg, giving his occupation as a photographer and carrying $100.[15] It is likely that he attempted to follow a career as a photographer, but this did not work out. Eventually he became an interior decorator and decorated the homes of many American millionaires on the eastern seaboard. He also turned his hand to restoring works of art.[16] Later, the success of his daughters on Broadway after 1910 must have secured lucrative introductions for these ventures.

After two years, the 12-year-old girls arrived in New York with their mother on 30 May 1905 from Hamburg.[17] 'How perfectly grand it seemed when we steamed majestically up the harbour past blooming Bensonhurst where we later were to have a summer home,' remembered Rosie. Travelling second class and not steerage on the liner the *Hamburg* must have made an enormous difference in terms of comfort, but the legendary immigration procedure on Ellis Island that often took an entire day must have been daunting. Rosie jested about 'the warmth of the greeting of welcome at the dock where the government agents were waiting' and the inspection of their luggage to discover how much duty they would levy on their collective ward-robe, not to mention being examined by the agents of the Children's Society.[18]

Once ashore, the family settled down to life at 11 Rivington Street on the edge of New York's Lower East Side, a neighbourhood settled by immigrants from all over Europe throughout history. It was a crowded place with big tenement blocks and by 1910, for example, there were 1,000 people per acre. Although poor, it was a hive of business activity, as people took their first steps on the road to the American dream.

The promise of a better life was proving elusive for their father, and the girls could see how hard he struggled to make ends meet. He wanted them to continue their education, but they felt that this was impossible because their knowledge of English was far from perfect and they would have had to start in classes for younger girls in order to catch up. Instead, it was reluctantly decided that they should help contribute to the family's depleted finances.

Despite Margarethe's earlier reluctance to encourage her daughters' theatrical aspirations, their financial predicament swayed her judgement. Dancing was in their blood, and the sisters aspired to a career as dancers more than anything, so they were delighted with this new opportunity, even though the impetus was primarily financial. Margarethe paid for ten lessons at Claude Alviene's famous dancing school in the same building as the Grand Opera house on 8th Avenue at 23rd Street, where they were also allowed to practise every day because there was no room at home.[19] She also took an active role in their training, giving them valuable help and advice, and she began to investigate performing opportunities in New York.[20] Her job was instantly thwarted by what had become known as 'the Gerry Society'. The Society for the Prevention of Cruelty to Children (SPCC) and its leader Eldbridge T. Gerry had campaigned to remove child performers from the professional stage and, beginning in New York State, had managed to impose a ban in 1876 that grew into a nationwide crusade. The Dollies were not allowed to perform in New York until they were 15 years old.

Margarethe discovered that the manager of the Berlin Wintergarten, who had wanted to help them in Europe, was in New York, and she went to see him. This was probably Baron Max Hoffman,[21] who tried to use his influence to get the sisters work in New York but to no avail. However, he was able to organise some appearances out of town, which included a Sunday afternoon special show in Boston in early 1906.

When the girls and Margarethe arrived in Boston with their wardrobe tied up in a sheet, they were thrown into confusion by the musical director. He asked for the orchestral parts of their music, but, because they had a repertoire of only two dances, all they had was a single violin part of one Hungarian piece of music. Undeterred, they carried on. Rosie did an Isadora Duncan barefoot dance and then Jenny did a 'robe' dance, but after a few steps she forgot what she was doing; in desperation she repeated what she had done, but got stuck again. The audience laughed, and she became more confused and got tangled in the old couch cover she used as the robe. The audience howled with mirth and demanded encore after encore. Afterwards the manager asked, 'Why in the world didn't you girls tell me you had a real comedy act?' They were not entirely happy that the seriousness of their first act had been misinterpreted as burlesquing a sister act.[22] Jenny's misfortune was the earliest example of something that was to become a much-talked-about theme later and one that was firmly entrenched in their mythology: a sense of rivalry between the two sisters because Rosie was always regarded as the lucky one and Jenny as the less fortunate.

With Margarethe undoubtedly as chaperone, Baron Hoffman arranged further appearances for the twins with his wife in a show that played the vaudeville circuit in the first half of 1906 but escaped the rules of the 'Gerry Society' because the tour was outside New York. Gertrude Hoffman was a versatile performer who had begun her career as a speciality dancer and then became an impersonator, often outshining the people she parodied. She was also provocative and her 'Dance of the Seven Veils' from *Salome*, which made her famous, was at the time considered indecent. As her stage career waned in the 1920s, she became one of the first female choreographers, and her troupe of girls became famous worldwide.

Gertrude Hoffman took quite a fancy to the young girls and was in a unique position to train the young dancers. Because she thought they looked cute, just like little dolls, she called them 'the Dollies', and this evolved into 'the Dolly Sisters'. Something that was initially used as a description became firmly fixed as their stage name. Ultimately their new 'American' surname became Dolly and replaced Deutsch in common usage.[23]

Jenny and Rosie were not tall but were extremely pretty, and their dark skin, shoulder-length dark hair and gypsy eyes proved an asset. This 'foreign' look made them ideal for wide-ranging roles, and because of their appearance Gertrude Hoffman gave them small parts in a 'Japanese' and 'Russian' section of her show.[24] They toured successfully and, by June 1906, for example, at the Bijou Theatre, Memphis, Gertrude Hoffman won great praise for her impersonations, songs and dances.[25]

As the vaudeville tour ended and before the girls were 14, sometime in late 1906, they accepted an offer from Hoffman or another New York agent to go to Cuba and dance for four weeks under the supervision of their mother. Cuba had been through an unstable period, with open rebellion against the unpopular president Tomas Estrada Palma, but, with his resignation in September 1906, and the establishment of an American-led government, the country became stable. It must have been after these events that the Dolly Sisters arrived in Havana with home-made costumes and self-invented dances, which Margarethe supervised.[26] They became known as 'Las muñecas Americanas' or 'The Little American dolls'. They performed in Havana for the National Theatre and other places in the Perfecto district and were so successful that the initial four-week contract stretched over several months. In mid-1907 they returned to New York, where they were now old enough to perform and were ready to see if Broadway would take a liking to them, as Cuba had done. They were not disappointed.

They were immediately signed by the producer Mortimer M. Thiese for the chorus in *The Maid and the Millionaire*, his new musical production at the Madison Square Roof Garden with Toma Hanlon as a young woman who is helped on her way to stardom by a stage-struck tycoon. The venue was the city's newest and fanciest roof-top restaurant, which had opened the previous summer with *Mamzelle Champagne*.[27] This show had become more significant because Harry K. Thaw, the deranged husband of musical comedy star Evelyn Nesbit, shot Stanford White, her lover and the architect of Madison Square Garden, during one of the early performances. There was no lurid scandal to darken the launch of the new summer show that opened on 15 June 1907 with the Dolly Sisters as two of the eight chorus girls in the pony ballet.

The famous English choreographer John Tiller had created the concept of the dancing troupe – several young girls who performed precision dancing in unison. George Lederer booked a John Tiller troupe to perform one of their famous routines – the 'pony ballet' – sometime after 1900 in New York. The diminutive chorines swiftly laid the foundation for the chorus line that became a common fixture of stage productions, and the pony ballet was copied relentlessly.[28] The reviews of *The Maid and the Millionaire* were not favourable, and the show was regarded as uneventful and slow and lasted only a few weeks through the summer heat.[29] But it was a good start and obviously gave the Dolly Sisters valuable experience in a legitimate New York production, even if it was only a summer roof-top show.

Thiese then secured the rights to 'The Belle of Ave A', a sequence from a production by A.H. Woods, which he evolved into a touring show called *The Strolling Players*.[30] Once again he used the talent of Toma Hanlon, with the Dolly Sisters among the chorus of sixteen. The show was launched in September 1907 and toured the country through the spring of 1908, but, like *The Maid and the Millionaire*, it was not viewed favourably. 'The best that can be said for the Strollers is that it is free from coarseness and has half a dozen bright spots to counterbalance a good deal of dullness.'[31]

According to the sisters, on the tour of the West they did twenty shows a day at $40 a week. They could not speak good English but just about managed to make their own bookings. All they could manage was 'Coffee and rolls please' – and they wondered why they did not get big meals like everyone else around them.[32] But they quickly came to the fore in their speciality segment, and one review observed 'it is said that they will create a New York sensation before long'.[33] Shortly before the 'Strollers' disbanded, the sisters left the cast and embarked on their own extensive tour of the Keith Circuit's vaudeville establishments in the spring of 1908.[34]

Benjamin Franklin Keith reportedly invented the phrase and concept of 'vaudeville' in an attempt to rechristen variety shows with a more elegant-sounding name to dispel part of their disreputable image. Keith began staging shows in Boston in the early 1880s and by 1885 had gone into business with fellow New Englander Edward Franklin Albee. They built an empire of theatres and the United Booking Office or UBO, which booked and coordinated the routing of acts. They believed that vaudeville must be a scrupulously pure form of entertainment for all the family with three vital components: no offensive material, continuous performances from 9.30 a.m. to 10.30 p.m. and luxurious theatres with palatial interiors. Their formula was so successful that through the 1890s and early 1900s they expanded rapidly, with a chain of theatres on the east coast in Boston, Philadelphia, Jersey City, Brooklyn and elsewhere, including the Colonial, Alhambra and Union Square in New York. By March 1913, when they opened their new offices in the flagship Palace Theatre, they controlled virtually every big vaudeville house in America through the Keith and Orpheum Circuit. The Keith Circuit was not without its competitors – namely, Hammerstein's Victoria (at the corner of 42nd Street and Broadway), regarded as the undisputed queen of variety theatres, and the Hippodrome and Madison Square Garden venues owned by the Shubert brothers.

Shows in the Keith houses, like most other vaudeville theatres, were changed each week, with the aim of presenting a variety of performers and material with a fast pace. Any act given a route on the Keith Circuit could look forward to anything from forty to eighty weeks' work. Each bill usually consisted of up to nine acts that were carefully chosen and well balanced with one headliner (although later at the Palace Theatre there was often more than one). The first act was called a dumb act with dancers or trick animals, next came a song-and-dance team to settle the audience, then something dramatic such as a mini-musical or revue, a named performer like a concert singer with accompanist, and another big name or named band before the intermission. The second part comprised a good monologuist or mime comedian, a one-act play with a legitimate star or a short comic play, and then the headlining slot of a popular jazz singer or star performer, followed by something solely visual such as an acrobatic act, trick animals or trapeze artists. With such a vast array of acts, it is not surprising that vaudeville became the training ground and model for the Broadway revue and its greatest reservoir of talent.[35]

The Dolly Sisters started at $50 a week, but this had to cover all their expenses. Before they reached their first port of call, their mother had already spent over $30 on railroad fares and hotel bills and she was $30 short at the end of the week.[36] Finances must have improved, as they continued through 1908, and they got used to the routine and devised ways of economising. By the summer of 1909[37] they had polished their performance and were making more of an impact nearer New York, appearing in some of the major entertainment palaces clustered along the Atlantic Ocean between Coney Island and Manhattan Beach in Brooklyn. 'The girls have about the liveliest little sister act shown in some time,'[38] said one critic of their ten-minute singing-and-dancing act. Their singing was described as not too strong but 'good enough for what little is required', and their costumes were admired as being prettier than usual. This was a trend of description that was to become standard for many years. Their sparkle and vitality did not go unnoticed, and they were poised for greater things.[39]

FAME ON THE GREAT WHITE WAY

T he Dolly Sisters had arrived on Broadway (called the 'Great White Way' because of the electrical signs that spanned the theatre district) when traditional musical comedy was being challenged by revue, with dancing a vital ingredient. Revue has a French ancestry and blossomed during the nineteenth century. Its main ingredients were satire, song, dance, monologues and humour conceived to reflect contemporary events and incidents. It was not long before this formula was copied in England and America with the addition of spectacular effects. On Broadway the revue came to fruition with the *Passing Show* of 1894 drawing on an ancestry of minstrel shows, variety, burlesque and vaudeville. But it was Florenz Ziegfeld's sumptuous *Follies of 1907* that became the basis of all revues thereafter, with the major shows opening in May or June designed to liven up the summer doldrums followed by a regional tour in the autumn. The Shubert brothers became equally renowned for their extravaganzas, and, as the Dolly Sisters made a name for themselves, they switched easily between the two.

The Dollies became successful because they were a novelty dancing act, with the allure of being identical twins. There had been sister acts before them, most famously the Hengler Sisters (May and Flo), society child protégées who made their mark at the turn of the century in America and Europe. But the Dolly Sisters were the first twin sister act to become famous and paved the way for future twin acts.

They entered their first true Broadway show after it had been launched. *The Midnight Sons*, a summer musical revue staged by Lew Fields and the Shubert brothers as the first attraction at the Broadway Theatre, opened on 22 May 1909. It was an elaborate production called 'the biggest musical play ever staged', and Lew Fields's imaginative scenes started the moment the curtain rose, when the audience beheld another audience in another theatre with an orchestra, balcony, gallery and boxes. The vast cast of 125 players, singers and dancers was largely recruited from vaudeville and headed by Blanche Ring, Norma Brown, Lotta Faust and Vernon Castle, later to be part of the headlining dancing team with his wife Irene.[1]

The Dolly Sisters had been spotted by Lee Shubert one night in vaudeville, and he gave them a try-out performance at the Shuberts' Herald Square Theatre to appear in *The Midnight Sons*.[2] Before they were signed, their parents brought them into the theatre to see Lew Fields and told him that they were clever. Fields and the rest of the principals saw that they looked alike as the proverbial two peas and took a great liking to them, and so they were taken on and initially added to the beauty chorus. They readily acknowledged that it was Lew Fields and Lee Shubert who gave them their first Broadway chance.[3] Fields with Joe Weber was part of the famous team of Weber and Fields that became the prototype for all future comedy teams.

The three Shubert brothers were legendary for their eccentric behaviour and uncanny business sense. Sam (who died in 1905), Lee (the dreamer and schemer) and Jake (who was ultra-practical) had developed their theatrical business empire from its early beginnings in Syracuse to become the largest theatre-management and producing operation in America. By 1910 the Shuberts owned over seventy major theatres around the country, including thirteen in New York, and held booking contracts with many more.[4]

The Midnight Sons ran for thirty-six weeks in New York before embarking on an extensive tour. During the run, Fields and the Shuberts kept an eye on their talented young charges, and at some point they progressed from the chorus line to their own routine.[5] They also understudied Lotta Faust and took some of her matinée performances.[6] When Faust left the cast, Jenny replaced her and with grace and spirit danced the Spanish bolero wearing a Carmen costume designed by Melville Ellis.[7]

Sometime in 1910, as the girls neared their seventeenth birthday, Margarethe left her daughters under the watchful eye of their father. She returned to Hungary and when she returned she brought back a son, Edward, aged 11, arriving in New York on 26 August 1910 aboard the SS *Pennsylvania* from Hamburg.[8] Strangely, Edward was listed as US born and later even claimed to have been born on 25 October 1898, the same day and month as his 'sisters', in Brooklyn.[9] If he was a son of Julius and Margarethe, and if his age is correct, he must have been born in Budapest, because they did not set foot in America until 1905. If we are to believe that Eddie was born a Deutsch, he must have been left in Hungary when his mother and sisters moved to New York in 1905. In a few later press interviews the Dolly Sisters stated quite clearly that they did not have any siblings. And yet, by the early 1920s, Eddie was being described as their brother. It helped that he was dark-haired and dark-eyed and bore some resemblance, and perhaps the fact that he was taller and bigger built was explained by the fact he was a boy. In all likelihood Margarethe rescued the son of a close relative on a trip back home to give him a better life in America and by the 1920s Eddie had become a fully-fledged Dolly and an actor, dancer and successful choreographer.

In the meantime, during the late summer of 1910, the Dollies were engaged at $90 a week for Charles Dillingham's singing and dancing frolic *The Echo* at the Globe, a showcase for Bessie McCoy. The Dolly Sisters had their own speciality spots and were aided in their endeavours by George White (later to become a rival to Ziegfeld in the staging of spectacular revue) and his partner Ben Ryan. According to White, whose nickname was 'Swiftie', Dillingham asked him to teach the Dolly Sisters some new dance steps.

> It was on account of the Dollies that my partner and I split up. Ryan and I had a fight about a close formation step we did with the girls. Ryan stepped on Jenny's foot and she protested. After they had finished dancing an argument started. I am always partial to the ladies, so I sided with Jenny. For the rest of the season Ryan and I were not on speaking terms.

And so ended the team of Ryan and White.[10]

Despite impressive staging and exotic costumes made in Paris from designs by Serge de Salomko of St Petersburg, *The Echo* was a short-lived affair running from August to October, although it did tour well into 1911. One of the stops on the tour was Indianapolis, where, in February 1911, Jenny met Harry Knight (1889–1913), the 21-year-old fearless motorcar driver. He already knew Bessie McCoy, who unknowingly played Cupid to the pair. By May 1911 there were rumours of an engagement, as Harry arranged for a private box for Jenny to see him in the 500-mile international sweepstakes event at an Indianapolis speedway.[11] Although love was in the air, it clearly could not compete with events in New York, and it was at this time that Florenz Ziegfeld took an interest in the sisters as he was preparing the fifth edition of his Follies, and the first to bear his name.

Ziegfeld was undoubtedly the most innovative and energetic new force in American theatre, and became recognised as America's greatest showman. The Chicago-born son of a German immigrant, he made his name at the turn of the century by becoming the promoter of Sandow, the world's strongest man, and by introducing the European star Anna Held to Broadway and turning her into a crowd-drawing celebrity. Each autumn Ziegfeld staged increasingly spectacular vehicles showcasing Held's talents, culminating with *The Parisian Model* in 1906, which co-starred the flamboyant dancer Gertrude Hoffman immediately following her vaudeville show with the Dollies. The show was a massive hit on account of the incredible sets, the fabulous costumes and most of all the erotic glimpses of the showgirls. Ziegfeld had made his mark by taking elements of popular entertainment and turning them into a sophisticated new form. On Held's advice Ziegfeld decided to stage a new form of show with Parisian qualities adapted for American taste. The informality of the New York Theatre roof garden was transformed into a typical Parisian café concert and evocatively renamed the Jardin de Paris. Here the first Follies starring Anna Held was staged in July 1907, a fast-paced sequence of comedy, parodies of celebrities, dancing and elaborate production numbers with, of course, the most vital ingredient, an abundance of beautiful women in stylish settings.

Not surprisingly, the Follies established itself as the most popular summer entertainment in the city and was followed by the incomparable vaudeville star and singer Nora Bayes, who introduced 'Shine on Harvest Moon' (1908). For the 1909 edition, Lillian Lorraine – 'the most beautiful girl in the world' – was the star, and in 1910 it was the brilliant young singing comedienne Fanny Brice. For the 1911 edition Ziegfeld engaged the beautiful dancer Vera Maxwell, the Australian comedian and dancer Leon Errol and the great black comic Bert Williams, along with Fanny Brice and Bessie McCoy. On the advice of McCoy, Ziegfeld saw the Dollies in *The Echo* and hired them[12] along with George White. In his shrewdness, Ziegfeld, like Lee Shubert, saw that the Dolly Sisters had a certain something: a tantalising sparkle that could only invigorate any production. 'You can't do much, but you're cute,' he said.[13] At the time their mother was still arranging all their business dealings. They had been earning $90 a week. When Ziegfeld asked what they were getting, their mother said $300. They settled on $350 a week[14] – more than enough to start saving for their dream home in Bensonhurst.

The Dollies had at least four major appearances in the *Ziegfeld Follies of 1911*, which opened on 26 June 1911 at the Jardin de Paris/New York Theatre roof. Wearing costumes by William H. Matthews and Tryce, they danced with Vera Maxwell, did the bumble-bee dance in a Californian poppy field, did a dance in a cabaret setting on New Year's Eve in San Francisco and a scene where they appeared as Siamese twins sharing a skirt while dancing. The critics had been unanimous in saying that each of the first four editions of the Follies had been better than its predecessor, but this was not the case with this edition. *Variety* was far from impressed, saying it was slow and had little life.[15] Of the thirteen scenes, the biggest applause was given to Bert Williams and Leon Errol, Bessie McCoy in 'Tad's Daffydills' and Dave Abrams, giving a clever and ludicrous impersonation of a frisky French poodle.

The show closed its Broadway run on 2 September and opened the regional tour in Chicago. Fanny Brice roomed with Vera Maxwell and the Dollies, and wherever possible they took a big travelling salesman's room with two beds. In Indianapolis they were invited to a party in the country, where the dress was blue jeans and straw hats. One wonders whether the speedy Harry Knight was the host, eager to romance Jenny again. Vera and the Dollies found the party dull, but Fanny was enjoying herself and stayed when the other three walked back to town. When Fanny returned to the hotel in the middle of the night, she found her trunk in the hall and was not allowed in the room until she had banged on the door for half an hour. Despite this minor altercation, the Dollies were to remain friends with Fanny Brice throughout their lives. The show toured through Philadelphia at the New Year and finally came to a close outside New York on 30 March 1912.[16]

Next the Dollies were signed for the second Dillingham–Ziegfeld collaboration *Winsome Widow*,[17] which opened at the New York Theatre, renamed the Moulin Rouge, on 11 April 1912, one day before the tragic sinking of the *Titanic*. It was in essence a series of vaudeville turns featuring such stars as the singer Emmy Wehlan, the singer and dancer Elizabeth Brice, the comedian Harry Conor, the blackface comedian Frank Tinney, Leon Errol and a young Mae West, who appeared as the baby vamp La Petite Daffy.

Ziegfeld's impeccable flair added some beautifully produced numbers, including a spectacular masquerade carnival and a magical ice-skating scene. The Dollies' act was a 'mixed dancing speciality – a sort of terpsichorean

Russian salad . . . in the main a pretty modification of the prevailing ragtime, embellished and refined with a dash of Hungarian paprika'.[18] The *Winsome Widow* was described by *Variety* as a 'regular Ziegfeld show'[19] and proved 'breathtaking and a monster hit' – so big a hit, in fact, that the new edition of the Follies that was to replace it was postponed.[20]

In an interview around this time Jenny explained that she was the spokesperson: 'Rosie makes me talk because I am the older.' She also discussed their dancing philosophy, echoing Isadora Duncan:

> We are like chameleons, absorbing colour here and there from what we see that is really good and novel. I don't like the term ballet nor the wooden artificiality it stands for. A dancer has got to feel her own impulse in what she does. That is why we sometimes hear a new piece of music in a restaurant or at a classical concert, or maybe in a ragtime piano shop and then we just get that and put it into a dance of our own that is as different as the music is. That is the modern idea of dancing, don't you think? We are always looking for something new and we dance a great deal more away from the theatre than here on the stage.[21]

In another interview Jenny added: 'as for the stage the Turkey Trot and others are a thing of the past. Last year to dance well you had only to imitate someone else. This year to be a successful dancer in the drawing room as on the stage you must have imagination and originality.'[22]

Their early years must have been difficult – Rosie once said it was tough 'living in cheap boarding houses, saving every penny we could'[23] – but their originality and hard work paid off, because in the summer of 1912 the Dolly Sisters had earned enough money to buy a house in Bensonhurst, a lovely seaside area in Brooklyn, Long Island, where they moved with their parents.[24] They came up to town for performances, then went home at night in their own car. 'We like the animation and sparkle of Broadway, and have lots of jolly friends in the profession, but a little of the Great White Way is enough and we can hardly wait to get back to the seashore where it is so quiet and sunny and breezy. We don't take anything else very seriously – except of course our business contracts.' Perhaps during their first summer at Bensonhurst, when they were appearing in the *Winsome Widow*, they did retire 'most' nights to the delights of the suburban seaside, but certainly this quiet secluded lifestyle is at odds with what we know about their love of New York nightlife. Equally bizarre are their comments about love. When asked about their love affairs, they said emphatically 'pouf! love affairs . . . If these are serious to anybody it isn't ourselves. Besides we haven't time.'[25] And yet Jenny had already experienced one documented close encounter, and Rosie at the time was in the throes of a romance herself and within a year was married, with Jenny not far behind.

3

DIAMOND JIM, THE LOBSTER
PALACES AND CABARET

By the time they approached their twentieth birthday in October 1912, the slender and graceful Dolly Sisters had blossomed into beautiful and attractive young women. They were all but identical, with only slight differences. Jenny was fractionally taller and Rosie was more petite in face and figure and weighed 21 ounces less – although where this difference in weight lay no one knew because they wore each other's clothes with perfect ease.

To those who knew them well, there was also a difference in their smiles. When amused, Rosie's lips extended in parallel lines, while Jenny dropped her lower lip a trifle. Also, when listening to a conversation Rosie would indicate her absorption with wide-open eyes and closed lips, while Jenny registered her interest with lips slightly apart. Their expressions differed a bit when dancing. Jenny always smiled, while Rosie, according to one interviewer, appeared to be in a dream, 'wearing an expression that reminds one of an enthralled pagan goddess and her art is her religious rite.

The only other woman on whose face I have seen the same expression is Sarah Bernhardt.'[1]

They also had quite different characters. Rosie always said that Jenny was smarter, and Jenny declared that Rosie was more artistic. These were good generalisations. Jenny was a romantic butterfly, reckless, pleasure seeking and more gregarious. Always smiling, she was a natural comedienne. She was the eldest and, because she was regarded as the boy of the pair, became the tomboy, took the lead and made the curtain speeches. Rosie was more stable and shunned the limelight. She too was romantic, but cautious and quiet, a dreamer immersed in poetry, music and art and constantly thinking of new steps. At school Rosie had been a literary whizz, and Jenny a mathematical shark, so Rosie would double for Jenny in composition while Jenny helped Rosie with figures.[2] And yet, as time went on, Rosie gained a reputation for being a very smart businesswoman, and she discussed all the business dealings and contracts.

As the Dollies embarked on their stage career, they effectively became creatures of the night. The rigours of their regular afternoon and evening performances meant that they started work late and ended late. Dinner, taken very late, more like supper, was followed by a period of fun and frolics into the small hours, bedtime was early in the morning and breakfast was at noon.

One of the advantages of being a Ziegfeld girl was the chance to look alluring for an audience of New York's richest and most eligible men. And one of the most famous stage-door Johnnies of the time was the legendary millionaire Diamond Jim Brady (1856–1917), who took an immediate interest in the Dollies.[3] Brady was the son of a New York saloon-keeper who made his fortune by selling railroad materials and becoming a nationally respected financier. An extremely large man, he was flamboyant, genial and thoughtful, and his heart was as generous as his girth. Rosie later remembered him by puffing out her cheeks and stretching out her arms in front of her to indicate a big pot-belly; in her words: 'He was a fat man . . . he ate himself out of shape, ate himself out of health and everything else.'[4]

Diamond Jim was renowned for his limitless appetite, his relationship with the actress Lillian Russell and for being quite simply the flashiest person around, always covered in diamonds. 'If you're gonna make money, you've got to look like money,' he once said.[5] He had complete sets of jewels, one for each day of the month. Each set comprised a watch, watch chain, ring, scarf pin, necktie pin, necktie clasp, pen, pencil, cufflinks, belt buckle, eye-glass case and pocketbook clasp, not to mention shirt studs, collar buttons and even underwear buttons.[6] When everything was in place, he looked like an excursion steamer at twilight. Sometimes referred to as 'the gay 90s playboy', Diamond Jim attended all the major theatrical first nights and after the shows he was a regular at all the major New York eating establishments and knew everybody in the business, both performers and producers.

From the 1890s through to 1912 nightlife flourished along Broadway. Delmonico's, long the favoured social mecca, began to face competition from the newer, more vibrant restaurants such as the Waldorf Astoria, Bustanoby's, Churchill's, Martin's, Maxim's, Murray's Roman Gardens, Rector's, Shanley's and Reisenweber's. These luxurious venues became known as 'lobster palaces' because of their elegant décor, which imitated European regal and imperial splendour, impeccable service and excellent cuisine, which favoured late-night lobster suppers. Diamond Jim took full advantage of all of them.

When Diamond Jim went out, he always entertained, and he loved to be surrounded by handsome men and beautiful women. But few could match his eating habits. He would start the day with a breakfast of beefsteak, chops, eggs, flapjacks, fried potatoes, corn bread and milk. A typical lunch at 11.30 consisted of two lobsters, devilled crabs, clams, oysters and beef. This would be followed by several pies. Dinner at 4.30 would comprise two or three dozen oysters, six hard-shelled crabs and bowls of turtle soup. The main course would feature two whole ducks, six or seven lobsters, a sirloin steak, two servings of terrapin and a variety of vegetables. Dessert of pastries and a 5lb box of chocolates or candies would complete the repast, which was all washed down with a least three or four of the largest carafes of orange juice.

As a result of his vast appetite, Rector of Rector's, the world-famous eating establishment that was Brady's favourite, pronounced Jim 'the best 25 customers I ever had'.[7]

At the age of 54, Diamond Jim noticed the Dolly Sisters before they really became famous when they appeared in *The Echo*. He began escorting them about town and introduced them to the pleasures of the best that New York could offer in terms of dining and nights out. And he gave each of them a diamond chain and a six-carat diamond ring. If a boyfriend entered the picture, he would be invited too, and sometimes there might be a group of five in his entourage. Brady's attention was purely platonic; he simply loved their invigorating company. Explaining his fondness for them, Rosie said:

> He used to say that if we hadn't parents he should have adopted both of us. And he would always urge us on to greater exertion. . . . he never let us smoke . . . nor drink . . . and if a person started to tell an off-colour story, Jim would order him away from the table. Jim had lots of envious critics but I'd match his moral code against that of anybody in New York.

When they did become named stars in the *Ziegfeld Follies of 1911*, a boy came to their dressing room and told them he had a present from Mr Brady. Bring it in, they said. But he declined and told them that they would have to go outside to see it. Excitedly they did as he said, and there at the kerb was a Rolls-Royce wrapped up in ribbons.[8]

By the time the Dolly Sisters began sampling the pleasures of New York on the arm of Diamond Jim, the concept of cabaret was changing the face of evening entertainment. In the spring of 1911 Henry Harris and Jesse Lasky opened the Folies Bergère, a theatre-restaurant designed to reflect Parisian bohemian style, but it had no opportunities for dancing and the idea failed. The Shuberts were more canny, and, when they opened the Winter Garden Theatre in March 1911, they included a venue called the Palais de Danse, situated in the south wing on the second and third floors with a restaurant and Persian

Ballroom, where entertainments were staged in conjunction with dining.[9] This was regarded as the first true nightclub in New York, modelled after the famous establishment in Berlin, and 'people went wild about the idea'.[10]

The Dollies and Diamond Jim would have visited these new venues, and, at the Folies Bergère, for example, marvelled at the dancing of Harry Pilcer, one of the principals of the show *Hello Paris*, who later became the dancing partner of Gaby Deslys and a good friend of the Dollies in Paris. The Dolly Sisters had started their Broadway career at an auspicious moment in New York nightlife, just as things began to change and dancing, their forte, became *de rigueur*, as cabaret proliferated.

The cabaret – watching an entertainment and dancing during dinner or a social drink – evolved out of the desire for novelty and a means of increasing trade. It was instrumental in breaking down the old formal barriers, as social conventions became blurred and men and women mixed freely. Stage entertainers were transferred to the floor of a nightclub or restaurant and as a result became more accessible to the public in this intimate and informal setting, where personality became a valuable asset.

Equally, the success of the new cabarets was due to the explosion of the dancing craze from 1912 as the new rhythm epitomised by Irving Berlin's ragtime music created the need for new dances. The strict regulation of ballrooms was abandoned in favour of freer expression in nightclubs where an extensive floor was needed not just for an entertainment but as a stage for the hundreds of new dances such as the Apache, Turkey Trot, Grizzly Bear, Texas Tommy, Bunny Hug, Lame Duck, Foxtrot and Tango. These celebrity gathering spots became dominated by the theatrical world, but the first real stars of cabaret were not stage stars but dancing stars, who, by introducing new dances to an eager public, found instant success. None was more popular than Maurice Mouvet and Florence Walton, and Vernon and Irene Castle.

With Diamond Jim, the Dolly Sisters became part of the core of a new fast set that turkey-trotted and tangoed up Broadway via Murray's, Claridge's, New York Roof, Rector's, Healy's, Churchill's, Reisenweber's and then the

400 Club until 4 a.m. This was followed by breakfast at Ciro's or Jack's and then finally bed at 6 a.m. Diamond Jim decided to learn how to dance all the new steps and spent thousands of dollars being taught by Maurice and Walton and then the Castles. But, because of his size and age, he always danced in the same grave way and 'showed more earnestness than grace'.[11] His lessons with the Dollies were less formal and formed part of his entertainment for the evening with supper thrown in. Despite his limitations, Brady and his entourage, which frequently included the Dollies, became the essential ingredients of any 'good night out' and often as important as the cabaret performers themselves.

Besides his zeal for eating, Diamond Jim also had a great passion for horse racing and owned a colt called Golden Heels. When he was not dancing up and down Broadway, he frequently escorted the Dollies to the races. They were spotted one summer at the Empire City race track in Yonkers under his supervision, where they were reported to have had a profitable afternoon. 'You certainly pick out good horses for us to bet on,' said one of the sisters to Diamond Jim. 'Oh it isn't that,' replied a ponderous Diamond Jim, with a grace many tons lighter than himself, 'but no thoroughbred would be ungallant enough to lose a race knowing that two such pretty girls were betting on him.'[12]

Not only did they visit Yonkers; they also patronised the Coney Island race tracks at Brighton Beach, Sheepshead Bay and Gravesend during the racing season from May to October. There was also an extensive array of luxury hotels, restaurants and music-hall attractions such as Henderson's that they often frequented as a perfect end to the day.[13]

Diamond Jim, like the Dolly Sisters, was unacceptable to high society, so he spent much time in Saratoga, Florida. Besides the opportunity for a flutter on the horses at the most beautiful race track in America, there was the added bonus of a casino. It was under Diamond Jim's influence that the Dolly Sisters began their love affair with gambling, which was to reach a pinnacle of obsession on the Normandy coast and the Riviera in the 1920s, not to mention their love of the ponies in Paris.

The Dollies were clearly admired and sought after by many others besides Diamond Jim. Some were definitely not shown the same kindness and appreciation, because their motives were suspect. The sisters clearly knew what to do when Senor Don Cabellero y Fuenterabia of Cienfuegos of Cuba tracked them down. He had seen them during their tour of Cuba and had become deeply enamoured, finally locating them in New York and expressing his admiration. He firmly believed that the focus of his attention should be Rosie, whom he invited to lunch at the Knickerbocker Hotel. It became apparent that a proposal of marriage was in the air. Jenny was displeased: 'I want luncheon too,' she pined – so the sisters decided that they would both have lunch at his expense and thwart his intentions.

Rosie arrived and ordered a vast lunch, which included Canadian melon, steak, salad and French pastry. After eating her way through the entire ensemble, she announced she must make a phone call and disappeared through the restaurant to the designated meeting point. Here the two sisters met and Rosie quickly outlined their conversation to her identically dressed sister. As Jenny went back in, the Don Juan asked her if she would like something else to finish – a Benedictine, or a coffee, perhaps. But instead she announced she was still hungry and ordered the same again. The Don Juan was more than astonished but too well bred to protest. He grew flustered and was keen to terminate the lunch without further ado. As he paid the bill and Jenny washed her dainty fingers in the finger bowl, she smiled gracefully and said: 'Is there anything else you want to say to me?' 'No,' he replied emphatically, clearly with the thought in his mind. 'My income is large, it is sufficient for two. I would gladly marry but I can't be eaten out of house and home.'[14]

After appearing in Ziegfeld's *Winsome Widow*, the Dollies jumped ship and rejoined Lee Shubert. Their attachment to the Shuberts was solid, and they expressed their appreciation clearly. 'We are Shubert protégées and proud of it. Mr Lee Shubert has been one of our best friends. We cannot tell you how much he has done for us and how grateful we are.'[15] Along with the American dancer Dazie (born Daisy Peterkin), regarded as America's most popular ballet danseuse, they appeared in a reworking of Johann Strauss's comic opera *Die Fledermaus* retitled *The Merry Countess*, which opened at the Casino Theatre in August 1912. The rest of the company comprised the original English cast from the Lyric Theatre, London, including the leading lady Jose Collins, a young singer the same age as the Dollies who had inherited her talent from her mother Lottie Collins, a famous music-hall star.

The Shuberts added lavish sets and costumes to give the show a polish that gleamed, and *Variety* believed it was the classiest thing in comic opera that had hit Broadway.[16] Jose Collins drew huge praise for her performance, and equal praise was allotted to the Dollies. With Martin Brown, another dancer for the Shuberts, as their partner, they danced gracefully to a medley of Strauss waltzes and the polka. 'He and the Dollies surpassed themselves,' said the *Evening Sun*,[17] while *Variety* enthused: 'the way the girls did it with Brown was astonishing. They looked well and danced better.'[18]

Even though they had already appeared in the *Ziegfeld Follies* it was in *The Merry Countess* that the Dollies hit the big time. One of their equally crowning achievements was the attention they received from Cornelius Vanderbilt, the wealthy financier. He attended the opening performance of *The Merry Countess* and was so enchanted by the Dollies' beauty and grace that he was determined to engage the girls to present their dances at the ball he was about to give.

Because of their popularity, the Shuberts would not allow the girls to leave the show even for one performance. Vanderbilt would not give up and continued to press the Shuberts to change their minds. Eventually after much discussion the Shuberts agreed to close the Casino Theatre for one night, at a cost of $4,000 before expenses, and give a special gala performance at his ball in his Newport home.[19] Since the Vanderbilts were 'the royal family' of America, this was a shrewd move, and the large fee more than compensated for one night's loss of earnings.

The cast were transferred by car from New York to Newport, travelling through the night, and arrived at the Vanderbilt home in the afternoon with their stage dresses over their arms covered in sheets. As the motley crew approached the front door, the butler dispatched another servant to intercept them and usher them to the servants' entrance. 'We felt more than outraged at this insult,' Jose said, and, ignoring the servant, marched up to the front door, announcing indignantly: 'I may be an actress, but I am not going to enter this house by the servants' entrance.' She was followed by everyone else, including the Dollies, as she swept past the flabbergasted butler into the magnificent hall, demanding to know where they were to dress. 'In those days, of course, stage people were looked down upon,' Jose explained, but she continued to fume at their treatment. 'Never has my pride been so injured as it was that night, although everything was done to make us as comfortable as possible.'

The evening, described as an Arabian Nights party, was a lavish affair. Yet segregation was still enforced, and, after their performance, the players were not allowed to mingle with the guests but instead had their supper served to them on gold plates in their own separate marquee. The party continued until breakfast time the next morning, but they left at 5 a.m. to be back at the Casino Theatre for the evening show. The Vanderbilt interlude was immediately reported extensively in the press and was exceedingly good for business thereafter.

The Merry Countess company was a 'very united family', and they had a happy time together. Nearly every night after the show the players, headed by Jose and the Dollies, along with the cast of another English show, popped into a local café called the Kaiserhof with an excellent black jazz band, and they used to have fun getting up and giving impromptu turns.[20] One Sunday afternoon in October 1912 the entire cast and other specially invited guests descended on the Dolly household at Bensonhurst for the sisters' twentieth birthday party.[21] But, although the celebrations must have been wonderful, change was in the air, and the Dollies were set to move into another clearly defined stage of their lives.

4

SEPARATION AND MARRIAGE

After a four-month run in New York, *The Merry Countess* toured for five months, ending in March 1913. It was during the tour that something rather momentous happened between the sisters. A decision was made that the time had come for them to perform separately. Exactly who made this decision and why is unclear. Lee Shubert is sometimes given responsibility, while the sisters themselves also claimed it was their idea. Rosie said: 'If we were ever to have distinct individualities, it was necessary for us to work separately . . . and while it was hard to bring ourselves to do it, it was necessary. From an artistic standpoint, our decision was wise.'[1]

As a result, Jenny returned to New York on her own to get ready for the launch of her first solo appearance in a new Shubert musical, *The Honeymoon Express*, in advance of Rosie's return and her debut in *The Beggar Student*. The separation was traumatic, and Rosie said: 'For the first two weeks after my sister left me in Boston with *The Merry Countess* I could neither sleep nor eat. I shall always remember that stay in Boston as a horrible nightmare.'[2] Jenny must have felt the same way.

There are several possible explanations for their separation. The most obvious, and the one they themselves proposed, was professional necessity. They had reached the age of 20 and had become well-known performers, but they needed to improve, diversify and maximise their individual potential. Although they both loved dancing, the two sisters had different aspirations. Rosie explained: 'Some day I hope to stop dancing and become just a nice plain actress. Once I played the part of a little French milliner and the stage manager said if I had been in a shop I could have sold him a hat at any old price. Sis wants to stop dancing too and become a prima or a secondary donna.'[3] Lee Shubert clearly agreed with their aims and gave them the break they needed.

Alongside these professional aspirations, lay other, more personal motives that only became obvious after their separation as an act. Like so many identical twins, they had developed a competitiveness that manifested itself in their relationships with the opposite sex. At the time they were discussing their future with Lee Shubert, Rosie was involved with the songwriter Jean Schwartz, and Jenny with the dapper comedian and singer Harry Fox. The men had been friends since Jean Schwartz had written songs for Harry Fox,[4] and so a double love affair had begun. Within less than two years the two couples would be married. They may have believed that the Dolly Sisters as an act would have to end once they were married, and so it was sensible to diverge and follow their individual dreams.

Jenny's solo debut was in the star-studded cast of *The Honeymoon Express*, along with her friend Fanny Brice and Harry Fox. Harry Fox (1882–1959) was born Arthur Carringford in Pomona, California. A music publisher liked his voice and hired him to sing songs from the boxes of vaudeville theatres in San Francisco. After the 1906 earthquake, he settled in New York, appearing in vaudeville before being taken into the Shubert fold, and was described as 'a genuine relief from the stereotyped book-form light comedian'.[5]

The Honeymoon Express was launched on 6 February 1913 and had some catchy, bright music by Jean Schwartz.[6] Al Jolson, a singer who had the remarkable ability to seduce and enthral an audience, was one of the stars of the show. He shared top billing with the incomparable French performer Gaby Deslys. The darling of London and Paris, she had made her Broadway debut in the Shuberts' *The Revue of Revues* (1911), followed by *Vera Violetta* (1911). Deslys was partnered by Harry Pilcer. He and Deslys formed a famous dancing partnership, and his innovative and uniquely American style took her and later Europe by storm.[7] A spectacular farce, with a minor plot revolving around a butler (Jolson) whose master must postpone a divorce in order to receive an inheritance, *The Honeymoon Express* was a smash hit, taking over $30,000 during the first week, and was notable for an amazing feat of staging that gave the show its name. As the house was darkened, the audience witnessed the race between a car and an express train, lights blazing, winding in and out of the mountainside, through devious turns of the road and down through valleys and tunnels, until finally, with incredible light and sound effects, they both appeared to burst into the footlights.[8]

The production did not run smoothly, because of Jolson's animosity towards his co-star. Allegedly this was because of her top billing and higher salary,[9] and the ill-feeling was very unsettling for Deslys and the rest of the cast. It was exacerbated by Sime Silverman, editor of the trade newspaper *Variety*. Sime (as he was known) had a passion for vaudeville and launched *Variety* in December 1905. He had a compulsion to speak the truth as he saw it and believed his comments were frank rather than offensive. Not surprisingly, he made serious enemies along the way. Even so, *Variety* became the number one theatrical paper and exerted a powerful influence on American show business. As Sophie Tucker observed, 'If *Variety* liked you, boosted you, you couldn't miss getting to the top.'[10] But if *Variety* did not like you, it was bad.

Variety did not like Gaby. Sime first of all attacked her for the $50,000 worth of costumes she had bought with her from Paris, implying that her performance had more to do with glamour than talent. He thought that, in comparison, Jenny Dolly 'looked really sweet' in her two gowns designed by

Melville Ellis 'and showed up the overdressed Gaby, who came after'. Finally, after a performance cast entirely from the understudies, Sime decided that Jenny in Gaby's role was better and observed slyly: 'to state she was good would be putting it mildly . . . should Miss Deslys ever, through illness or other causes, miss a performance, there is a treat in store.'[11]

When Rosie finished the tour of *The Merry Countess* in the early spring of 1913, she returned to New York and appeared in a revival of an old favourite. *The Beggar Student* was a three-act opera produced by the Gilbert and Sullivan Company at the Casino at the end of March 1913 for a short run. Rosie's performance, with Émile August (formerly ballet master at the Alhambra Theatre in London) as her dancing partner, was regarded as 'a decided hit', and, even though their style did not particularly fit into the scheme of an opera, it was enjoyed.[12]

But far more important than Rosie's solo debut was her marriage. Just a year after saying 'pouf to love affairs', Rosie eloped and tied the knot with Jean Schwartz. At 33, Schwartz was fourteen years older than Rosie. He too was originally from Budapest and had been married to Alice Davies in 1903 but divorced in 1908. He and Rosie had first met at a theatrical party when Schwartz was writing all the songs for Al Jolson. 'Jean played for us and I lost my heart,' Rosie recalled. 'I did not see Jean for some time but I was secretly in love with him.' This may have been during the run of the *Ziegfeld Follies of 1911*, for which he had written some of the music.[13] Rose said that at first they used to be just pals. She admired his music and he admired her dancing. 'We used to talk over our ambitions. He thought I could help him in his work. And I knew he could help me in mine, for he had been writing beautiful music for my dances. It was rather sudden when we decided to marry. We spoke of it one morning and that afternoon . . . we were married.'[14]

There was great surprise when Jean whisked Rosie off by car to Greenwich, Connecticut, to be married on 10 April 1913. The only guests for the ceremony and breakfast at Wolf's Inn, Larchmont, were Harry Fox and Jenny. Amusingly, the wedding provided another wonderful case of mistaken identity.

After the ceremony, while the bride was putting on her coat and the magistrate had received his fee, he turned to Jenny to present her with the certificate and asked her for the customary bridal kiss. Later, when they had finished the bridal breakfast, some people who were also at the inn and had learned that it was a bridal party threw handfuls of rice at Jenny and Harry, thinking they were the happy couple, while the real bride and groom walked out behind them chuckling with glee.[15]

After the secret ceremony, which Harry Fox explained, rather enigmatically, was imperative because it had to do with 'a large amount of money', Rosie returned to her dressing room that afternoon for her matinée performance in *The Beggar Student*. 'Calmly the 21 year old bride of a few hours entered her dressing room. Casually she greeted her waiting mother. Nonchalantly she explained her absence as a trivial thing. Slowly she took off her hat and rice fell all over the floor. The secret was out.'[16] To say Margarethe was disappointed was an understatement. 'She had wonderful ambitions. She used to say 'a millionaire at least my Roszika; a millionaire at least', and Rosie would reply, 'I am willing . . . but there aren't many of them. Astors and Vanderbilts are scarce and don't grow on bushes.'[17] Later that evening, after his new bride's performance, Schwartz entertained a party of theatrical friends and family at his apartment.[18]

Jean Schwartz (1878–1956) was born on 4 November 1878. His sister had been a pupil of the composer Franz Liszt, and she taught Jean to play the piano when he was young. When he was 13, his family emigrated to New York, where they lived in the Lower East side in poverty. Jean did all sorts of jobs, mostly musical. One job was as a sheet-music demonstrator in a department store, another was as a staff pianist and song plugger for a Tin Pan Alley music publisher. In 1899, at the age of 21, he published his first song 'Dusky Dudes' and in 1901 met the well-known lyricist William Jerome. This started a fruitful songwriting partnership, and for twelve years they wrote many hit songs, including 'Rock-a-Bye your Baby with a Dixie Melody'. Their first complete score for Broadway was the musical comedy show *Piff, Paff, Pouf* (1904). As a team they became a natural act for vaudeville, where they were headliners for many years. In 1913 the team of Schwartz and Jerome came to an end, and Jean branched out on his own with other lyricists.

Blissfully happy, Rosie moved into Jean's apartment, and when in New York, Jenny frequently stayed with her sister instead of driving home to Bensonhurst.[19] The fact that she was also enjoying a love affair with Harry Fox may have influenced her decision to stay in the city.

After the short run of *The Beggar Student* Rosie joined forces with Martin Brown once more in a headlining act at Hammerstein's Victoria Theatre, the premier New York vaudeville institution. Their new and original musical comedy, offering clever songs, wonderful dances and fine gowns, was clearly designed to capitalise on their success at the Casino in *The Merry Countess*. Rosie received a massive salary of $2,000 per week for a limited season of two weeks from 12 May 1913.[20] For the new portion, Martin Brown sang and introduced three different styles of dance – the minuet, waltz and Spanish tango – which he danced with Rosie. Martin Brown was regarded by one critic as 'without doubt one of the most graceful male ballroom dancers that has ever graced the vaudeville boards', and Rosie's dances were described as 'the acme of perfection'. Another critic thought that their act eclipsed all past performances of dancers in their particular line.[21]

However, Sime of *Variety* was a little sharp about the new act. He made it plain that he did not think Rosie's performance duplicated her success in *The Merry Countess* and thought the setting was cheap and did not impress. He was equally unflattering about Rosie's gowns.

Meanwhile, all was not well in the cast of *The Honeymoon Express*. Harry Fox and Jenny Dolly had their feathers ruffled by the arrival of Ina Claire, the chic singer, dancer and clever mimic, who probably stole their limelight. They promptly left the show in early June 1913,[22] and, since they had been immensely popular, it was no surprise that they were immediately signed for the Keith Circuit to headline in a hefty twenty-four-week vaudeville tour.

They made their debut at Shea's Theatre, in Buffalo, where they were a decided success,[23] and then made their way to the Brooklyn riviera and played three weeks at the summer venues of Henderson's, Rockaway Beach and the Brighton Music Hall, before heading south at the end of July to the Savoy Theatre in Atlantic City.

Unlike Sime's unpleasant comments about Rosie's vaudeville turn, he found something good to say about Jenny and Harry Fox. 'If there is a better two-act in vaudeville it hasn't made its appearance hereabouts up to date.'[24]

It was soon time for the annual warm-weather summer revue, and, on 16 June, Rosie and Martin Brown stepped out of vaudeville and into the *Ziegfeld Follies of 1913*, the first Follies to appear in the sumptuous and exquisite New Amsterdam Theatre, where the Follies would remain for the next fifteen years.

Rosie felt completely at home with old friends Leon Errol, Jose Collins and Elizabeth Brice. The cast also included the new rave – the dimple-kneed dancer Ann Pennington – who became another friend of the Dollies. At a mere 4 feet 11½ inches tall in high heels, she was nicknamed Tiny, and would subsequently enliven seven editions of the Follies and become one of Ziegfeld's biggest dancing sensations.[25]

For some it was not one of the better Follies, but, because of Ziegfeld's usual taste and imagination, it far outstripped the other revues on offer that season.[26] One of the most popular dance numbers was called Turkish Trottishness, an entertaining spoof of the current craze for the Turkey Trot, a face-to-face dance that necessitated the flapping of the arms; hence its name. Martin Brown and Rosie, however, took the audience by storm with a range of other dances and scored a big hit as they imitated famous ballet dancers in the Palais d'Danse scene,[27] although Sime again proved difficult to please.[28]

While Rosie appeared in the *Ziegfeld Follies*, Jenny and Harry Fox were deep into their extensive vaudeville tour, and one interview at the time claimed that this enforced separation created considerable emotional distress between the twins. From the moment Rosie said goodbye to Jenny at Grand Central

Station, until they were reunited, neither knew a moment's peace or happiness. They both felt the separation to be a horrible nightmare, even worse than the one they had had to endure at the beginning of the year. They spent half the day on long-distance telephone calls, and the rest of the day in weeping and grieving. Both suffered ill-health, both lost weight, and after eight weeks both decided that life without the other was unbearable. Harry Fox explained the rather dire situation to the organisers of his tour and was able to terminate their engagement and return to New York. When they were finally reunited after more than nine weeks, Rosie and Jenny vowed never to be separated again for such a long period of time.[29] Thereafter, Jenny and Harry headlined in local vaudeville and made appearances at the exclusive '400 affairs', the social events given by the top 400 names in American 'society'. Offers of work outside New York were politely declined, even when an international vaudeville agent offered them a season in London, St Petersburg and Paris.[30]

With this new regime, Rosie decided not to become part of the traditional regional tour of the *Ziegfeld Follies* and instead also stayed in New York, joining the cast of the Shuberts' operetta *Lieber Augustin* staged in September 1913 at the Casino. It received a lukewarm reception: the public thought that, since the play had a German title, it would be in German, and as a result it played for only a poor five weeks in New York. The star De Wolf Hopper persuaded the Shuberts to retitle it *Miss Caprice* to correct this misunderstanding, and it was restaged at the Studebaker Theatre in Chicago in November. Despite their earlier outburst about how difficult their separation had been and the assertion that they would never endure anything remotely similar again, Rosie went with the show to Chicago. Almost as an excuse, it was made clear that, 'wherever they were, the invisible bond that links these two identities together, like Siamese twins was never broken'.[31]

One particular night Rosie became very agitated.

I was so lonesome that I thought I couldn't stand it without calling to Jenny and hearing her voice in answer, though there was nothing particular we had to communicate. So while I was thinking how much of a telephone talk I could afford at a dollar a minute, a messenger ran up saying 'Miss Dolly, you're wanted on the long-distance'. It was Jenny in New York, feeling exactly as I felt, at the same moment.[32]

Rosie's unease was swiftly terminated. Even the repackaged version of *Miss Caprice* could not do business, and the show was closed after a short run, enabling Rosie to return to New York and spend Christmas at home in Bensonhurst with her husband Jean, Jenny, Harry and her parents.[33] Rosie was then cast in a new Shubert extravaganza at the Winter Garden Theatre back in New York.

The Whirl of the World was a lively, elaborate musical revue launched on 10 January 1914 with the added glamour of the Ziegfeld star Lillian Lorraine and the Russian dancer Lydia Kyasht. Running for a respectable twenty weeks, the show was noticeable for Martin Brown's absence as Rosie's partner. He had, in fact, been lured to Europe, where he spent almost a year in London and Paris and appeared in the second edition of Albert de Courville's *Hello Tango* at the London Hippodrome.[34] Rosie's new partner was Lester Sheehan, who may have been a promising chorus boy in the Shubert stable. It was his only major Broadway billing, and he later resurfaced as the character 'Lester Queen' in Mae West's controversial homosexual comedy drama *The Pleasure Man* (1928).

The plot of *The Whirl of the World*, which centred on a marquis who places a bet that he can win thirty girls in thirty days, getting each of them to sign her name in his little red book as proof, enabled introductions to a wide range of female talent. The show was advertised as the 'dernier cri in dance craze' and dancing was clearly the strong point, with every style from ballet to the Turkey Trot featured, with appropriate music by the new composer Sigmund Romberg.[35] Sime was clearly having a good day with the Shuberts when he wrote his review, because, although he had some criticism, he liked the staging: 'It was expensive . . . extravagant, in people, production and dressing . . . the Winter Garden is going to do business with this show.' Another critic thought that the show was the best the Winter Garden had staged, primarily because of the dancing, and greatly admired Rosie, saying 'everything she does is delicious'.[36]

Melville Ellis's costumes caused a stir and on the whole were extravagant in concept, except for Rosie's ensembles, which were admired by *Variety* as 'a contrast to all the gloss'. However, there were no kind remarks from Sime, who thought she looked weak in contrast to the classiness of Lydia Kyasht, and he complained bitterly: 'They let Miss Dolly sing. And she can't sing.'[37]

Jenny, meanwhile, was appearing with Harry Fox in a new vaudeville tour around New York. Their debut was at the Palace Theatre on 23 March 1914 for the theatre's first anniversary bill,[38] followed by the Colonial, Hammerstein's and the Alhambra in April and May. At the Palace they shared the top spot with the dancing of the glamorous but diminutive Mae Murray and the versatile singer, dancer and actor Clifton Webb.

Adding to their individual nightly performances in vaudeville, the Dollies were reunited for a few weeks at the Jardin de Danse, a hugely successful late-night cabaret, in the roof of the New York Theatre at Broadway and 45th Street. The roof garden had become a hit the previous summer when it became a dance cabaret with full restaurant service. Downstairs, the theatre had been converted into a movie house, and, as an added attraction, the management decided to try vaudeville acts between the film shows. This was a strategy that would eventually find full expression in the mid-1920s with the combined film show and revue presentation policy across the country.

Harry Fox and a company of 'American Beauties' were selected to put on a dancing act to meet the current huge interest in ballroom dancing, and it became a big success. But even more successful was the dance that Harry developed that was to bear his name – he was doing trotting steps to ragtime music that was referred to as 'Fox's trot', and as the 'Foxtrot' it became one of the most original and exciting of the newly invented dances. The elite of the dancing world soon tried to capture the unusual style of movement, and it became one of the most significant developments in ballroom dancing.[39]

By September 1914 all the dance instructors in New York were advertising Foxtrot lessons, including Vernon and Irene Castle, who believed that they had invented it.

At the same time as Harry was Foxtrotting downstairs, the Dolly Sisters, together again on the stage after a separation of over a year, opened on 9 May 1914 and created 'the greatest sensation Broadway has known in many seasons'.[40] The Dollies' reappearance came at the end of the day at a time when Jenny was rehearsing for the new Winter Garden production in the mornings and was then doing two shows a day in vaudeville with Harry Fox. Rosie was also appearing in *The Whirl of the World*. Their cabaret appearance was therefore an addition to their usual daily routine and was not viewed as a permanent arrangement.

The New York Theatre Roof Garden had been a Ziegfeld establishment and previously the home of the *Ziegfeld Follies* from 1907 to 1912, and the Dolly Sisters had been there in the 1911 edition. The opening of the Jardin de Danse was not an isolated development but part of a scramble to capitalise on the still burgeoning desire for new night-time frolics with an emphasis on dancing. At the end of 1913 the Castles had opened a small club in a basement on 42nd Street called Sans Souci, which was designed after Parisian models and was the first cabaret not associated with a pre-existing lobster palace. After a year they moved to the roof of the 44th Street Theatre, where they inaugurated the highly successful Castles in the Air. Ziegfeld opened the Danse de Follies on 1 June 1914 in the roof of the Amsterdam Theatre so that visitors to the Follies downstairs could follow their evening theatrical excursion with drinking and dancing. Quickly following suit, the Shuberts remodelled their cabaret venue Palais de Danse in the Winter Garden Theatre, turning it into Chez Maurice with the star attractions of Maurice and Florence Walton.

The nightly debut of the Dolly Sisters was 'a sensational ensemble of costume novelty dances' with Carlos Sebastian, one of the most successful ballroom dancers of the time. Their première was a veritable triumph: 'So brilliantly beautiful and daintily diaphanous is the costuming of these fascinating young feminines that they have been christened the Heavenly Twins.'[41] Prominent society folk and theatrical celebrities crowded the rectangle of private boxes about the dance floor with the stage actress Ethel Barrymore, sister to actors Lionel and John, friends Gaby Deslys, Nora Bayes and Diamond Jim Brady, the ballroom dancer Gertrude Vanderbilt and the silent-screen actresses Mary Pickford and Blanche Sweet among the glitterati of notables.[42]

According to *Variety*, all the dances were new and caused quite a stir. The introduction was a fantastic dream, with just the Dollies wearing modernised Grecian gowns of golden yellow, 'a fluttering affair in gauzy material', which enabled them to give bewildering high kicks. For the Papalatsa, an exotic fantasy and sort of Spanish Maxixe, Jenny danced with Carlos, who looked just like a Castillian. Carlos next made his entrance carrying Rosie, who wore a fringed shawl dress, and they danced the Havana Rumba, a thing of gymnastic whirls, which was a tropical triumph. The Arhumba was a mix of Hungarian and Mexican movement, with Carlos Sebastian dressed as a Mexican. But the *pièce de résistance* was the High School Gallop, described as 'a transcendence of terpsichore', which eclipsed anything of the kind ever attempted. *Variety* thought it was 'the best thing as a novelty dance that has been shown in a very long time', and it was later named the pony trot. Sebastian in a coach hat, evening and driving dress carried a whip and drove the two Dollies with quaint black masks and odd animal ears as ponies around the floor making them leap over four low hurdles, which brought 'the most sincere applause New York has yet heard'.[43]

The Pony Trot was an extension of the pony ballet devised by John Tiller in about 1910: the girls were grouped in two sets of four dressed as ponies and imitating the animals' movements. The tallest girls were chosen as drivers and simply trotted behind, reining in the other ponies.[44] Apparently the Pony Trot as a dance had been originated on the New York roof in April by the team of Le Roy and Mons, who got very upset when their successors Seabury and Shaw copied them.[45] The Dollies and Sebastian obviously pinched the idea but turned it into an even more appealing novelty dance by having two twin ponies and a trainer. It became one of the Dolly Sisters' trademarks during the 1920s in Europe, but was equally adapted by many others.[46]

For the run at the Jardin de Danse, the Dollies were being paid $600 a week and Carlos Sebastian $400. It is, therefore, no surprise that after a few weeks they moved the entire act to Hammerstein's Victoria on vastly increased salaries of $1,500 each per week from 22 May 1914. It was certainly this production that established the Dolly Sisters' style and routine, which were to become such important facets of their performance in later years – exotic and impeccable dances brought to life with innovative and glamorous dressing.

During the Dollies' run at Hammerstein's it was announced that Harry Fox had been granted a divorce from his first wife, Lydia, who alleged adultery with another woman, presumably Jenny.[47] When he was asked by the Divorce Court judge if he would pay his ex-wife $25 per week maintenance, he replied: 'With much pleasure.' On leaving the court, he told reporters: 'I like the way they do business here. I'm always coming here for my divorces in future.'[48]

The divorce allowed Jenny and Harry to plan their wedding,[49] although it was nearly three months before they were married on 28 August 1914, shortly after Britain had declared war on Germany, plunging Europe into turmoil. The delay was partly due to the fact the Harry had to undergo surgery on his throat followed by a period of recuperation with Jenny at the Long Island resort of Long Beach, which was one of his favourite summer haunts.[50]

The marriage took place in Greenwich, Connecticut, starting with a wedding breakfast at the Hotel Claridge. Afterwards a big limousine loaned by Diamond Jim Brady took the party for the ceremony shortly after noon. It was a small family affair, with Jenny's parents, Jean Schwartz, Rosie and their brother Eddie.[51] Margarethe, Jenny's mother, was apparently heartbroken by the marriage. First Rosie and now Jenny. She thought they were both too young to marry and that their marriages would mean the end of their careers.[52] She must have been relieved when her initial anxiety proved to be misplaced. The Dollies were also pleased that they did not conform to type, since they always believed that, once they had become famous, they would marry millionaires, 'like all successful actresses are supposed to do eventually and retire from the stage – live happy ever afterward – like real society ladies'. Despite the numerous opportunities to follow their initial objective, they in fact both married for love and certainly not for money, something that they claimed made them proud. Of course, as the years rolled by, things changed, and millionaires became a rather more important requirement.[53]

Shortly after Jenny's marriage, the two couples moved into adjoining apartments on Riverside Drive, Central Park West. This scenic north–south boulevard, which generally runs parallel to the Hudson River, was, and still is, one of the most coveted addresses in Manhattan. Everyone was interested in how their husbands managed to identify the right wife. Apparently every precaution was taken against any mix-up – Jenny's room was pink and Rosie's blue (back to the ribbons tied on their legs when they were little girls), and they made a point of dressing differently so that Harry would never mistake Rosie for Jenny and Jean would always be able to identify Rosie, no matter how early in the morning he returned home.[54] Jean Schwartz said that, in order to identify his wife, he made Rosie eat an onion every morning, and Jenny wore an antique ring given to her by Harry. Jean was also believed to possess a sixth sense by which he could always tell the sisters apart.[55]

Whatever the means of identification, sometimes one of the husbands got it wrong. The sisters were taking an afternoon siesta on a big divan one day when Jean tiptoed toward the slumbering twins, intent on giving his wife a soft kiss goodbye. He looked at both of them and was a bit perplexed, but decided he knew which was which and leaned over Jenny by mistake. But just as he was to plant his kiss on her cheek, she put her hand up to ward him off, laughing: 'Here cease! Kiss your own wife!'[56]

With the marriage of Harry Fox and Jenny, the press described the sister act as at an end, just as their mother had feared. Rosie would be appearing in vaudeville with Martin Brown for a few weeks before joining a new Broadway production and Harry and Jenny announced that they would also return to vaudeville before appearing in a new Shubert show at the Winter Garden.[57]

Harry and Jenny began their new tour at the Palace Theatre in early September 1914.[58] On the same bill was the young Laddie Cliff, advertised as 'the little English boy comic', who in six years' time was to partner the Dolly Sisters in their London debut. By mid-October Rosie was once again teamed with Martin Brown in a new twenty-eight-minute act entitled *Danceland*, which was launched at the Palace Theatre and was regarded as 'the finest dancing entertainment ever shown' and 'one of the classiest dancing acts in vaudeville'.[59]

When the purple velvet hangings were drawn aside, Rosie and Martin were seated in an alcove draped in a flowered cretonne fabric and James Moore as a Pierrot announced each dancing number with his singing. Martin and Rosie presented several old-fashioned dances before embarking on classical waltzes and then more up-to-date creations, including the Galop Brazilian. Clearly money had been no object: there was a superb setting (they had clearly noted Sime's criticisms of their act at Hammerstein's Victoria in May 1913), and Rosie had splashed out on an impressive wardrobe of gowns from the famous New York couturiers Frances and Hayden. One dress was a hoop skirt with lace pantalettes, there was a pink charmeuse caught up at the hips showing an elaborate lace petticoat and for the tango dance she wore a cloak of solid sequins, beneath which was a shawl dress with the usual fringe and purple boots.[60] *Variety* decided that Rosie was now 'talented to a degree', that she made 'a stunning appearance'[61] and that both would henceforth gain a reputation for staging a class act.[62]

Rosie and Martin Brown were finally in favour[63] and scored another hit in their next show, George M. Cohan and Sam H. Harris's *Hello Broadway*, which opened on Christmas Day 1914 at the Astor Theatre. Described by *Variety* as 'a regular musical hit',[64] it was, in fact, an innovative revue, since it dispensed with the opulence of the Ziegfeld and Shubert productions, returning to the simpler tradition of burlesque made famous by Fields and Weber.[65]

Cohan was the star, writer, director, producer and composer, and had, in fact, changed the look of the revue by liberating it from any pretence of plot. The result was a crazy patchwork of scenes threaded together with words and music that satirised American institutions, particularly the stage. Rosie wore some sumptuous costumes designed by Cora MacGeachey, and her dancing numbers with Martin Brown were described as 'one of the remarkable features of the show. . . . they have conceived some breakneck whirlwind dances that are graceful as well as artistic and unusual.'[66]

The success of Rosie and Martin Brown's *Danceland* vaudeville act and their performance in *Hello Broadway* must have been the catalyst that convinced the Universal Film Company to film them dancing in its studio in New York or New Jersey. It was regarded as a novelty for their weekly magazine series, which showed serials and topical film reviews. And so, on 23 February 1915, *Dance Creations* was released, screening five of their vivid dance interpretations: a Chinese fantasy called 'Chopsticks', a Spanish dance called 'Habanera Hesitation', a polka set to a Southern antebellum theme in crinoline, the clown trot with novelty Pierrot costumes and a classic waltz.[67]

After a few months in the cast of *Hello Broadway* Martin Brown was suddenly forced to retire with a serious heart problem and was replaced by Harry Delf, another talented dancer.

Jenny became one of the featured artists in the new Winter Garden production *Maid in America*, launched on 18 February 1915 by the Shuberts with a string of other vaudeville stars including the comedian Joe Jackson, Charles J. Ross, friends Nora Bayes and Dazie and, of course, her husband Harry Fox. The show played up to the growing strength of feeling about the European war.[68] Harry Fox and Jenny Dolly did their vaudeville turn, and Jenny with Lew Brice, the brother of Fanny Brice, gave a wonderful impersonation of Vernon and Irene Castle.

Variety thought that 'Jenny Dolly never looked better'. One of her dancing frocks by Harry Collins was made entirely of feathers, shading from the palest to the darkest blue, with a dazzling headdress of diamonds and bird-of-paradise feathers.[69] Thinking of the future, Harry Fox and Jenny planned a new act with Nora Bayes, and the proposal with a fee of $3,000 a week was considered by vaudeville managers in March 1915, but the idea was not taken up.[70]

Through Jenny's influence, brother Eddie joined the cast of *Maid in America* in April 1915 as a bartender and dancer. Not yet 18, Eddie aspired to be a comedian, but like his sisters he found it difficult to break out of the dancing mould.[71] After a falling-out with new cast member, Ina Gould, Harry and Jenny decided to leave *Maid in America* just before it departed on tour. Immediately, Harry had an offer to appear in Ziegfeld's new edition of the *Midnight Frolic*, and there were also offers of more vaudeville engagements.[72]

As Harry considered his options, Jenny opted to star in her first movie, *The Call of the Dance* – one of the Kalem Company's four-act Broadway Favourites Features, filmed in July and August 1915 in New York. Directed by George Sargent, it was the story of the love affair between a dancer and a cop with menacing themes of underworld entanglement, white slave trade and murder. Jenny played an East side girl whose inborn talent for dancing raised her out of the slums onto the stage. When the film was released on 20 September, *Variety* was not impressed: 'Of all the cheap, sordid, conventional and sanguinary melodramas ever filmed, this one is entitled to first position.' But it did have praise for Jenny and her dancing as 'the only thing worth while'.[73] Sadly no print survives today.

Jenny enjoyed her experience as a movie star and expressed interest in continuing a film career. She said she had been made various offers,[74] but vaudeville and not films or the *Midnight Frolic* intervened, and by the late summer of 1915 the popular headlining act of Fox and Dolly was back on the road in and around New York. The new act differed little from what had been presented before, but much attention was paid to Jenny's attire. *Variety* exclaimed that she was 'one woman on the stage who is not stingy with her clothes. Every time she joins a production . . . she never fails to display a new and nifty wardrobe.' During this time Harry Fox was secured as one of the leads for Charles Dillingham's production of *Stop! Look! Listen!*, launched at Christmas 1915 with a glittering cast and music by Irving Berlin. In the lead, Gaby Deslys was partnered by Harry Pilcer, and in a minor part was Marion Davies; it was here that she was first noticed by the multimillionaire media king William Randolph Hearst before her appearance in the *Ziegfeld Follies*. Despite the marvellous staging, *Stop! Look! Listen!* had only a short run, closing in March 1916 before embarking on a regional tour.

Shortly after *Hello Broadway* closed, Rosie set off on a new adventure. In late June 1915, while Jenny was filming *The Call of the Dance* in New York, she took what was supposed to be a short trip to the West Coast. With Jean Schwartz, she went on what was described as a business trip for Jean and a holiday for Rosie as guests of Diamond Jim Brady. After a five-day journey in Diamond Jim's private railway car to Los Angeles,[75] Rosie, Jean and Diamond Jim checked in at the luxurious Alexandra Hotel at Fifth and Spring – 'all crystal chandeliers, marble columns, potted palms and oriental rugs' – and began to entertain lavishly. The Hollywood Hotel on Hollywood Boulevard at Highland, which had opened in 1903, had been the focal point of the embryonic movie colony until the opening of the Alexandra in 1906, which became the new meeting ground for movie professionals and a natural gathering spot for the emerging movie aristocracy. As Gloria Swanson noted, 'It was where the snobs dined and had their fancy parties.'[76]

Diamond Jim renewed his friendship with one of the greatest screen legends of the time, Charlie Chaplin, and immediately gave one of those fancy parties at the hotel to introduce Rosie and her husband to the Hollywood elite. The guest list included Chaplin, the actress Carlotta Monterey, the film star Lou Tellegen (Sarah Bernhardt's leading man), the silver-screen darlings Blanche Sweet and Mabel Normand,[77] the producer Mack Sennett, regarded as the father of American slapstick comedy, who was having an affair with Mabel Normand, and Nat Goodwin, nicknamed 'Marrying Nat' because he had been married eight times. Nat was considered one of the greatest light comedians of the stage and a great friend of Chaplin. He was equally well known as the owner of the Pier Café at the end of Hollister Avenue, billed as a high-class cabaret with a sun parlour, roof garden and ballroom.[78]

Many have been under the illusion that both Dollies and husbands were in Hollywood at the same time, when in fact it was only Rosie and Jean Schwartz. Charlie Chaplin claimed that he met both sisters in Hollywood and thought that they 'were sensationally beautiful', which must refer to seeing them together in New York, not in Hollywood.[79]

Following Diamond Jim's party, the three companions attended the opening performance at the beginning of July of Oliver Morosco's *So Long Letty*, starring the beautiful dancer Charlotte Greenwood, at the Morosco Theatre; it later transferred to New York.[80] They then made a trip with prominent Hollywood screen artists to San Francisco for a Grand Ball at the Municipal Auditorium in the Civic Centre.[81] Suddenly Rosie decided to cut the trip short and return to New York, but a couple of business propositions brought about a change in plan. Rosie signed a film contract with the newly formed Triangle Film Corporation to appear in the feature *The Lily and the Rose*, while Jean Schwartz considered writing a score for the next Oliver Morosco production.[82]

It became evident that Rosie would be staying in Hollywood. Given the trauma the two sisters claimed to have faced at being separated before, it is interesting that Rosie decided to stay in Hollywood for more than three months, despite having vowed categorically that a long separation would never happen again. From the perspective of the ever-dependable Jenny, it would have been the second time that she had been deserted by the more impulsive Rosie.

It was equally strange that both sisters made their feature-film debut at about the same time. This 'coincidence' probably highlights a degree of competitiveness between the sisters. As Jenny secured her film contract, Rosie accepted a Hollywood film deal so as not to be outdone by her sister. A more cynical view might also suggest that Rosie was rebelling against Jenny's desire for them to stay together and that Rosie was in fact indifferent to any periods of separation. Whatever the true interpretation, Rosie clearly continued to have a ball in tinsel town without Jenny.

Hollywood in 1915 was not like Hollywood today. The Cahuenga valley from which Hollywood emerged was a frostless belt covered with orange and lemon groves. The few streets that had been created were lined with beautiful trees and few were paved simply because there were hardly any cars. It was completely undeveloped. The two-hour drive from Hollywood to Santa Barbara, for example, was one long unspoilt stretch. This Garden of Eden had only recently been found by the movie industry, with visitors filming there from 1907. The first studio was opened by the Nestor company in 1911; other pioneering companies such as Selig, Biograph and Vitagraph promptly followed suit.

The location was favoured for four main reasons: the climate was ideal, with a sunshine quota of over 350 days a year; there was an exceptional range of natural settings; labour costs were half of those of New York; and Hollywood offered an escape from the monopolistic control of movie production and distribution in New York. By 1915 several companies had established permanent studios in Hollywood. These included Universal on the north side of the Hollywood Hills run by Carl Laemmle; Mutual-Triangle at Sunset and Hollywood Boulevards used by D.W. Griffith (often called the father of motion pictures and Hollywood itself), where he filmed his best-known early features *The Squaw Man* (1914), *The Birth of a Nation* (1915) and *Intolerance* (1916); the Jesse L. Lasky Feature Play Company at Selma and Vine; and Mack Sennett Comedies in Edendale.

In July 1915 a new conglomerate headed by Henry Aitken, who wanted to lay the foundation for a new movie empire, formed the ill-fated Triangle Corporation with D.W. Griffith, Thomas Ince and Mack Sennett and built a new studio at Culver City, later to be occupied by MGM. Aitken had been involved in various aspects of movie production, created the Mutual Film Company in 1912 for the distribution of independent films and worked with D.W. Griffith. It was agreed that Griffith and Ince would supply the dramatic pictures and Sennett the comedies. To build a stock company of bright new talent to augment existing stars that joined the fold, Aitken went on a secret spending spree through Broadway during the season of 1914–15 and engaged a host of stars, who were brought to Triangle for the summer season with huge salaries,[83] including Constance Collier, the British actress who became one of Hollywood's most famous acting coaches; Billie Burke, the red-haired beauty and toast of the London stage and Broadway who had just married Florenz Ziegfeld; Sir Herbert Beerbohm Tree, the most famous British actor-manager of his time; and Douglas Fairbanks, the young, dashing, Broadway favourite who became the screen's most famous swashbuckling hero, and who later married Mary Pickford.

When Rosie arrived on Aitken's doorstep, she was the perfect choice to play a dancer opposite Lillian Gish in her new movie. Lillian was the protégée of D.W. Griffith and the star of his greatest early works, including *Birth of a Nation*; she was also sister to the equally famous Dorothy. Rosie was signed to a contract earning a salary of $750 per week for one picture. In a discussion about movie salaries, *Photoplay* decided that 'these are golden days for the performer with a reputation'. Average salaries of $1,000 per week were common for limited engagements of one or two picture deals, although the really big, established stars got more. For example, Charlie Chaplin and Mary Pickford earned $2,000 per week, but also got bonuses with yearly salaries in excess of $150,000. The biggest salary paid at Triangle was to Sir Herbert Beerbohm Tree at $3,000–$4,000 per week for *Macbeth*.[84]

The first crop of movies from Triangle released in 1915 included three with Douglas Fairbanks, two with Mabel Normand and Mack Sennett and two with Dorothy Gish. The first movie from D.W. Griffith was *The Lily and the Rose*, released on 6 December 1915 . Directed by Paul Powell, the film had a plot that followed the usual melodramatic nonsense of the time. To the dismay of her adoring neighbour, Mary (Lillian Gish), an unsophisticated country girl, falls in love and marries a handsome former football star, but he soon becomes infatuated by the charms of the vampire Rose (Rosie), an exotic dancer. It all ends in disaster.

During preproduction for the film, Lillian Gish and Rosie Dolly were sent by Griffith to study with Ruth St Denis, the film's choreographer. St Denis was a 37-year-old American actress and dance star whose name still had drawing power at the box office. She had opened a school for the dramatic arts in Los Angeles, known as the Denishawn School of Dance, in late 1914, just after she had married Ted Shawn, a virtually unknown 23-year-old ballroom dancer.[85]

She gave Lillian and Rosie tuition in the art of making expressive gestures and posing for the camera. This was based on 'Delsarte', which was a 'language' of theatrical gestures, facial expressions and posturing that had been popular in the 1890s. St Denis combined it with dance steps and dramatic poses taken from well-known artworks in order to 'act out' plays that were performed without the use of speech. St Denis was a valuable asset because her method was so appropriate for silent-film production. D.W. Griffith saw that St Denis's technique could be developed into an acting style for the silent screen that would overcome the lack of spoken dialogue and convey meaning through physical expression. His belief in this was so strong that he sent his entire stable of actresses to St Denis for training, as did others.

In addition to training Lillian and Rosie in 'Delsarte', St Denis was also responsible for creating the dances that both would perform in the film to represent their separate characters: Lillian, blond and fragile, was the pure element in the leading man's life, and Rosie, dark and sultry, the evil element. St Denis delegated the job of choreographing Lillian's dance to Shawn, who devised a demure minuet-like number that was cool and gentle. For Rosie she created a provocative and sensual oriental number, one that D.W. Griffith thought looked appropriate for Rosie's character as the wicked cabaret dancer. Despite this training, in later years it became 'Dolly policy' to declare that they never had dance lessons in their life and that they thought dancing was more effective if it was spontaneous and not taught by a master.[86]

Rosie confided in St Denis and Shawn that she 'might not be a great artist' but she knew from experience that she was a 'great business woman'. All summer she shook her head over their slapdash bookkeeping, their extravagance and the generous gestures that she could afford but they could not. On their wedding anniversary Rosie sent them a huge bouquet of flowers in a basket on which were perched a pair of stuffed pure white doves, which she explained was symbolic of wedded bliss and of their innocence in money and management matters.[87]

Rosie described her thoughts about acting in front of a camera: 'The difference between the speaking stage and the film drama as I see it is that in motion pictures you can't really act. You just have to be natural.'[88] She must have done rather well, because one reviewer praised her performance by saying that she was a 'really wonderful dancer and entertainer' and, 'discounting her apparent uneasiness before the camera, sprinkles enough pepper throughout the film to lift it from lassitude'.[89]

Throughout her stay in Hollywood, Rosie punctuated her work schedule with a string of social engagements. She spent a lot of time with her friend Mary Pickford, the most famous film star of the time. Rosie and Mary had in fact met in New York before Rosie's Hollywood trip. Mary had appeared in the David Belasco fairy tale *A Good Little Devil* staged at the Republic Theatre in January 1913 along with Lillian Gish. One of the other cast members had been Edward Dolly, the brother of the Dolly Sisters, probably in his first stage appearance at the tender age of 12.

Perhaps because of this association, or because Mary saw the Dollies dance in other productions at the time, she expressed an interest in meeting them socially, and they finally met one afternoon for tea in the Biltmore Hotel. They had a pleasant chat, and their acquaintance blossomed into a firm friendship.[90] Mary continued to be a great friend to both Dollies, particularly Rosie, with whom she kept in touch well into the 1940s. Rosie also became friends with other famous movie stars, including Norma and Constance Talmadge.

Rosie was one of the guests at a dinner-dance held in the Hotel Alexandria on Saturday 4 September in honour of the three new vice-presidents of Triangle[91] and shortly afterwards she played a scene from *The Lily and the Rose* with her co-star Lillian at a party at the Triangle Studios for a group of close movie friends, including Mabel Normand and Blanche Sweet.[92] There must have been excursions to favourite Hollywood night spots such as Nat Goodwin's Pier, the Ship café, which was built on a pier in Venice Beach, and Baron Long's Vernon Country Club, which had opened in 1912 with an integrated floor show, orchestra, dancing and chorus girls and was viewed as the birthplace of Hollywood nightlife.[93]

Sometime in September, Rosie and her husband took the train back east, and at Rochester they were met by Jenny and Harry Fox at the station. Rosie said to waiting newsmen that she did not particularly like film work and was eager to return to the stage, because 'applause is the stimulant I desire'.[94] This was a good sentiment, because, while Rosie had been enjoying the pleasures of Hollywood, Jenny had been busy negotiating new deals, and the Dolly Sisters were soon to become reunited and once again the toast of Broadway.

The Two Identical Rhinestones Reunited

After nearly three years of separation, the Dollies were reunited on the New York stage at the beginning of 1916. Initially they were engaged by Cohan and Harris to appear with Raymond Hitchcock (a comedian who had become well known in a variety of musicals) in a new revue, but Hitchcock decided to accept an offer in London and so instead they found themselves back with Florenz Ziegfeld.[1]

What precipitated this move and was it accidental or deliberate? Had their solo careers run their course? Their double act at the Jardin de Danse in 1914 had been a huge hit, and they must have realised that they were clearly more valuable as a double act. They had also repeatedly expressed their discomfort at being apart and had vowed not to be separated for long periods again.

On their return to New York in the autumn of 1915 they were made two offers that they simply could not refuse. First came a marvellous opportunity to join Ziegfeld's *Midnight Frolic* and then the offer of starring roles in Al Woods's production of *His Bridal Night*, a play that had been specially written for them. It just so happened that everything came together to ensure that they became the Dolly Sisters again.

It was only at the end of 1914, by which time the ragtime dance craze had made cabaret profitable, that owners realised the earning potential of more elaborate shows with 'star' headliners rather than just exhibition dancers. The extra expense of theatrical licences, star salaries and an array of chorus girls with sets and costumes precipitated higher admission charges and menu prices, but it did not appear to perturb the punters. One of the first supper entertainments to be staged as a mini-revue was the *Midnight Frolic* launched by Florenz Ziegfeld in January 1915 in the roof of the New Amsterdam Theatre. The sumptuous show, which started at midnight, was an instant sensation with New York high society, setting the style and pace of future night-time entertainment that many others tried to copy.

With audience participation encouraged and the major attraction of the twenty-four glorious girls interacting with guests, in exotic and sometimes brief attire, the *Midnight Frolic* emerged as a year-round dinner and entertainment venue, with sixteen shows staged between 1915 and 1922 until Prohibition forced its closure. The first edition was staged at the beginning of January 1915 with *Nothing but Girls* starring Nora Bayes, charging an unheard of $3 per person cover. This was followed by *Just Girls* with popular comedian and satirist Will Rogers on 23 August 1915. The third edition, which opened on 24 January 1916, starred Will Rogers once again, together with the added glitter of the Dolly Sisters and the strikingly beautiful Olive Thomas, who immediately became another close friend.

It was at this point that the Dollies began to be dressed by the already famous couturier Lady Duff Gordon, a lively, witty, British redhead known as Lucile; they continued to use her for the next six years.[2] Abandoned by a philandering husband, Mrs James Wallace (born Lady Lucy Christiana Sutherland in London in 1863) scandalised her well-bred family by obtaining a divorce and working as a dressmaker. She opened her first branch of Lucile Ltd in London (1896), followed by branches in New York (1910), Paris

(1911) and Chicago. Lucile married her second husband, Scottish landowner and sherry heir Sir Cosmo Edmund Duff Gordon, in 1900. Elder sister to the equally flamboyant novelist Elinor Glyn, Lucile notoriously escaped the *Titanic* disaster in a lifeboat she allegedly commandeered for herself, her husband and secretary.

With the dawn of 1915, Ziegfeld, persuaded by his wife, Billie Burke, acquired the services of Lucile to costume most of his shows, beginning with the *Midnight Frolic*. Although patronised by international society and royalty, Lucile had made her name in the performing arts. She had carefully moulded the image of the major exponents of ballroom dancing: Irene Castle, Florence Walton and Mae Murray and film stars such as Mary Pickford, Lillian Gish and Marion Davies. It soon became clear that, as actresses were seduced by Lucile's spell, their fame as performers was matched by their reputation as fashion trend-setters. Once this relationship was understood, it greatly increased Lucile's appeal.

Lucile's hallmark was delicate and luxuriously feminine designs based on rococo and neo-Greek lines conceived in pastel shades of chiffon, crêpe de Chine and taffeta, which formed trailing, diaphanous gowns and equally romantic, if racy, lingerie. The attractions of Lucile's creations were manifold. First and foremost, Lucile's vision was synonymous with the emerging concept of the new woman, which advocated fashions that were comfortable and practical and yet absolutely feminine. Equally, her gowns were less restrictive and allowed freedom of movement that matched the mood of the time with the explosion of the dance craze.

Although the Dolly Sisters had already been dressed well in their various stage appearances by a variety of designers up to 1914, they had paid little attention to the importance of fashion as a means of making their mark and using an effective wardrobe to enhance their performance. The success of their act at the Jardin de Danse in the summer of 1914, where they had clearly invested in extremely expensive and impressive gowns – with no designer credit, although I suspect Lucile's touch – must have made them realise that, in future, an investment in furs, feathers, frills and finery was of the utmost importance. With their appearance in the *Midnight Frolic* in Lucile creations, their image and costumes became a major facet of their performance. As Randy Bigham makes clear, the Dollies after 1916 were continually 'dressed to the "*n*th" in some of Lucile's most audaciously romantic creations and their dainty songs and dances and daintier Lucile finery drew crowds'.[3]

The dramatic opening number of the 1916 edition of the *Frolic* was 'The Girls of New York Town', with the chorus costumed to represent some of the principal thoroughfares such as Riverside Drive, Central Park and Washington Square.[4] Another big scene was 'A Girl's Trousseau', in which a singing lingerie salesman shows the audience a series of drawings in which the women wear progressively less lingerie. As he sang, live models dressed in these garments stepped through the drawings. When the last and seemingly nude model was about to appear, the audience gasped, until Will Rogers stepped through as a masked marvel![5] Despite these numbers and various speciality acts, *Variety* thought that it lacked 'the snap and ginger' of previous editions, but declared the Dolly Sisters 'the one high spot'.[6]

The Dollies appeared in at least five numbers and became the saving grace of the show: 'The bright particular moments . . . were when the Dolly Sisters came on the floor. These girls ran away with all the class of the show. . . . Those Dollys can look, dance, and dress.'[7] They first did a golfing or new polo dance and were as 'graceful and agile as ever'.[8] They were also dressed in blue and gold dancing frocks for their foxtrot to 'Underneath the Stars',[9] and grass skirts for the 'Fascination of Hawaii' hula number called 'Luana Lou' with Oscar Shaw,[10] which pre-dated the new craze for Hawaiian orchestras and hula-hulas that swept Broadway in late 1916.

Besides appearing in the *Midnight Frolic*, they were also lured back to vaudeville dressed in Lucile finery and in mid-February returned to the Palace Theatre with Rosie's husband Jean Schwartz at the piano as accompanist amid the adulation that recognised them as 'the entertainment idols of the Great White Way'.[11] The new act proved so popular that they were held over for several weeks, changing the routines and frocks regularly. During their third week they wore seaside attire of vivid yellow for a song about bathing beaches, performed a Chinese dance with fans and embroidered parasols, and finally gave a lively duet in dashing gowns of orange and silver.[12]

But all was not well at the Palace, and discord swiftly ensued when the management added two other top dance acts to headline with the Dolly Sisters – not a shrewd move on the part of the management in view of the other two acts' reputation for jealousy. Immediately an argument developed between the dancing acts of Franklin and Green and Maurice and Walton over their billing,[13] which spilled over onto the footlights as they tried to outstage each other. On the first night, at the end of her act with Maurice, Florence Walton introduced the audience to Charlie Chaplin, who was occupying a box. The obvious (and planned) resultant hysteria completely overshadowed the following performance from Franklin and Green. There were fireworks, but throughout the debacle the Dolly Sisters were exemplary in their behaviour and steered clear of taking sides.

In the course of these performances they turned down an offer from the international film company Pathé Frères to appear in a movie serial – a popular movie format that had been made famous by Pearl White in her *Perils of Pauline* series – but were considering a contract from the Fox Film Corporation.[14] After their run at the Palace, they appeared at the Alhambra, Orpheum, Brooklyn, Colonial and Prospect from mid-March through April, and in the last few weeks doubled up rehearsing in the morning for A.H. Woods in *His Bridal Night*.[15]

When Al Woods first approached them, their reaction was, 'Oh no! Speak lines on the stage! We can't do it.' They had only uttered one line each before: Jenny saying 'Hello everybody, are you waiting for me?', which she had delivered in her piquant accent in *The Midnight Sons*, and Rosie had announced: 'I'm going to quit this minute if I can't do as I please' in *The Merry Countess*. But after reading the script they loved the idea, and Margaret Mayo, one of the writers, spent some time studying them and as a result redrafted the script so that their speaking parts were foolproof.[16] The theme of mistaken identities with the need for a set of twins in the lead roles meant that *His Bridal Night* became a perfect match for their talents. The story was highly confusing but revolved around a young husband, his bride, her sister and a jealous lover. Any attempt to explain the plot would need a pictorial graph, but suffice it to say that neither the husband nor the lover can quite be certain which of the sisters is the true object of his affection and that it all ended happily ever after.

After lengthy rehearsals, *His Bridal Night* was presented by Al Woods in Atlantic City before moving to Washington, DC in early May 1916. The audience in Washington loved the show and filled the house with uproarious laughter. Florence Yoder from the *Washington Times* observed: 'Although Miss Mayo's art and the good book by Lawrence Rising have much to do with the success of the first venture of these two famous dancers into the speaking drama, they themselves are largely responsible. Wonderfully clever mimics and natural actresses, they have humour enough to make them even better farceuses than they promise today.'[17] However, another critic said that it must not be forgotten that the Dollies were really twin sisters and that in their moments of greatest naturalness and ease they were simply living their everyday lives.[18] This qualification aside, *His Bridal Night* had a significant effect on their career and the way in which the public and theatrical management viewed them. They stepped out of the ranks of just being able to dance well and look good and ventured into more sophisticated realms, where they were required to do more as performers.

The New York opening was at the Republic Theatre in August, and the Dollies were adored: 'They are charming from rise to fall of the curtain, full of "pep" with that exquisite grace which only adepts in the art of Terpischore display on the stage and they blossom forth as the daintiest comediennes imaginable.'[19] The Dollies were Broadway stars, as the *New York Review* explained: 'The Dollys twinkle as brightly as any stars along the Great White Way and deservedly for they have placed themselves where they are by talent and hard work in the face of many handicaps, which included originally a very limited knowledge of English.'[20] Before their debut there had been much speculation and gossip about the talent of the Dollies and their ability to perform for Woods in dramatic and speaking parts. One critic thought that those who scoffed were most pleasantly disappointed. 'True the twins are not Sarah Bernhardts, but considering the fact that they have had little if any training as actresses . . . they did remarkably well.'[21]

The dozens of gowns created by Lucile for the Dolly Sisters caused the 'sartorial sensation of the season', confirming the belief that the Dollies had now become as famous for their gowns as they were for their performance. Their oriental tea gowns with magnificent riots of colour, some cut with turkish trousers, evoked gasps of admiration from the audience,[22] and the bridal ensembles, including the bridesmaids' dresses of white tulle and satin, lace petticoats and wreaths of orange blossoms, were advocated for all brides getting married that season.[23] One bride who may have succumbed to the charms of Lucile's bridal attire as worn by the Dollies was Wallis Warfield (later to become the Duchess of Windsor). Wallis saw the production as she was planning her wedding to Earl Spencer, her first husband, and on the big day she wore a Lucile wedding dress that looked remarkably similar to her creation for the Dollies.[24]

In an interview during the run of the show, Margery Burr asked: 'Are your clothes all alike?' 'Most of them,' Rosie replied, 'we order doubles of everything. Poor Lucile complains that she loses interest when she has to repeat herself so frequently. But sometimes one of us gets a pretty thing that the other covets and then . . .' 'the first one up is the one best dressed!' broke in Jenny with a laugh.[25]

David Belasco, the legendary playwright, theatrical manager and producer known as 'the Bishop of Broadway', who placed great importance on natural acting styles, saw their performance and was so impressed that he went backstage and offered them a long-term contract to be under his tutelage, eventually becoming Belasco dramatic stars – an offer that was not taken up.

They were at the time immersed in the idea of being taken seriously as actresses rather than simply dancers. Asked how she liked acting, Rosie answered: 'I feel it is a great art of which I know but very little yet, but its possibilities are inspiring to me and I shall try and realise some of them. I wish that I could feel as much at home acting as I do dancing, but I must confess that at present I don't.' Jenny, however, was more at ease and said:

I think I enjoy acting more than Rosie does, for I can make people laugh and that is my ambition. I would rather be a clown than anything else, but as that is impossible, I will try and become a comedienne. I am going to stick to acting. Mr Belasco says that I have great talent and wishes to coach me, so I am going to work in earnest and try to do some big things.

When asked about Rosie, she said simply: 'I suppose as we grow older we will not be so much alike. Rosie may become an emotional actress but I won't, I am sure.'[26]

Jenny once again took on the role of spokesperson and comes across as the driving force in terms of their career development. But the interviewer made it clear, almost to downplay this dominance, that, like all twins, the Dollies adored one another. They made great pains to say 'be sure and say that we love each other' and 'we have been through a lot . . . but in spite of it all we have always been true to each other'.[27]

Whatever tensions bubbled beneath the surface, the Dollies were now fully settled in New York in a hit of a show that became one of the lasting successes of the year before touring well into 1917. They were happy to be together again and continued their delightful excursions through the myriad attractions of New York nightlife. 'We both enjoy going out to cabarets, restaurants and places like Castles in the Air. We meet everybody we know and dance and have a good time. We find it positively refreshing.' It can be no surprise that, given their effervescent personalities, they became the leaders and the essential prerequisite of Broadway festivities. 'No gathering of Broadway society is complete without the sisters . . . and no girls are more popular than they are.'[28] But in order to go out every night to late night suppers and dances and always look fresh and beautiful their one beauty secret was temperance: 'We never drink a drop of alcoholic beverage of any kind and we are both moderate in indulging in fancy dishes and sweets . . . and dancing gives us plenty of exercise.'[29]

The scale of their popularity can be observed when, at the end of October 1916, they gathered fifty friends and family with an impressive guest list that included Diamond Jim Brady, Olive Thomas, Marion Davies (in the early stages of her love affair with Randolph Hearst), the actor George MacFarland, the dancer and actor Joseph Santley, Raymond and Flora Hitchcock, the actor and writer William Collier, Mr and Mrs W. Randolph Hearst, Nora Bayes, Lottie Pickford (the sister of Mary) and Irving Berlin for a beefsteak dinner at Healys Restaurant on 66th Street to celebrate their twenty-fourth birthday.[30]

Shortly after their party they became the subject of further cases of mistaken identity that made the news. Jenny was having lunch in a fashionable New York restaurant when she noticed a woman who turned out to be Mary Pickford bowing at her. Jenny thought that she was bowing to someone else nearby and so ignored her. 'I'm sorry Rosie that a little New York success has so gone to your head that you have forgotten our nice friendship in Los Angeles,' Mary barked. Jenny apologised and had to explain who she was. 'I had to make her feel like a fool by explaining that I was Jenny and not Rosie.' A similar incident happened with Mack Sennett at about the same time. Mack had also been good friends with Rosie in Hollywood and insisted he could tell them apart because he believed it was all press agent bunk that they looked identical. One day Jenny saw a man making faces at her in a New York café. She thought he was drunk or a fool and she was most distraught when he came toward her, leaned over her shoulder and said: 'Kiss me Kid – I told you you couldn't fool your uncle Mack!'[31] Needless to say Uncle Mack had been fooled too!

As the years rolled by Diamond Jim's health deteriorated, and in November 1916, shortly after the Dollies' birthday party, he was suffering badly from gastric ulcers. His doctors told him that surgery was not possible because of his diabetes and coronary artery disease and advised him to retire somewhere quiet where he could rest and follow a rather rigid diet. Jim decided to move to Atlantic City, his favourite seaside resort, halfway between New York and Baltimore and the place where all the new shows were tried out before arriving on Broadway. At least, even on a diet, he thought, he would be able to have a little bit of fun. So for nearly six months he lived at the Sherbourne Hotel, paying $1,000 per week for his lavish ocean-front apartment and for an additional $36,000 had a glass-encased veranda built around it. One must assume that the Dolly Sisters went to see him during this period, but this new regime was not fooling anyone. Shortly before America entered the First World War on 13 April 1917, Diamond Jim lost the battle against angina, pectoris, diabetes and severe kidney complications; his funeral took place on 16 April in New York. The bulk of his estate went to various philanthropic enterprises, and many of his possessions were auctioned, but there were $1,000,000 worth of bequests, including a string of sixty-five pearls to Rosie, a pearl ring containing one pearl as big as a marble and eight diamonds to Jenny, a ring set with a sporting crystal and fourteen diamonds to Harry Fox, and a scarf pin set with sporting crystal and twenty-two diamonds to Jean Schwartz.[32]

Rosie remembered Diamond Jim with a great deal of warmth: 'a fat man', who would invite them 'all the time to go out to places where – frankly we couldn't afford to go. Just to dance. . . . he ate himself out of shape, health and everything else . . .'[33] In an interview after his death, the twins expressed their fondness for him. 'He was just like a father to us. And when he was dying and could have had us at his bedside as soon as he sent the word he demonstrated his unselfishness by insisting that we go ahead with the show [*His Bridal Night* tour]. His great ambition was to have us succeed in fullest measure,' said Rosie.

'He was a wonderful man,' said Jenny.

'He wrote us the loveliest of letters,' said Rosie.

'I think that they are really the nicest things he has left behind . . .'

The interviewer gazed at the enormous nine-carat diamond rings on each of their fingers as large as teaspoons and queried 'the very nicest?'

'Yes,' insisted Jenny emphatically tossing her head defiantly, ignoring the interviewer's attempt at humour.[34]

On their return to New York after the lengthy tour of *His Bridal Night*, Jenny was faced with a bit of a shock when someone showed her a cheque signed by her husband Harry payable to another woman and was told that other things had been going on in her absence. Jenny got very angry and did not discuss the situation with a single soul, 'not even me', added Rosie aggrievedly, 'and you know we've always told each other everything'. Believing the worst, Jenny immediately filed for divorce in the High Court on 9 June 1917, alleging adultery and naming the woman as Miss Fay Atkins. It was so unexpected that theatrical circles gasped. For the next week Rosie felt the emotional torture of her sister. She could not sleep because Jenny could not sleep nor could they eat or function properly.

The strange mental sympathy existing between the Dolly Sisters was a well-known fact in Broadway circles. There was one story of how Jenny, separated for a night from Rosie, suddenly awakened with a headache and knew that her sister was suffering from the same ailment. There were various other trivial instances that suggested that telepathy existed between them. These feelings could not be explained, but they just 'know that it is there'. In this particular instance the pain that Rosie felt became so unbearable that she decided to find the woman to whom Harry had given the mysterious cheque and had caused Jenny to file for divorce. Later Jenny said that Rosie's determination to solve the situation by becoming a regular detective 'was the cleverest thing. I'd never thought of it at all. But she did.' Rosie found the woman and discovered to her astonishment that it was someone Harry had known years ago who was old and sick and he had just wanted to help because he was 'so wonderfully good hearted'. Harry had given people money before and Jenny had remonstrated about it, so he had started to use stealth and secrecy, which is why he did not tell Jenny. 'I thought I had uncovered something dreadfully clandestine and was furious and saw my lawyer. But Rosie's detective work saved the day.' It was all a silly misunderstanding, the divorce was off[35] and the reconciled couple left for a second honeymoon in French Lick – a resort and spa in Indiana noted for a great hotel, beautiful gardens, hot springs and gambling.[36]

With this emotional upheaval behind them, the Dollies announced that they were going to retire from the stage in five years' time, before they were 30 (in the early 1920s), while they were still in their prime. This was because they wanted people to say that the Dolly Sisters are good and subsequently that they were good. 'But never, positively never, that they had been good once.' At the same time they decided that they wanted 'to raise babies – lots of them. Wouldn't it be adorable if we should each have a pair of dear little twins! It's sometimes hereditary, they tell us. We're going to rear families on a fine big country estate. We are going to have houses side by side and a nice winter apartment in New York. That's why we are so ambitious and so eager to earn enough to provide for the youngsters.'[37] They were clearly very sincere about their future plans at the time, but neither the retirement at 30 nor the birth of numerous babies would come to fruition.

His Bridal Night proved enduringly popular, and another tour commenced in August 1917 with the Barr Sisters, who had been playing at Maxim's cabaret in New York in the place of the Dollies.[38] During the summer the Dollies' representative Harry Weber was busy trying to place a vaudeville act comprising the Dolly Sisters, Harry Fox and Jean Schwartz, but this did not materialise, and instead only the Dolly Sisters returned to headline at the Palace Theatre in July 1917. Harry Fox, unable to join the sisters at the Palace, opened in an act of his own with Lou Pollard at the Majestic Theatre, Chicago, at the end of August. He also signed a contract for $1,000 per week with J.L. Saks to appear in a London revue at the beginning of 1918, but he was refused a passport and had to cancel.[39]

The Dollies made a triumphant reappearance at the Palace Theatre and were greeted by an enormous audience with much applause and many floral tributes. They demonstrated new dances of artistic grace and skill. Sime at *Variety*, however, had a different view: 'It is far from the best the Dollys have presented . . . many people believe the Dollys are the Dollys and accept them in that way regardless of their singing or dancing, the former not considered at all and the latter seldom changing.' Sime thought that they looked too demure for the Dollies and too much like a 'sister act'. The Greater Morgan dancers, six black girls, acted as maids in one number then became a female jazz band: 'their shrieking discords took all the class away from the Dolly turn.' Patsy Smith on the women's page of *Variety* went further: 'The Dollies are no better dancers, no better singers or no better performers than they were before. It is well they have the judgement to make hay while the sun shines and capture the prize salaries now for they sure seem to have their limitations.'[40]

This was a rather nasty and hostile attack from *Variety* on two fronts; were they really that bad or was there another agenda? Sime and his colleagues were not always objective, and, as a consequence, Sime, in particular, as head of *Variety*, made numerous enemies, most notably E.F. Albee, who ran the Keith Circuit. A deep enmity arose between the two, and as a result derogatory news stories and bitter editorials about the Keith Circuit, the Palace Theatre and Albee's performers flowed from Sime's acid pen. Albee in retaliation banned any act that advertised in *Variety* from working on the Keith Circuit.[41] The Dollies were great favourites and great friends with Albee and his family, which may explain why Sime's comments about the Dollies at this time were so critical. In contrast, other publications expressed the usual adoration: 'They are, if anything prettier, brighter and more entertaining than ever,' said one.[42] Lucile's costumes once again were regarded as the real fashion show of the season.[43]

Many years later, after the death of Sime Silverman, Rosie recalled their long-standing feud: 'Don't get me wrong, I loved Sime and he loved me – but he thought Jenny and I were pretty awful on the stage and I tried to tell him I thought his paper was awful, just to get back at him.' At one point during one of their vaudeville engagements for the Keith Circuit, perhaps in 1917, Rosie called him up and invited him to a champagne supper. It was a grand meal 'and before we left he kissed me and he kissed Jenny and said, "you are two darlings. I love you both. You are wonderful"'. Two days later *Variety* came out, and Sime had written dreadful things about them.[44]

By August the Dollies had revised the act, which *Variety* decided was more versatile than before, with 'more expressive gowns, which made a world of difference'.[45] Another critic for the *New York American* was more appreciative: 'The sisters are dancing like slim sylphs . . . their frocks are confections assembled by a genius, their little songs are cute and altogether the Dolly Sisters are adorable.'[46] Whatever the criticism, they must have been highly popular with the public, who still demanded to see them week after week at the Palace before they ventured out to other notable Keith theatres in Washington and Philadelphia. Then a little fracas broke out with Al Woods.

He had them in mind for a new musical piece, teaming them with the comic actor Henry Bergman, to be launched in the autumn. Woods claims he gave the Dollies permission to play four weeks in vaudeville and told them that, if they played the vaudeville tour routed for them, he would consider his contract calling for exclusive services breached.[47] The Dollies appear to have taken no notice and carried on regardless and spent the rest of the season in vaudeville,[48] and then there were rumours that they were talking to Raymond Hitchcock about starring in a new revue or appearing in a tour of his popular show *Hitchy-Koo*.[49]

Back at the Palace, but also doubling up at other theatres such as the Colonial and Alhambra, they began to threaten the record of their old friend and vaudeville star Nora Bayes[50] and they soon notched up a record-breaking run of twelve weeks.[51] This time Jean Schwartz joined them on piano, an ideal addition, since when they made costume changes he indulged in reminiscences of his own compositions. The Dollies performed four dance duets, a bridal waltz, a cute summertime number in plain white dresses with large red capelines and liberty blue ribbon girdles, the Danzon (a Russian ballet dance) in orange gowns trimmed with peacock blue beads and dashes of extravagance and finally a patriotic dance in red, white and blue to the tune of 'Over There', specially written for them by Jean Schwartz. Lucile's creations – three of which were named 'simplicity', 'oriental influence' and 'young dignity' – were regarded as 'a triumph of sartorial art' and 'the acme of smart simplicity and grace'.[52]

Finally, the rumour of their association with Raymond Hitchcock was confirmed, and in November it was announced that they would be the stars of his new revue *Words and Music*,[53] which was destined to follow *Hitchy-Koo* at the 44th Street Theatre. Shortly after this announcement another followed, saying that they had withdrawn from the revue because they were dissatisfied with the parts assigned them and were contemplating a further vaudeville tour.[54] But the truth may be that they had been made an offer that they simply could not refuse – to star in their own movie – although they must have kept the offer already made to them by the United Booking Office for a forty-week run on the Keith Circuit at $1,550 per week in reserve.[55]

As these negotiations continued, the Dollies filled in time by dancing in the Grill Room of the Hotel Knickerbocker. Moreover, since America had declared war on Germany in April 1917, everyone was mobilised to help in any way they could, and the Dollies also appeared for the benefit of the Christmas War Fund at Murray's Roman Gardens, a plush restaurant-cabaret, with its French exterior, Roman interior and revolving dance floor.[56]

Continuing their activities for the war effort, the Dollies travelled to Palm Beach, Florida, in January 1918 to perform for the Red Cross.[57] It would not have taken much persuasion for the Dollies to go to one of the most-talked-about resorts and the most exclusive enclave in America, and they also had the pretext of charity work to explain their winter excursion! Mixing with America's elite must have been a far cry from their treatment at the Newport home of Cornelius Vanderbilt in 1912. This was the prelude to the time when their visits to the resorts of the social elite on both continents would be made under their own steam and on their own terms.

Angelina, the fashion correspondent for *Theatre Magazine*, was with them as they decided to pack and was enthralled with the ease of the process as the maid was instructed to bring out the two wardrobe trunks. As the packing began, all three sat down for a chat with a jolly box of bonbons making the rounds. All the suits and frocks were changed from the hangers in their wardrobe straight onto the hangers in the vast wardrobe trunk. All their lingerie, hats and shoes were placed neatly in the accompanying chintz-covered drawers. As a result, everything was guaranteed to emerge at the other end of the journey in the same unwrinkled fresh condition in which they started. Hey presto, packing was simple![58]

While Newport, Rhode Island, was the summer colony of many of America's oldest families and multimillionaires, who were building their huge white marble villas along Ocean Drive, in the winter the playground was transferred to Palm Beach, which had been built on a strip of land between the eastern shore of Lake Worth (a lagoon and ideal harbour for all the private yachts) and the Atlantic. Miles of silver beach, the bluest water, stately palms and a profusion of flowers in all colours made this a paradise. The Dolly Sisters swiftly adjusted to the daily life of beach activities and swimming, entertainment at the Beach Casino, tea and dancing at the Coconut Grove, part of the Royal Poinciana Hotel, gambling at Bradley's Beach Club and golf and memorable dinners at the Everglades Club.[59]

Tearing themselves away from the sun, sand and sea, the Dollies rushed back to New York to start filming their first moving picture together. Leonce Perret (1880–1935), the celebrated French director, had seen them dance at the Palace Theatre in late 1917 and 'was caught by their lithesomeness, their personalities, the sheer expressiveness of their twinkling feet, their nimble bodies and their provocative faces'. He firmly believed that they were born for the screen and persuaded them to appear together in a film that he had specially written for them, called, rather appropriately, *The Million Dollar Dollies*,[60] and filming began in February 1918.[61] Perret had been director-general of the Gaumont film company in Paris for fourteen years and had written or produced over 300 feature films mostly before the First World War but had now made his American debut with *The Silent Master* (1917).[62]

Produced by Emerald Pictures and distributed by Metro, *The Million Dollar Dollies* was released in April 1918 as 'one of the ocular gems of the year',[63] with the Dolly Sisters described as 'New York's greatest stage attraction'. It was a romantic fantasy with a silly plot about the Dollies, maharajahs and a million dollars.[64] It was a picturesque tale with extremely good sets, which evoked the right atmosphere of the mystery of the East and included a replica of the ultra-fashionable Sherry's restaurant. In essence, the film showcased the Dollies as the Dollies, 'varying in behaviour from pouty and pert to coquettish and kittenish'.[65] It was a vehicle to display their dancing and, of course, their amazing wardrobe, which allegedly comprised forty-eight different costumes created especially for them by Lucile.[66]

The Dollies breezed through their unique offering like a 'saucy gust of wind',[67] and there was not a minute that did not 'fascinate the eye'. When the film was released in London in the spring of 1920 to capitalise on their success in the stage show *Jigsaw* at the Hippodrome, it was described as 'typically American in its dash and sparkle . . . a very bright and pleasing entertainment', which showed the Dollies 'had the charm and talent of two very dainty comediennes'.[68]

To fill in time before their next big project, they accepted an offer from the Shuberts to appear for a few weeks from 23 May in *The Midnight Revue* at the Century Grove, the roof garden at the Century Theatre at Central Park West and 62nd Street. The cabaret, under the management of Elliott, Comstock and Gest (who were later to produce *Oh Look!*), was highly regarded: 'There is polish to all the number productions . . . they are the best produced . . . of any cabaret show in New York.'[69] Joined in the cast by George White, with whom they had worked in *The Echo* (1910), the Dollies performed eccentric dances in scenes called 'The Bing Boys of Broadway' and 'Chickawaka Indian Jazz', assisted by a little-known dancer called Kuy Kendall,[70] and in one number they were also dressed as the American flag.[71]

With success on the stage and screen, the Dollies had become a highly visible commodity, and new offers from vaudeville, other motion picture companies and theatrical agents from London and Paris came flooding in. Their popularity was widely recognised: 'Their rise has been more rapid than that of any other girls on the stage. Their remarkable grace and beauty combined with their rare ability as dancers made a strong popular appeal.'[72] Much to the surprise of everyone, they chose to sign as co-stars with comedy duo Weber and Fields for their forthcoming reunion in *Back Again*. The only explanation for this strange business move was to show their support and appreciation to Lew Fields, who had given them their first Broadway chance in *The Midnight Sons* in 1910.

Weber and Fields had revised and brought up to date the musical comedy *A Peck of Pickles*, which they renamed *Back Again* and launched at the Chestnut Theatre, Philadelphia, with the idea that it would be restaged in New York for the Shuberts at the New Apollo with the added benefit of the Dolly Sisters. It must have been very frustrating for the Dolly Sisters to agree to join this production as early as February 1918, putting all other offers on hold, only to be kept waiting until the summer and then told that the show had been postponed indefinitely because of dissatisfaction with the book, and finally that it would not be staged at all.[73]

Despite this fiasco, the Dollies were signed at the last minute to headline with Harry Fox in a revamped version of *Oh Look!*, which opened at the Belasco Theatre on 14 July 1918.[74] A musical version of James Montgomery's *Ready Money*, a farce produced in 1913, it had been turned into a two-act play that had originally opened at the Vanderbilt Theatre on 7 March 1918 with Harry Fox as the male lead but had run for only sixty-seven performances. *Variety* thought that the original production had not succeeded because there was a lack of punch in the leading women and a lack of showmanship in the handling of the production, but added that it could be made into a smash hit if produced properly.[75]

The production team of Comstock, Elliott and Gest, who were known for producing 'class, cleanliness and cleverness',[76] did just that with a major revamp. This included the casting of the Dolly Sisters and made *Oh Look!* one of the biggest musical-comedy hits of the year. During a smart, intimate weekend on a Long Island estate, a young man (Harry Fox) on the verge of bankruptcy is given a loan by a friend until his gold mine becomes profitable. The new money proves alluring to many new friends, but they all disappear when the money is found to be counterfeit. Luckily, the young man's girlfriend (Jenny) and her sister (Rosie) do not desert him, and, as the mine makes money, the happy couple sing a duet knowing they will soon be very wealthy. The flow of the story was punctuated with dancing and eight musical numbers, including Harry Fox singing 'I'm Always Chasing Rainbows', which became a huge hit.

The arrival of the show in Chicago in August 1918 was the biggest opening from the standpoint of gross receipts the La Salle Theatre had ever seen. The show was adored, and the only criticism was that neither Harry Fox nor the Dollies were 'A-class' singers.[77] In Philadelphia the singing did not appear to be a problem, and here they received rapturous applause: 'The Dolly Sisters are revealed as musical comedy artists of the most pleasing type acting with much charm and rendering their several music numbers to the thorough delight of the audience.'[78] After they had appeared in Kansas City, there was more praise: 'They are so dainty so graceful so fun loving so sincere yet so individual and genuinely charming that one's ears and eyes are pleased alike all the time they are on the stage.'[79]

During the Dollies' successful stay in Chicago, the journalist Ashton Stevens interviewed them one afternoon in the middle of the frivolity of a bathing-suit luncheon at the world-famous Edgewater Beach Hotel with Harry Fox, William Elliot (one of the Dollies' managers) and two 'Dolly fireside companions', the actresses Peggy O'Neil and Mabel McCane.

'We loathe being twins,' observed Jenny.

'We never get ourselves up as twins except when we are being paid to be twins,' added Rosie.

'Twins is our business not our pleasure,' said Jenny.

'You'll never catch us at home or in the street in the same kind of clothes. Nothing could induce us to dress alike off the stage,' said Rosie.

'Being a twin is the hardest thing I do,' Rosie sighed.

'The awful jokes we have to hear,' Jenny moaned.

'Hasn't being twins any advantages?' Ashton Stevens asked.

'Mighty few,' Rosie replied sharply.

'Perhaps you think it's funny being forever taken for somebody else. Well it isn't. It's awful,' Jenny concluded firmly.[80]

These harsh words should be treated cautiously: there is no other evidence that they really did not like being twins – after all, deep down they adored each other. Perhaps this conversation was at a point in their lives when mistaken identity was proving a little difficult for them. Despite this unease, it was certainly paying the bills, and they were doing very well out of it. *Oh Look!* toured right through 1919 and into 1920.

During a break in the summer of 1919, the Dollies must have been in need of rest, because they turned down a staggering offer of $2,500 per week to appear at the Pennsylvania Hotel in New York.[81] By December it was announced that they would star in a new revue on Broadway[82] for Comstock and Gest to follow the enormous success of *Oh Look!* When it became clear that this would not happen until the autumn of 1920, they decided instead to accept an offer of a six-week contract from the theatrical producer Albert de Courville to appear for a season in London.[83] They finally closed their thirty-one-week tour of *Oh Look!* at the Grand Opera House, Wilkes-Barre, Pennsylvania, in early April 1920 and began preparations for their first trip to Europe. This would be a defining phase of their lives and would have a profound effect on their personal relationships. It would also completely change their profile as entertainers and make them international celebrities and stars.

It is strange that they accepted Albert de Courville's offer in the first place. Apart from the wonderful opportunity to visit and perform in London, something else must have clinched the decision. Rosie said that, when they decided to go to London, both husbands were furious. 'We went anyway and that was how our marriages went on the rocks. We never went back to our husbands.'[84] But their going to London could not have been the only reason for the failure of their marriages. Throughout their early career on Broadway they had consistently tried to portray themselves as virtuous by marrying for love and not for money, and cultivated a wholesome 'good-girl' image (despite some hiccups, such as Jenny being named in Harry Fox's first divorce). This would have been in sharp contrast to many of their friends in the business who were being plucked from stardom to become the wives or mistresses of the rich and famous.

Despite the fact that the Dollies were allegedly blissfully married, they had been continually pampered by Diamond Jim Brady, who had provided them with every indulgence. They had been in a unique situation, able to enjoy the best of both worlds. With Diamond Jim's death in April 1917, the sparkle of his generosity evaporated. His absence would have been nothing short of a devastating blow – they had lost their main benefactor and the source of their extravagance and luxury. This gaping void in their lives would have put their marriages into a new perspective.

The Dollies were rather tight-lipped about what actually happened. Rosie made it quite clear that before they left New York their spouses were getting jealous of their fame: 'Two people who are married and doing the same kind of work are liable to become jealous of each other,'[85] implying that their relationships were already on rocky ground. Talking about her husband and her marriage later in life, Rosie believed that she had been 'a silly young girl ignorant of the facts of life'. Even though she was 20 at the time she married, she clearly felt that she had been too young and too immature, and had married for the wrong reasons.[86] After her divorce, Jenny was completely honest about her marriage to Harry Fox. 'I realised it is a mistake for an actress to marry an actor. We are still congenial . . . He's a dear, sweet boy, but I just knew it was a mistake to have a husband in the profession. Road trips force husband and wife apart, temptations follow and lonesomeness is bound to bring new friendships.' She then added: 'I would never advise an actress to marry an actor.' The interviewer agreed and said: 'It's much better to marry a banker and take him and a cheque book right along with you.'[87]

The London engagement was both a marvellous career opportunity and a means to an end. Within a year of arriving in England, both sisters were seeking divorces. As they settled down to life in London without their husbands, they quickly overcame their initial loneliness and were swiftly engrossed in the excitement of new surroundings and people. Their innate rivalry, contained for several years, resurfaced, and they became more competitive with each successive flirtation and love affair. The sisters had suddenly lost their innocence, grown up and were discovering that far more interesting marriage propositions that linked love with cheque books could be found.

6

THE LONDON DEBUT

Europe in 1920 was vastly different from what it had been at the onset of the First World War in 1914. Empires had been dissolved, monarchies overthrown and the victorious allies were recovering from social and economic upheavals. Life was not easy, however, with a growing disparity between prices and wages that led to industrial strife. Populations had been decimated by the loss of young men, and with a shift in the moral climate a radical new woman had been born who had the opportunity to be less constrained by old conventions. The stage had also blossomed with the new sensation called revue, aided by a fascination with all things American – cocktails, nightclubs, jazz and cabaret. When the Dolly Sisters arrived in Southampton aboard the *Baltic* in the late spring of 1920, they were poised to reap the benefits of the new changes in society and were, once again, magically in the right place at the right time.

Despite their excitement at being in London, their first few weeks were far from happy, and they were terribly lonely. When they moved into their rented apartment in fashionable Mayfair, they knew very few people and had no letters of introduction.[1] Even though everyone they met was extremely polite, they were left very much on their own. They simply divided their time between the theatre and the apartment, because they did not feel able to go out on their own, only visiting the American Express Company to get cables and letters from friends at home. Their apartment overlooked the gardens of a town house belonging to a prominent London family.[2] Frequently they would see lines of cars drawing up for social functions, see guests strolling in the garden and could hear music and laughter, which made them feel neglected. They were so close to a wonderful social life, the kind of life that they had been accustomed to in New York, but here in London it was denied them.[3]

The rehearsals for the show went badly. The rainy weather, draughty theatre and a damp, unheated apartment brought them to the verge of pneumonia. Rosie reproached herself for signing the contract and for urging Jenny to sign too. They cried themselves to sleep night after night. Rosie had longed to visit London, but when she arrived, it was not the London of her dreams – to her it appeared as a dark and gloomy place with continual rain.[4]

With this sense of malaise, they made their London debut on 16 June 1920 as the stars of *Jigsaw*, Albert de Courville's tenth lavish revue at the London Hippodrome, described as 'an English salad with American dressing'.[5] De Courville devised a novel way of introducing the Dolly Sisters, who were so nervous on their first night that they could hardly speak. A stage set was created to represent the 'graceful fancy'[6] of a huge black velvet lady's hat. As an artist sang 'Trimming the Hat', showgirls emerged, taking their positions around the brim in specially designed costumes by Hugh Willoughby representing a variety of trimmings such as lace, red and blue leather, cherries and bird of paradise. Then the crown of the hat was slowly raised to reveal a lady's boudoir with the Dollies holding a large mirror at a make-up table. The idea was to deceive the audience into believing that one sister was admiring her reflection in the mirror. The illusion ended when they both rose and performed a waltz before returning to the hat as the crown was lowered once more. The audience applauded so much that they did not notice that Jenny dropped the mirror just as the crown of the hat covered them again.[7] This scene was followed by the extravagant intoxication of 'Perfumes', with the perfume girl introducing an array of chorus girls representing all the choicest samples of perfume to be found in a Bond Street shop window.[8]

The Dollies then appeared in several other scenes, wearing a series of exotic gowns created by Lucile. In 'Limehouse Nights' they were able to do something a little different, showing that they were 'more than just mere song and dance artists' by becoming 'actresses of no mean quality'.[9] Jenny played a Chinese boy and Rosie a poppy with Nancy Gibb singing 'Poppyland' in a sequence associated with Chinese opium dens. This evoked the continuing public fascination with the 'hidden' world of drugs that had been brought to the fore by the tragic death by an alleged drug overdose of the actress Billie Carleton after the armistice-night revelries at the Albert Hall in November 1918.

Their biggest hit, however, was in 'Sports' with the Pony Trot, the famed dance that they had first performed with Carlos Sebastian on Broadway in 1914. Here they danced as a pair of spirited ponies, plumed and prancing, with Laddie Cliff (with whom they had shared billing in a vaudeville show in 1914 in New York) as the nimble coachman in charge of whip and reins. Their nervousness was compounded during the Pony Trot. Just before they ventured on the stage, the American Dooley brothers, acrobatic dancers, were hissed off, which increased their anxiety. They heard roars, hoots and whistles from the audience. 'When we reached the wings we were crying. Then I shall never forget Laddie Cliff saying "They aren't hissing, they're cheering you". Neither of us could believe it.'[10] The number brought the house down night after night and was described as 'the best thing in the show';[11] it became one of their most enduring showpieces. At the end of the first-night performance they were showered with applause and flowers, which they donated immediately to a local hospital.[12]

The reviews of *Jigsaw* were mixed. Some felt it was 'the show of the year', with scenes of 'dazzling splendour'.[13] Others were more subdued: 'a palatable dish',[14] said *The Stage*, while *Eve* thought it was 'mediocre' and then observed 'the production is not one tasty sandwich, but a high pile of sandwiches, unfortunately the meat tastes frozen, the bread stale and the crumbs come obviously from the table of the richer'.[15] Everyone, however, was full of praise and admiration for the Dolly Sisters. *The Stage* decided that they had unmistakably clicked with the London audience,[16] and *Eve* thought that they were one of the redeeming features. 'They move with a perfect ensemble, which is partly explained by the fact that they are twins – the rest of the reasons is talent and practice . . . . two of their turns are worth ten of the revue.'[17]

They had felt utterly desolate on their arrival and during rehearsals; now their anxiety had been partly alleviated by the reception they had received from the audience and critics on opening night. 'The success of our revue naturally contributed to our happiness. Success is a wonderful thing but it is not everything.'[18] They were still unhappy about not being able to go out and enjoy London's nightlife, but gradually things would change.

The flaws in *Jigsaw*, particularly the fact that the Dollies did not appear in enough scenes, were obviously seen at the box office, and it was not surprising that the show drew to a close in December 1920. For Albert de Courville this was the last production that he would stage at the Hippodrome. The Dollies' association with *Jigsaw* did not last until the close of the show. They had a contract for six weeks, which must have been renewable, but they really did not like Albert de Courville and were not happy about the way in which they had to work. 'All I ever knew about was giving two shows a day. And I thought over there it would be the same. But no!' said Rosie. 'They wanted us to do three, four shows a day. So I pretended I fell down and hit my head in front of the audience. They took me out of there, put me in hospital for a week and we never went back to the show again.'[19]

Out of work, they must have been looking around for something better to do rather than return to New York, where they were booked to star in a new revue by Comstock and Gest to follow *Oh Look!* with Harry Fox.[20] Something better came in the form of the famous British producer Charles B. Cochran, who immediately took them under his wing with plans to star them in his next big production in 1921.

Once released from *Jigsaw*, the Dolly Sisters embarked on a period of fun and frolics and by the end of August were enjoying their first, extended trip to France. They visited Deauville for the first time at the height of the season, and it was reported that Jenny had won the colossal sum of $160,000 at the casino, thus starting a frenzied interest from the media in her winnings and losses.[21] In Paris, they must have visited their old friend Harry Pilcer, who was running an extremely fashionable open-air dancing venue called L'Oasis, situated in the garden at the rear of Paul Poiret's couture house on the rue d'Antin.[22] At the same time they would have enjoyed seeing old friends Norma and Constance Talmadge, Joseph Schenck and Mary Pickford, who had arrived in Europe with Dorothy Gish, Douglas Fairbanks and Anita Loos, for an extended trip that included visits to both London and Paris.[23]

Besides these famous movie stars, the Dollies also met their old friend Olive Thomas, who was staying at the Ritz Hotel. But their meeting was marked by unexpected tragedy. Since her days working for Ziegfeld, Olive had been snapped up by Hollywood and had become the star of numerous films. She was introduced to the suave, handsome Jack Pickford, brother of Mary Pickford, and it became a case of love at first sight. Their affair was stormy, with clashes of temperament, but they married in 1917, and in September 1920 they arrived in Paris for a second honeymoon.

On the night of Saturday 5 September Olive and Jack had dinner with a group of friends and then visited some Montmartre nightspots, including the Abbaye de Thélème in the place Pigalle, formerly a church and the oldest and most chic venue in the area, the Rat Mort and perhaps other key places like Zelli's and Florence's. They returned to the Ritz at about 3.30 a.m., and, as they prepared for bed, Jack found Olive in the bathroom of their suite having digested mercury bichloride, which he claimed had been done accidentally. She was rushed to the American hospital and, after five days of dreadful suffering, died at the height of her career on Thursday 10 September.

Since her arrival in Paris, Olive had not been feeling well and had complained of fatigue and insomnia, but she still went out on the town. Jack was well known as a womaniser before and after his marriage to Olive. He was rumoured to have syphilis and had infected Olive and was undergoing treatment with mercury bichloride. According to one account, she swallowed a large amount of mercury bichloride, thinking it was a sleeping potion. Another version claimed that she was so upset with Jack over his philandering that she deliberately ended her life, while another speculated that Jack poisoned her.

It was never established whether Olive's death was an accident or suicide. Whatever the truth, it became one of the first big scandals that rocked Hollywood, to be followed by the Fatty Arbuckle rape scandal of 1921 and the murder of William Desmond Taylor in 1922. Rosie, clearly upset, commented:

> I knew Olive Thomas very well. In fact, I was invited to the party on the fatal night. I was not able to go and did not see Olive until afterward at the hospital. She was devoted to Jack . . . as she dragged out the agonising hours before her death she kissed his hand repeatedly and told him how much she loved him. Personally I am certain that Olive could not have committed suicide.[24]

On their return to London, the Dollies acted as a pair of Cupids for their friend, the actress Jose Collins. Jose was appearing at Daly's Theatre in *A Southern Maid*, which had opened on 15 May 1920. Her dressing room was open house, and one evening in walked the Dolly Sisters, announcing that they had just arrived back from Paris and had brought an old friend to see her. This turned out to be the dashing and distinguished Lord Robert Innes Ker, or Robin as she called him. Jose had first met him in 1917 during the run of *The Maid of the Mountains*, when he was introduced to her by a friend in the theatre during a period of leave from France, where he was serving with the Irish Guards.

At first Jose did not want to see him but not wishing to embarrass the Dollies allowed him in. The meeting went well and the Dollies suggested that the four of them should meet again the next day. This 'foursome' soon became a regular occurrence, and they met at Jose's dressing room, at the Dollies' flat, at parties, at the races and at other functions. Then Jose began to see Robin on his own and soon they were married.[25]

As Jose's love affair developed, so romance also blossomed for the Dollies. Something, or more likely someone, significant prevented Rosie from joining Jenny on her return to New York on the liner the *Adriatic*, leaving 15 October 1920 from Cherbourg. It was a short trip of a few weeks, and, once at the Waldorf Astoria Hotel, Jenny smoothed over the relationship with Comstock and Gest, started divorce proceedings from Harry Fox and, on Rosie's behalf, chased up divorce proceedings against Jean Schwartz. Love was also in the air for Jenny, who announced that, as soon as her divorce from Harry Fox was finalised, she intended to marry an English duke.[26] So who on earth was the lucky chap? And what, or rather more importantly who, was keeping Rosie busy in London?

On Jenny's return to London they were interviewed by the *Picturegoer* and were described as 'two excited young chatterboxes':

'We love London,' said Jenny 'we are just crazy . . .'

'. . . about it,' said Rosie. 'But do you know that when we first came here to play at the Hippodrome we didn't like it a bit? The people, the atmosphere of the place seemed so different. I felt we should never get across our act. I . . .'

'. . . I cried', said Jenny, 'and wanted to go home again and . . .'

'. . . offered to refund our passage money,' said Rosie, 'but Mrs Cochran . . .'

'. . . persuaded us to stay, and . . .', said Jenny,

'. . . we are real glad that we stayed . . .', added Rosie.

'Good . . .', said Jenny,

'. . . bye,' said Rosie.[27]

COCHRAN'S LUSCIOUS
PAIR OF LOLLIPOPS

After their rather unsettling relationship with Albert de Courville, the Dollies must have been delighted to be 'adopted' by the impresario Charles B. Cochran, who became their London mentor. Affectionately called 'Cockie', Cochran was short, stocky and red faced and had charm, persuasiveness and cool authority. He was everything to be expected of a master showman. He had great dignity, being immaculate in manner and dress, with impeccable taste even down to his vast cigars.[1] Cochran, who did everything with flair, earning him the name of the British Ziegfeld, had a gift for spotting new talent and bringing together well-known names in the most innovative way. His shows were a byword for glamour, beauty, spectacle and star names. The French actress and singer Alice Delysia was his first major star in *Odds and Ends* (1914), as he embarked on a series of intimate revues that made his unique mark on the London theatrical scene. This was augmented by seasons featuring the great Russian ballerina Anna Pavlova, the grande dame of French theatre Sarah Bernhardt, the Russian ballet of Serge Diaghilev and the work of the famous French writer and actor

Sacha Guitry. He made the London Pavilion his headquarters, and in 1920 presented *London, Paris and New York*, a show marked by style and taste that outclassed de Courville's *Jigsaw*.[2]

Rosie said that they liked Cochran because 'he was like Ziegfeld – not at all like that man at the Hippodrome [Albert de Courville]',[3] and Cochran liked them, realising their potential in a way that had simply eluded de Courville. He once remarked: 'Two more electric personalities it has never been my fate to meet. They radiated personal magnetism, vibrant energy or whatever you like to call it and any revue benefited enormously by their presence on the stage. . . . On the stage and off the Dolly sisters were unique.'[4]

The purpose of Cochran's visit to New York in the autumn of 1920 became clear when he starred the Dolly Sisters in *League of Notions*, launched on 17 January 1921 at the New Oxford Theatre. Cochran brought producer John Murray Anderson from New York to stage the show, described as an 'inconsequential process of music, dance and dramatic interlude', and had taken the items he had liked best from two of Anderson's previous New York productions. Anderson had been a pupil of the famous British actor and stage manager Sir Herbert Tree at His Majesty's Theatre in London before visiting New York and becoming a dancer and producer of spectacular shows, with the much applauded *Greenwich Village Follies*.

Cochran also secured the talents of the sisters Helen and Josephine Trix, who were popular vaudeville singers in New York, the dancer Earl Leslie, destined for stardom in Paris, a team of collie dogs that he had seen in a chorus number of a Charles Dillingham show and, of course, some lovely new showgirls. He also added Fortunello and Cirillino, two Italian clowns who had been spotted by Rosie at the Olympia Theatre in Paris during the summer of 1920.[5] At the same time as his vast investment in the cast and production, he had also spent $400,000 renovating the Old Oxford Music Hall ready for the new show and the inauguration of the New Oxford Theatre.

All was going well until in the middle of rehearsals Cochran became ill, leaving Anderson in control, which proved to be almost a disaster, since

Anderson had no sense of time or money. Things got worse as postponements led to mounting salary and rent costs. The Dolly Sisters saw that Anderson's behaviour could ruin Cochran and so decided to intervene by advising him what was happening and ensuring that Anderson kept to a schedule. Of course Anderson was not pleased with them, but they saved the day. 'If it hadn't been for the Dollies the revue would not have been produced when it was . . . they saved me thousands of pounds . . . I can never sufficiently express my gratitude to those splendid artists and wonderful women,' said an appreciative Cochran.[6]

The revue opened with a curtain, a gleaming creation of silver tissue that rose to reveal a theatre manager in a fog trying to find a plot. A pierrot, columbine and harlequin disperse the fog and take him to a tailor to discuss the issue as the stage becomes full of beautiful girls representing music, dance and youth and other ingredients of a popular show; and so the excitement began.[7] Throughout, Cochran made much better use of the Dolly Sisters than de Courville had done, and they appeared in no less than ten scenes. Their first, 'The Art Students', showed them in gorgeous night attire as they sang 'I Love Thou Lovest' in Lucile negligées. One of their biggest hits was 'The Dollies and their Collies', where they shared the stage with a pack of handsome and intelligent collie dogs trained by Jud Brady, which followed the sisters in their various steps. They did an exotic Persian Dance in 'The Garden of Dreams', and in 'On the 'Alls', a witty pastiche of old-time music-hall artistes of a decade ago, the Dollies wore black top hats and coachmen's silken cloaks. For the finale, 'The Bridal Veil', they appeared as the Bride of the Future and the Bridesmaid of the Future, in gleaming gowns with headdresses of astonishing complexity.

Since the bulk of the show had been imported from New York, most of the costumes for *League of Notions* were created by the American designers James Reynolds and Robert E. Locher. However, the costumes for the Dolly Sisters were created for them in Paris, where they had to endure endless rounds of fittings besides all the night-time fun in the autumn of 1920. Paul Poiret created their exotic bridal gowns, and their costumes for 'The Dollies and their Collies' and the Persian Dance were executed by Max Weldy. Most probably these latter costumes were designed by Dolly Tree, one of London's leading stage designers, who became a great friend and working colleague of their brother Eddie.[8]

League of Notions was undoubtedly Cochran's most ambitious and lavish revue to date, attracting Prince George, the Duke of York, and Prince Henry, the Duke of Gloucester, to the première. David, Prince of Wales, also saw the show.[9] One reviewer opined that the *League of Notions* 'easily beats, for sheer magnificence, anything I have seen on the London stage',[10] while another said that it illustrated 'a sheer embarrassment of riches . . . and general spectacular effects'.[11] The reviews were astoundingly complimentary, and the Dolly Sisters, regarded as great favourites,[12] enthralled the audience with their magnificent costumes and sheer personality. 'It is impossible to assess the value of the Dolly Sisters as contributors to the show – they simply immerse themselves in the needs of the occasion and emerge in triumph.'[13] Charles Graves candidly observed that 'nobody would ever suggest that the Dolly Sisters were great artists, but they were certainly great troupers. They sang and danced with amazing energy . . .', and he firmly believed that the show 'pulsated with their personal energy'.[14] 'What are those twins made of?', Cochran asked at the time. 'Heaven only knows! Their vitality is staggering.'[15]

Another guest at the première was the father of the Dolly Sisters, Julius Dolly, who made his first visit to London with Jenny when she returned from New York in November 1920 and stayed until February 1921. It was strange that it was just Julius and not the rest of the family who made the visit, although they did all make the trip later in the year.[16] They must all have had a fabulous time on the opening night, because after the show C.B. Cochran gave a party for all the cast and specially invited guests at the Ivy restaurant.[17]

A few weeks after the opening of *League of Notions* the Dollies received a letter that was radically to transform their social standing and impression of London. The letter was from Sir Philip Sassoon, MP for Hythe in Kent, and brother of Siegfried, the war poet, inviting them to dance at a big charity entertainment in his London House at 25 Park Lane. Sassoon (1888–1939) was extremely wealthy and highly intelligent, and had been Private Secretary to Field Marshal Sir Douglas Haig, Commander-in-Chief of British Armies in France 1915–18 and was shortly to become trustee of the National Gallery. He moved in the highest social and political circles and was on good terms with the Prince of Wales.

The Dollies were thrilled, especially when they learned that Sassoon was one of Britain's richest and most eligible young bachelors, even though his sexuality was in doubt. His house was regarded as one of the finest in London, and they were told that everyone of importance in London would be at this particular ball. 'Perhaps London isn't so bad after all,' Rosie said, as they talked over the invitation. 'But we won't meet any of the guests,' Jenny observed; 'we'll be taken in through the tradesman's entrance and after we have finished our dance we'll be sent home. I don't see anything very wonderful in that.'

As they discussed this issue in their dressing room, there was a knock at the door, and they were introduced to Sir William Maxwell Aitken, better known as Lord Beaverbrook. The Canadian-born British newspaper magnate and political go-between was then a millionaire, 44 and in his prime. Although married, Lord Beaverbrook (1879–1964) led a somewhat separate social life from his wife and was known to have had several affairs. After making a fortune in Montreal as a financier, he moved to England and became active in politics as a Conservative. Beginning in 1916, he took over or founded newspapers, including the London *Daily Express*, *Sunday Express* and *Evening Standard*. Idiosyncratic and successful, he became a champion of individual enterprise and British imperial interests and held various high government appointments during both world wars.

Lord Beaverbrook had been sitting in the front row and had enjoyed their performance so much that after the show he asked to be introduced to them. The Dollies 'were delighted to be so highly honoured', and during the course of conversation they asked him about Sir Philip Sassoon's letter. 'You're quite right,' he said. 'If Sir Philip wants to entertain you in his home you should go as guests – not as entertainers. Especially if that's the way you feel about it.'

So that night they wrote and declined Sir Philip's offer to dance at his party. Sir Philip was so amazed at their refusal to dance that a few days later he decided to go and see them and discover for himself what kind of strange people they were. He told them this and added that he appreciated their point of view and as a mark of his appreciation he had decided to give a party in early March 1921 in their honour (perhaps Lord Beaverbrook had a hand in this decision). A week later he collected them from the theatre after their performance by car and drove them to his Park Lane home. He assisted them to the red carpet that ran from the entrance to the kerb.

'The Prince is here tonight,' he announced.

'You could have knocked me down with a feather and my sister later confided in me that she was never so flustered in her life,' said Rosie.

They were escorted into the ballroom, where about twenty guests were dancing to a jazz band. As the band stopped, a good-looking young man described by Rosie as 'a blond, pink-faced youth' rushed up to them. He was, of course, the Prince of Wales, later to become Edward VIII, who had returned to London in October 1920 from an extensive trip to Australia, New Zealand and the West Indies. He was to become one of their most ardent admirers.

Overwhelmingly charming, hence his nickname 'Prince Charming', Edward had an instinctive flair for public relations and could be tactful, eloquent and quick-witted when he wanted to be or duty called. And yet, despite his enormous popularity, he lacked confidence, and, according to his cousin Lord Mountbatten, beneath the veneer he 'was a lonely and sad person always liable to deep depression'. The Prince could be immature and reckless, and his lack of seriousness, dislike of royal duties and hectic hedonism precipitated grave doubts about his suitability as future king.

His continual battle against authority, and his father in particular, plus lack of attention from his mother, had a major influence on his private life in the form of a search for a mother-figure who would lavish love and affection upon him. This would later materialise most clearly when he fell in love with the American Wallis Simpson, for whom he relinquished his crown in 1936. From 1915 the Prince had been infatuated with Marion Coke, Viscountess Coke, daughter-in-law of the Earl of Leicester and fifteen years his senior. After two years she was replaced in his affections by Lady Rosemary Leverson-Gower, the youngest daughter of the Duke of Sutherland, whom he met in late 1916.

The Prince was dissuaded from continuing the romance and subsequently became entranced by Winifred (Freda) Dudley Ward, daughter of a Nottingham lace manufacturer. Petite, elegant and pretty Freda was the same age as the Prince. According to her friend Lady Loughborough, 'She was absolutely fascinating to look at, she had a good mind, a tremendous character, great loyalty and a wonderful sense of humour. She built one up and made one feel amusing and attractive.'

Freda had also been married for five years to William Dudley Ward, the Liberal MP for Southampton and Vice Chamberlain of the Royal Household, but lived a convenient separate life. After meeting the Prince of Wales in 1918, she became his passion, beginning a relationship with no future that endured for fifteen years even though it was interspersed with numerous other dalliances.[18]

It was into these circumstances that the Dollies blissfully danced at Philip Sassoon's party.

'So glad to meet you,' the Prince said to the Dolly Sisters, taking both of their right hands in greeting.

'I've seen you dance . . . and I think you're wonderful.'

'I want you to meet my brother,' he continued and beckoned to a slender young man who proved to be Prince Henry, the more reserved, amiable yet highly strung Duke of Gloucester.

The band struck up a foxtrot, and Rosie was asked to dance by the Prince of Wales as Jenny danced with Prince Henry. The Prince of Wales proved to be a capital dancer and he talked entertainingly while they danced. Rosie showed him some new steps; he must have been remarkably quick at learning them and delighted at mastering them, for he asked the band to repeat the number. He then danced with Jenny, as Rosie danced with Prince Henry.

'Pinch me, I'm dreaming,' Jenny said during a break; 'it's like a fairy book.'

They had a supper of caviar and champagne and throughout the evening met all Sir Philip's guests, including his sister Lady Rocksavage, and found everyone to be extremely cordial.

Then the Prince of Wales said to Rosie, 'You should teach those new steps to everyone here.'

So all the guests lined up in front of them and for half an hour Rosie and Jenny performed the steps and taught them to everyone. The evening was delightful and made them feel happier than they had since they arrived in London. As they got to bed at 6 a.m., Rosie said: 'London is wonderful, isn't it Jenny?'

'Too wonderful for words,' Jenny replied.'[19]

Philip Sassoon's party proved to be the turning point for them; at last they had been really noticed and admired by London polite society. 'I am sure we would not have remained in London if it had not been for the friendships we formed and the kindness which was shown to us on every side,' said Rosie.

They still had to follow protocol and listened to Lord Beaverbrook's wisdom as he told them to make themselves agreeable to personages of their own sex in high society and to accept invitations only from them. To be taken to exclusive homes by anyone of the male persuasion, no matter what his standing, might prove fatal to a successful social career. On the other hand, invitations from women would enable them to meet everyone in time. He also made it clear that in London it was always best to make haste slowly.[20]

Beaverbrook's keen interest in ensuring their social success was later explained by one of his biographers. A.J.P. Taylor believed that he loved to 'make' people. For example, Taylor believed that Beaverbrook transformed his mistress, Jean Norton, into a woman of the world.[21] The implication was that the same sense of achievement must have been his motivation with the

Dollies. However, Beaverbrook's attraction and desire for the sisters may well have taken precedence, as in his later affair with Tallulah Bankhead.

The Dollies took Lord Beaverbrook's advice wholeheartedly. 'We minded our Ps and Qs and found the initial advice that had been given to us enormously useful. The women in London society decide who is to be invited a second time – and that is the thing that counts.' Instead of being ignored and lonely, they were soon flooded with invitations. They had finally arrived among London's pivotal social group and devoted all their spare time to social activities. Luncheons, teas and supper parties in the most exclusive of London homes followed in rapid succession as they became acutely aware of the different way in which they were being treated.

Although they had been invited to many high-class homes in New York, they were received in London on a very different basis. Jenny observed that successful artists in London had a very different standing from their American counterparts. In New York actresses were still regarded as a separate class, and when society people invited actresses to functions they were expected to perform and were not invited just as guests. In contrast, actresses in London seemed to be viewed differently and had a higher social standing because the theatre was taken more seriously as a profession. It attracted a better class of people. It was not the mecca of the socially disappointed and it was freer from commercialism and vulgarity. Equally, Jenny also noticed a big difference with regard to alcohol; in London no one would ever drink to excess and lose decorum, whereas in New York, perhaps because of Prohibition, the majority of Americans simply did not know how to drink.[22]

One important and influential new friend was Freda Dudley Ward, whom they met at a dinner party, describing her as 'one of the most charming as well as the most beautiful members of "the Prince's set"'. She was well known as the Prince of Wales's mistress, so the Dolly Sisters, like everyone else, used the utmost tact in describing the liaison. The reason why Freda Dudley Ward extended the hand of friendship will remain a mystery. Freda's mother was American, so the Dollies assumed she was happy to entertain her 'fellow countrywomen'.[23] But this is far too simplistic an explanation. Did the Prince of Wales influence Freda to encompass the Dollies in her circle? Or was Freda perhaps jealous of his attention to them and so included them in her social events to keep an eye on them? By the summer of 1920, when the Dollies first met the Prince of Wales, his relationship with Freda had cooled as she tried to make it more platonic, but they still remained close. Freda may well have enjoyed their company, but keeping an eye on the Dollies would have meant she could keep an eye on the Prince of Wales at the same time.

Another new friend was Sir Thomas Lipton (1859–1931), the celebrated businessman, millionaire and founder of a grocery-store empire, who had made his money out of tea. Born in Glasgow, Lipton had established a nationwide chain of grocery stores and revolutionised the retail trade by developing marketing techniques that are still used by supermarkets today. To supply his shops, Lipton bought tea, coffee and cocoa plantations in Ceylon as well as English fruit farms, jam factories and bakeries. He became a household name through innovations in the tea business that included the development of tea bags. His fortune also enabled him to challenge consistently, but unsuccessfully, for the Americas yachting cup. He had no heirs on his death and left much of his fortune to the city of Glasgow, to aid the poor and to build hospitals.[24]

Later in life he enjoyed a considerable reputation as a ladies' man, but this was a carefully cultivated myth, and, although his name was frequently linked in the gossip columns with a variety of women, there was never any substance to the stories, and rumours of engagement were followed by denials. His true passion appears to have been William Love, his inseparable business partner, and obviously much more than his right-hand man. When they parted company in 1893, they remained on intimate terms, and he was seemingly 'replaced' by John Westwood, his private secretary for thirty years.

Like Beaverbrook, Lipton admired the Dollies' performance at the Hippodrome and introduced himself. Well into his seventies, Lipton was still romantically linked with prominent socialites, celebrities and actresses, including the Dolly Sisters, who said that 'our acquaintance soon developed into a warm and fast friendship'. They spent the weekend at Lipton's beautiful, yet rather old-fashioned, country home at Osidge, Old Southgate, Middlesex. Following their Saturday night performance in *League of Notions*, they were driven to his estate in one of his cars, which he sent for them. They left London at midnight and arrived at 1 a.m. and were taken to their rooms by a small retinue of Indian servants all in native costume. They were up bright and early and joined Lipton and his other guests, among them Sir Harry Lauder, the world-famous Scottish music-hall artist and his wife.

At Sunday lunch, Lipton told the Dollies that he had been deeply in love with a young girl and they were to be married, but she ran off and married a rich man twice her age. He had never got over it. 'I had a very bitter experience . . . I came to the conclusion that matrimony was largely a matter of money . . . I was convinced that it was my fortune and not myself that women were after.' He then chuckled and added: 'Yes I am a bachelor and I'm going to remain one. For you know, my dear friends, married men make the worst husbands.'[25] To maintain his reputation and the myth of his flirtatious nature, Jenny announced that the old charmer had lost none of his winning ways with the fair sex.

Through Lord Beaverbrook, Sir Thomas Lipton and other prominent, not to mention rich, members of English society, the Dollies stepped out into London nightlife, being wined, dined and entertained.[26] It would have been very different from what they had been used to in New York. There was dancing in the grand hotels such as the Savoy, Piccadilly and Cecil, but at the time there were few nightspots that catered for those in need of another type of rendezvous: nightclubs in London were very select, small and in essence smart restaurants with dance floors.

The most exclusive and sophisticated place, and a favourite of the Prince of Wales, was the Embassy Club at the Piccadilly end of Bond Street. The Embassy was a long basement, luxuriously furnished with sofas and tables along the walls, which held glass mirrors. In the centre of the room was the dance floor and at one end of the room, on a balcony, was the dance band.

Their first experience of this place would have been when Albert de Courville arranged a dance contest at the club on 8–15 July 1920. The Dollies were judges along with other stage celebrities.[27] After this event they became regular visitors, although other venues also beckoned. The Grafton Galleries were regarded as the home of dancing, with a vast high-ceilinged ballroom, but there were also the Riviera, overlooking the river on Grosvenor Road, Ciro's in Orange Street, modelled on the famous Ciro's of Paris, Rector's in the bowels of the earth below Tottenham Court Road, and Murray's Club, the only venue at the time with a cabaret floor show.[28]

Lord Beaverbrook became one of their regular escorts. Early in 1921 he was entertaining them at the Criterion one evening – dinner in the beautifully decorated dining room followed by dancing in the sumptuous Italian Roof Garden – when he was summoned by the Prime Minister, David Lloyd George, and offered the post of Lord High Commissioner of the General Assembly of the Church of Scotland. Beaverbrook told him he was not suited to the office. Lloyd George then said he would offer the job to 'Geordie' (the Duke of Sutherland). When Beaverbrook returned to the Criterion, to his surprise he found 'Geordie' dancing with one of the Dolly Sisters.[29]

During the run of *League of Notions* the Dollies were observed at all sorts of social and charity affairs. In April they attended the London Country Club's fancy-dress ball at Hendon,[30] and in May the Warriors' Day Ball in Covent Garden, where they won first prize in the fancy-dress competition representing Ciro pearls.[31] And, in July, at the Theatrical Garden Party in Covent Garden accompanied by two collie dogs, they sold dolls and were delighted to spend an enjoyable and warm afternoon in the company of the Prince of Wales.[32] Unlike de Courville, Cochran looked after them and ensured that they made friends with his other stars, including Alice Delysia, whose sparkling personality, provocative looks and glorious singing voice became the toast of London in the 1920s. He also introduced them to other visiting theatrical folk such as Sacha Guitry and his wife, the actress and singer Yvonne Printemps, during their seasons in London.

The Dollies also met the great French producer Jacques-Charles, from the Casino de Paris, and the magnificent yet difficult Mistinguett, who also arrived for a short stay in late 1921. The most dazzling of all Parisian entertainers, Mistinguett (1875–1956), or 'Miss' as she was known affectionately, was a lithe dancer and had a flair for style and glamour that gave her star quality. Her fabulous legs were reputedly insured for a million dollars. 'Miss' was relentlessly ambitious, had tremendous discipline and energy but was notorious for her tantrums and backstage feuding. Jacques-Charles once said that she was his dearest friend and his worst enemy; they frequently quarrelled only to make up later.[33] Mistinguett and Jacques-Charles saw *League of Notions* and both took an interest in Earl Leslie, who eventually became both Mistinguett's dancing partner and her lover and was secured to appear in the new Casino de Paris show *Paris en l'air* that opened in late 1921.

Mistinguett believed that during her trip to London she became great friends with the Dollies. She made some odd comments about them – for example, that they were 'fairly badly off' – and claimed that she once ironed and washed Jenny's only dress so she could go to a press party.[34] It is difficult to believe that the Dolly Sisters were badly off and that Jenny had only one dress. Either Mistinguett was being malicious or perhaps the Dollies had hatched a plot to dupe Mistinguett into believing they were poor – another of their games of deception.

The Dollies were also regulars at soirées hosted by British stage stars like Ivor Novello. Regarded as Britain's greatest genius of the musical stage and a matinée idol, he used to have parties from midnight, the perfect time for theatre folk. His flat was always crammed with famous stage personalities. Supper was often ordered from the Savoy Hotel, and there were frequent impromptu performances, where the Dollies would have been obliged to demonstrate their dancing skills.[35] They also acted as hosts and entertained a wide variety of guests at their own elegant rented flat in St Martin's Lane – secured for them by C.B. Cochran and a more suitable location than their first London flat in Mayfair – which they shared with a parrot, an Irish terrier and a Persian cat, all no doubt rented too.[36]

Towards the end of the run of *League of Notions*,[37] Cochran launched *Fun of the Fayre* in mid-October at the Pavilion, with the beautiful actress and singer Evelyn Laye, Trini, hailed as the most beautiful girl in the world, and Clifton Webb to replace the talent of Earl Leslie. The Fratellini clowns, whom Cochran had brought over from the Cirque Medrano in Paris, were also one of the attractions, but they flopped badly on the first night because of problems with props and disturbances in the audience because of rumours that they were German. The Dollies graciously saved the day by running from *League of Notions* and appearing in the finale with Clifton Webb doing the Pony Trot, which they revived from *Jigsaw*, proving an extremely popular addition.

They continued their round of social engagements with the smart London set. At one such event they met the Duke and Duchess of Sutherland and Mrs Richard Norton, who later became the mistress of Lord Beaverbrook. They were invited to go to one of the greatest social functions of the year – the fancy-dress Victory Ball at the Albert Hall attended by every prominent member of society on Friday 12 November. Freda Dudley Ward's plan was to have all her female guests dressed exactly like the Dolly Sisters 'and in that way add to the gaiety of the occasion' and selected an apache costume from *League of Notions* – a short plaid skirt with a red sash, white blouse and black hat. The idea was to have four sets of Dollies at the ball, and in order to mystify the other guests it was arranged to have them arrive one set at a time. Because of their performance schedule, however, the Dollies arrived late and joined the party in Freda Dudley Ward's box. Nevertheless, the ruse, as intended, caused much confusion and comment. Later the Dollies played a minor deception at dinner, or more accurately at a very late supper, on the young Lord Ashley (1900–47), son of the 9th Earl of Shaftesbury.

Lord Ashley had wagered £25 that he could tell Rosie from Jenny. 'It was a very foolish wager on his part,' said Jenny, 'for several times when I had gone to luncheon or dinner with him he had talked to me about things that had happened when he was with Rosie.' Since he was enamoured at the time with Rosie, he had supper with her. But Jenny had whispered her deception plan to

Rosie, and after supper Rosie excused herself, to be replaced by Jenny. Lord Ashley, of course, did not notice and so Jenny claimed the wager. Lord Ashley was still bewildered and could not believe he had been duped and said, 'the only way you can prove to me that you are not Rosie is to eat another supper . . . I know Rosie had supper with me and she did herself so well that I don't believe she could eat another.' Jenny obliged, and he admitted his mistake.[38] He clearly had a thing about showgirls, because he later married the lovely actress Sylvia Hawkes, referred to at the time as the 'latest recruit from the stage to the peerage'.[39]

At about the same time that Lord Ashley was enamoured with Rosie, rumours of a new love match for Jenny began circulating in Europe and America. At the time Rosie's divorce from Jean Schwartz had been finalised, and Jenny was on the verge of obtaining her divorce from Harry Fox.[40] The stories noted that a persistent admirer was Alexander Smith Cochran (1875–1929), the multimillionaire New York carpet king, sportsman and generous philanthropist and that an engagement was on the horizon. Smith Cochran had been called the most eligible bachelor in the world, but had secretly married the Polish opera singer Mme Ganna Walska in September 1920.[41] At the time of Jenny's alleged 'liaison' with Smith Cochran, he was separated and seeking a divorce from Walska and busy working on a project with C.B. Cochran to purchase a site in London and construct a new pleasure palace.[42] In London Jenny said, 'When I marry, Broadway will get the surprise of its life.'[43] Broadway must have been surprised, since nothing happened and the romance must have fizzled out, rather like the pleasure palace project itself.

Even though Rosie appeared to be romantically linked with Lord Ashley, there were other rumours that she was to marry George Brockbank, the millionaire son of a well-known English railway magnate, whom she apparently met at a house party given by Sir Thomas Lipton, and yet Rosie denied she even knew him.[44] Rosie's romances, like Jenny's, seemed to evaporate.

In the midst of all these rumours of romance, the rest of the Dolly family – mother, father and brother Eddie – arrived in London at the end of 1921. It was Eddie's first trip to London, and he enjoyed himself so much that he decided to stay. Tall, handsome and debonair, he was as vibrant a personality as his two sisters. It helped that Eddie was also an accomplished dancer, and the Dollies persuaded Cochran to give him a job orchestrating the dance numbers for the next Cochran show – a Christmas pantomime – with Stowitts, the multi-talented American dancer, decorator, painter, producer and film star.[45] Eddie 'had the kind of face that doesn't do too much to you, but you can't forget the twinkle in his eye. He couldn't leave the girls alone,' said Kit Peters, who worked with him in one of his shows.[46] Cochran used Eddie as choreographer on many of his shows, and he became well known in theatrical circles in London.[47] Although he led his own life, he frequently joined his sisters in Paris and on the Riviera.

After the closure of *League of Notions* on 26 November 1921, Cochran decided to stage his first pantomime and starred the Dolly Sisters in an elaborate production of *Babes in the Wood* presented at the New Oxford Theatre on 21 December.

The rich fruity humour for *Babes in the Wood* was provided by A.W. Bascomb as the elderly dame, while the Fratellini clowns, who had bombed in *Fun of the Fayre*, found their feet in such scenes as 'Where the Toys Come From', which showed living toys and a talking toy ballet. The show was staged and costumed with exquisite taste,[48] including some sumptuous dresses by Paul Poiret for the luminous moths in the wood scene and a ballet of cards. But the show simply did not go down well with the London public, who instead packed the Hippodrome to see the more traditional *Jack and the Beanstalk* presented by Julian Wylie, the 'King of Pantomime'.

Although Cochran thought that he had scrupulously respected all the old traditions, it was thought that there was 'a vein of refinement' running through the show, making it too sophisticated and striking 'a rather higher note in pantomime than is usual'.[49] The Dolly Sisters were described as being 'something more than charming' and in their lighter scenes were thought to be quite dainty and funny.[50] Their song 'Keep on Humming' also proved to be immensely popular. But Charles Graves rightly observed that a man of Cochran's experience and talent should have seen the incongruity of the Dolly Sisters playing the babes.[51] His loss on the brief run was over $35,000.

After the closure of *Babes in the Wood* on 21 January 1922, the Dollies should have taken a period of rest and relaxation before embarking on a new project. A short holiday somewhere would have been timely, but instead they recrossed the Atlantic to fulfil a short vaudeville season for the Keith Circuit to capitalise on their London success.

THE DANDY-LOOKING DOLLIES IN DIXIE AND DEAUVILLE

Once back in New York in early February 1922, the Dolly Sisters installed themselves in a magnificent duplex apartment at 33 West 67th Street that belonged to a film magnate of international popularity who had just departed on a European trip. To them, New York was now a different place, showing the full impact of Prohibition, which had come into effect on 15 January 1920. 'Even in the comparatively short time they have been away they have noted many changes which have come over New York and they have been spending considerable time in attempts to reacclimatise themselves.'[1] Denied the revenue from liquor, the majority of the original cabarets had become idle. In order to survive and continue to stage some form of show, those that did continue were forced to charge an entrance fee and raise prices. By the spring of 1922 nightlife had returned but in a different format.

Many of the new venues, mostly at restaurants or hotels, had orchestras, and dancing was the main preoccupation. There were some venues that staged floor shows, including Club Maurice, Healy's Golden Glades and the Strand

Roof, but mostly entertainment was provided by one or more principals, such as the dancing of Gilda Grey at the Rendezvous or Bessie McCoy at the Knickerbocker Grill. The Dollies would also have visited their friend Sophie Tucker, who was the main singing attraction at the Crystal Room of Reisenweber's. The employment opportunities were so difficult in the cabarets that the Dollies' offer to appear in one of the major venues (most likely Club Maurice) at $3,250 weekly was not taken up. Equally, their friend Harry Pilcer, who had been appearing in Albert de Courville's show *Pins and Needles*, had his request for $2,000 a week refused.[2]

There was no such slump in the Dollies' magnificent apartment, since they had brought a portable bar from London and, with no regard for Prohibition, shook their cocktail shakers and offered their guests a range of delectable concoctions. The Dollies had arrived, newly divorced, with forty-two dance numbers and forty-two changes of costume for their limited vaudeville engagement of five weeks at the Palace Theatre and two other Keith theatres each week. The productions were staged by Kuy Kendall, whom they had befriended when they appeared together at the Shuberts' *Midnight Revue* in 1918.

They made their debut wearing colourful coral dresses and yellow gowns at the Palace Theatre in mid-February in a twenty-minute segment doing three numbers with Kendall;[3] this was seen as 'something of an event along Broadway'. The crowd was overflowing and the front rows and boxes held many well-known people of the theatre. Once again Sime of *Variety* provided his usual sly comments. He felt that they did not quite meet the expectations of the audience, whose applause was desultory because much of what they saw was simply nothing new. Further, he thought that perhaps their success in London had caused them to be careless in composing the act for the Palace and an American audience, since they appeared to do very little, although he did concede that the orchestra 'did not help the girls'. Sime clearly did not appreciate them and did not understand why they were so popular. 'The Dollys for years have held an odd hold on the New York show-going public. . . . As two dandy looking twins who cannot be told apart with class and who can dance if they want to, the Dolly Sisters are always worth the price of admission just to look at.' Given that he had made scathing comments about them before, the review was nothing out of the ordinary in terms of its criticism, and yet the Dollies must have felt that they were not at their best, because by the evening performance their routine had been changed.[4]

By the second week they presented a completely new act of four dance numbers that had been Americanised and speeded up. Their first dresses were of grey velvet fringed with silver lace and lined in turquoise blue, with huge grey hats trimmed with osprey. The second number was tinged with jazz, and they wore fetching short-skirted gypsy costumes with silver bodices and fringes in many colours. The third dresses were very bride-like in white chiffon abundantly showered with brilliants and headdresses of white plumes and brilliants. Their final change was into deep orange chiffon frocks with silver bodices hung with bunches of cherries.[5]

Variety thought that the initial poor reception had undoubtedly hurt them professionally but had not damaged their drawing power. The fact that they had polished their act and found a more enthusiastic response meant they were now set for a five-week stay. They also appeared at the Riverside, on 96th Street, and Broadway, where another reviewer believed that their act offered something on a par with their reputation and popularity.[6] By the third week *Variety* decided that they had a 'nice act', and, although audiences had dwindled slightly at the Palace, they were still popular and doubled up at the Colonial and Alhambra. More new frocks appeared, including chartreuse net dresses with very transparent skirts showing long pants and hats of the same shade with long plumes in salmon, flesh-coloured union suits hung with a silver fringe and simple white gowns with red hats and sashes.[7]

For the latter part of their run they changed the act considerably, and *Variety* decided that they 'seem to improve with acquaintance'. They did a new opening number wearing dresses of fluffy red tulle, a waltz wearing new silk fringed dresses and novelty headdresses, and an old-fashioned clog dance wearing grotesque hats and short skirts. Wearing a full black skirt, tight bodice and red apron, Rosie appeared with Kendall in 'The Man from Montmartre', and Jenny, similarly dressed, did a modernised Apache dance with Kendall dressed in black velvet.[8]

Overall, their reappearance at the Palace was a success and well worth the $25,000 that they received for five weeks' work. Out of this they were forced to pay F. Ray Comstock, theatrical manager, the sum of $5,000 for non-payment of a promissory note signed and dated 15 April 1920. Even deducting the cost of forty-two frocks, they must still have netted a tidy sum, which would have made Mistinguett envious.[9]

After a brief rest, the Dolly Sisters returned to London aboard the *Aquitania*, arriving in Southampton on Wednesday 19 April 1922. Jack Dempsey, the heavyweight boxing champion of the world, was also on board, travelling to Europe on a tour accompanied by author Damon Runyon, who was writing stories for the American press. Dempsey clearly spent a lot of time being entertained by the Dollies, and when he arrived in London on the boat train, the British press were eager to find out about his voyage and his new friends.

'We hear Mr Dempsey, that you not only worked out in the gymnasium on shipboard but that you spent busy evenings with the singing Dolly Sisters.'

'They're nice girls,' he said, 'both of them.'

'Are you going to marry either of the Dolly Sisters?' he was asked.

'I'd have to be Solomon to choose and I'm not Solomon. I'm a prizefighter. Who could choose between the Dolly Sisters? I can't.'[10]

Clearly someone could tell them apart, because Rosie was on the verge of marriage, the tale of which Jenny revealed in a later interview. Originally the plan had been for the sisters to return to London and appear in Cochran's new revue *From Mayfair to Montmartre*,[11] which had opened in early March. During the run of *League of Notions*, Rosie had met and fallen in love with the Honourable Percy Brook, an attractive young Englishman of title.[12] Rosie's romance put an end to any notions of new starring roles on the London stage, but equally *From Mayfair to Montmartre* was not doing well and closed prematurely on 20 May. According to Jenny, as soon as Rosie arrived back in London, Percy proposed marriage, and Rosie impulsively accepted. Jenny remarked that 'marriage meant retirement from the stage and separation from me. So I counselled Rosie to be very sure of her own mind before making such a change in her life.' The upshot of Jenny's counsel was that Percy and his sister took Rosie on a long motoring trip to Spain and Morocco. They both agreed that it would determine the questions whether Rosie could be happy away from Jenny and whether Percy was the right husband. After a few weeks Jenny started to receive letters from Rosie indicating that she was not as happy as she had expected to be. Although Percy and his sister were charming and marvellous company, she missed the excitement of her career and, most importantly, so we are told, Jenny. Eventually she joined Jenny in Paris and the engagement was called off.[13]

With the end of Rosie's romance, their two-year love affair with London came to an end, to be replaced by the allure of Paris, the attractions of the Normandy coast and the Riviera, and a new source of wealthy admirers. Both sisters had been tempted by several offers of matrimony, but, even though they were newly divorced, footloose and fancy free and reaching the age of 30, the need to maintain their career and identity as the Dolly Sisters appears to have been of greater importance.

They had clearly discovered a new life, a life of independence where they were in control of their own destiny both professionally and emotionally and where enjoyment and pleasure outstripped the desire to settle down. They revelled in the attention of rich and titled men, the continual flow of expensive presents and the excursions to exclusive restaurants and nightclubs. Although many of their liaisons were fleeting, both Dollies appeared to be romantically inclined and with each affair believed they had fallen in love again. Yet this competitive cycle of falling in love, suggestions of engagement and then cold feet as the realisation that marriage would mean a separation and the end of their act caused difficulties. Each romance precipitated anxiety about how they would face the future on their own.

As Rosie's adventure with Percy Brook unfolded, Jenny was in Paris having a good time without her. One night in the New York Bar she was spotted dancing with Jack Dempsey, clearly renewing their acquaintance from the journey on the *Aquitania*. Between the end of dinner and 11.30 p.m., when the supper-dancing establishments opened, there was only one thing 'doing' in Paris and that was the cabaret beneath the New York Bar on the rue Daunou. It became popular in 1922, when two New York singers, Tommy Lyman and Roy Barton, arrived from an appearance at the Clover Club along with Maurice Mouvet and his new dancing partner, Leonora Hughes.[14] Dempsey had known them when they sang at Kelly's in New York, and it was his presence along with other celebrities that put the place firmly on the map.[15] On this particular night, among many other notable guests who included Maurice and Hughes and the film actress Murial Spring, Irving Berlin was playing at the piano and Jenny Dolly was asked to dance. She persuaded Dempsey to join her, and they performed a spirited jazz dance called 'Chicago'.[16]

Paris during the 1920s was the undisputed international capital of pleasure and extravagance and the cultural and artistic centre of Europe.[17] It was regarded as *the* place to be, and the wealthiest, the most gifted and the most beautiful people from all over the world flocked there to enjoy its unique atmosphere and its diverse attractions – fashion, art, café society, jazz and cabaret along with the wide availability of sex, drugs and alcohol. Americans in particular flocked to Paris because of its openness and an extremely favourable foreign exchange rate, not to mention the fact that Prohibition was left behind as soon as they disembarked. In 1919 the exchange rate stood at FF7 to the dollar, but by 1926 it had reached an all-time high of FF55, stabilising at FF25 in 1927. As a result, Americans could live well on very little money, and many led a rather self-indulgent, carefree life, enjoying all the benefits of one of the most exciting places in Europe, including an extraordinary frenetic nightlife: 'You didn't go out just one or two nights a week in those days. You went out every night. If it wasn't to a party, it was to the opera or the theatre or the Folies Bergère, and afterward you went to one of the Montmartre clubs. Parties began at 11, or even midnight and carried on until the early hours of the morning.'[18]

Paris was also a place of tolerance, where diversity was allowed free expression in terms of sexual orientation, colour of skin and background. Parisians maintained an open fascination with black culture, and black was beautiful and fashionable. This was highlighted by the successful staging of black revues such as *La Revue nègre* at the Champs-Elysées Music Hall in October 1925, which introduced the scantily dressed young black singer and dancer Josephine Baker, who swiftly became the toast of Paris and rival to Mistinguett in the popularity stakes. Edmund Sayag also imported the Lew Leslie show *Blackbirds* with the equally glamorous black singer and dancer Florence Mills at the Ambassadeurs in mid-1926. But before Miss Baker there had been a huge influx of American talent. Besides the Dolly Sisters, there was also the acrobatic dancer Nina Payne, the 'drag' trapeze artist Barbette, the dancers Harry Pilcer and Earl Leslie and the Gertrude Hoffman Girls, who competed with such home-grown talents as Mistinguett, Damia, Yvonne Gilbert and Maurice Chevalier. The Americans had also revitalised the night scene in Paris with a wave of American-owned nightclubs such as Zelli's, Mitchell's, Florence's and Bricktop's, which all flourished with much success.

Paris relished the notion that it was the home of the spectacular revue, and it was the theatre directors who forged this development into a coherent and dynamic whole between 1900 and the First World War. Of these, Oscar Dufrenne, Henri Varna, Leon Volterra, Jacques-Charles and Paul Derval were responsible for modelling the lavish revue into a spectacle that reached a pinnacle of extravagance in the 1920s. They believed that the future of French music hall lay, not with parochial Parisian material, but in the sumptuous international super productions that would attract tourists. So they gathered around them the leading talents of the day, including performers, costumiers, designers, choreographers, lyricists and composers, to help make their vision a reality.[19]

In 1917 Leon Volterra with Jacques-Charles took over the Casino de Paris and launched a series of historic revues with *Laissez-les tomber*, starring Gaby

Deslys, who had returned to Paris after a successful tour of America with Harry Pilcer. This vibrant new show set the tone for modern French music hall, combining the old music-hall charm with more modern ideas from the New World, featuring elaborate costumes, spectacular sets and a black jazz band. This marked the start of glamorous spectacle on the Parisian stage. By 1923 the Folies Bergère, Casino de Paris, Ba-ta-Clan, the Olympia and the Ambassadeurs were leading the lavish revue field.

After two months of parties it was time for Jenny to earn a living again, and in early June she became the star attraction at the newly opened Acacias dancing and eating establishment. The Acacias, a hall in the rear of the Hotel Acacias, near the bois de Boulogne, with a garden for the hot weather, was originally opened in the summer of 1921 by Maurice Chevalier and the singer-impressionist Saint-Grenier.[20] This incarnation was allegedly the unique conception of Elsa Maxwell, who was once described as the 'leviathan of the international café society'.[21]

Maxwell, a small, stout woman from San Francisco, was ebullient and overwhelming. Since she was physically unattractive, she used her only skill – a remarkable ability to organise things – to make her name as 'a licensed buffoon, a jester and doyenne of party-giving on two continents', and thus become socially acceptable.[22] Society became her life and her profession and she used her wide acquaintances to propel herself as a society hostess.[23]

Maxwell insisted that it was she who decided to open a high-class cabaret in Paris, described as 'Elsa Maxwell's Hot-Weather Haunt',[24] and quickly found a backer in the English couturier Captain Edward Molyneux. Maxwell secured him by suggesting that the venture would provide a major benefit – he could promote his salon with the clientele a chic nightclub would attract.[25]

When the Acacias opened, it had been redesigned in the style of a Southern plantation. In the kitchen a black Mammy cooked Southern dishes, and 'piccaninnies' served the guests. Jenny was partnered by Clifton Webb, fresh from his spell under Cochran's guidance in London, and the pair danced beneath the trees to the light of the moon and the electric lamps. Webb also sang songs from *The Music Box Revue* and *Good Morning Dearie*. Jenny was expensively gowned by Molyneux and made an entrance every night covered in a reversible cloak of silver cloth lined with black velvet and adorned with an abundance of white feathers together with a headdress of black and white paradise plumes worth a fortune. Underneath the cloak was a lacquered silver cloth gown with a wide girdle embroidered with diamonds and pearls.[26] She also wore a coral pink frock, a girdle embroidered with coral and pink steel beads and a cloak of steel-coloured lamé cloth embroidered with silver, and finally a gown of lacquered gold cloth with a wide girdle of diamonds and topaz and a headdress of grapes in shades of jade and cobalt. All smart Parisian society took tables for the great opening event: Baron and Baronne Rothschild, Cécile Sorel, the great French actress and doyenne of the Comédie Française, Elsie de Wolfe, the first lady of interior design, the Marquis de Castellane, the elegant man about Paris and social arbiter of France, the opera singer Mary Garden and prima ballerina Anna Pavlova were among the notable first-night guests.[27]

In fact, the Acacias was a duplicate of the New York venue known as The Plantation. This Broadway cabaret-restaurant formerly known as the Folies Bergère was located in the Winter Garden building and opened on 15 February 1922, with an all-coloured show in a Southern plantation setting staged and conceived by Lew Leslie. Going through a gate at the entrance you were immediately inside a big room where there was a log cabin with a big black Mammy cooking waffles. The 45-minute show had a Mississippi river set and was called *Nighttime Frolics in Dixieland*, starring Florence Mills from *Shuffle Along* and other featured performers and six chorus girls. The music was by the Red Devils' Jazz Band, who looked as if they came straight from a farm in Virginia playing Southern melodies. *Variety* observed that the New York night-going public did not mind the $2 cover charge, because it was a novelty and well worth watching.[28] The Plantation was a huge success and anticipated the rise of the Harlem nightclubs that were soon to proliferate, and Lew Leslie became the pre-eminent figure in their development.[29]

Despite the fact that Maxwell claimed the Acacias was her idea, she says nothing about where the Southern plantation idea came from. It is interesting that Jenny Dolly had been in New York at the time Lew Leslie launched the Plantation Club; she must have enjoyed the pleasures of this new venue. Did Jenny actually give Maxwell the idea in the first place? Maxwell also fails to mention in her autobiography that Oscar Mouvet was in fact the manager of the Acacias. Mouvet was the brother of Maurice Mouvet the dancer and became one of the best-known American entertainment entrepreneurs in Paris. After the war he spent some time as a manager for his brother and ran Maurice's Club at the Grande-Bretagne Hotel before running the Acacias.[30] After Maxwell had closed the Acacias, it was taken over by Harry Pilcer, and, with Molyneux again, Maxwell opened Le Jardin de ma Sœur (My Sister's Garden) on the rue Caumartin near the Opéra, with the first-floor show featuring Josephine Baker. Again Oscar Mouvet was the manager. Whatever the truth behind the opening of the new Acacias, it became the number one nightspot in Paris, with the social elite of Paris clamouring to get in.

Rosie arrived back in Paris from her abortive engagement trip with Percy Brook on the afternoon of the final appearance of Jenny and Clifton Webb at the Acacias and performed with her sister that evening. Molyneux was so entranced with the sisters that he decided to organise a dinner party for them and Clifton Webb with some very important guests. But he was told quite categorically: 'You simply cannot have the Dolly Sisters and the United States Ambassador to dine at the same time.' He took no notice and organised the dinner party, inviting not only the Ambassador but the aristocratic Conservative politician Lord Derby, who had been British Ambassador to France for two years until 1920, and the novelist Elinor Glyn, sister to Lucile the couturier, who had been a favourite of the Dollies. The party was a great success and lasted until 6 a.m. Some believed that Molyneux led the celebrity march into society by entertaining a 'mixture of everybody' at this dinner party,[31] but the Dolly Sisters had already started this process themselves by becoming 'agreeable' to London society.

Knowing that Rosie was to return to Paris, Jenny had been in discussion with C.B. Cochran for them to be the stars of a new show at the Palace Theatre in London to replace *The Co-Optimists*.[32] This was later described as a new variety show,[33] which was to follow the success Cochran was having with a similar venture at the Pavilion, staged by Eddie Dolly.[34]

As this idea was being developed, they arranged the dances with brother Eddie for Cochran's new show *Phi-Phi*, launched at the London Pavilion on 16 August with Clifton Webb and Evelyn Laye. But instead of a London engagement the Dollies accepted one of those very lucrative offers that was hard to refuse – a six-week contract from M. Cornuche to dance at his Casino in Deauville. Their love affair with the naughty pleasures of the Normandy coast had already begun in August 1920, but this time they set up residence in an apartment in M. Cornuche's Hotel Royal at the end of July 1922 and made an even bigger splash than before.[35]

Deauville, dubbed by author Basil Woon 'the city of spectacular sin',[36] had been a resort for the wealthy since the Second Empire. At the height of its popularity in the 1920s an American newspaper described it as the wickedest resort in the world. 'It is a maelstrom of human passion concealing thrills and excitement for those rich, incautious and careless enough to plunge in.' It also attracted a cosmopolitan crowd that included every rank and nationality from royalty to mannequins. Deauville owed its fame to Eugene Cornuche and the fabulously wealthy Letellier family. Cornuche had first made his mark with Chauvot and Maxime in the 1890s when they took the lease of a building in the rue Royale near the place de la Concorde and opened a café-restaurant named Maxime's that became the most famous venue in Paris. Eventually he became the sole proprietor but then sold out to an English syndicate. Just before the First World War he leased the Ambassadeurs restaurant and added an open-air theatre and dance hall, which became an instant hit. Then he bought the Concert Mayol and transformed it into a revue theatre. At Trouville he created a casino, but he was viewed with envy by the locals and so switched his attention to Deauville across the river. With the approval of

Henri Letellier, the popular socialite mayor of Deauville, Cornuche built the Normandy Hotel and a casino, which opened in 1913. The casino was a magnificent building in white stone with a façade reminiscent of Versailles; it contained a huge central dance hall and a theatre with a stage where an entire opera ballet could perform, another theatre, a moving picture theatre, a grill, a restaurant, two bars, a tea room, shops and the largest suite of gambling rooms outside Monte Carlo. Cornuche was also the first to put a dance orchestra in a café and changed bar society by allowing women into his drinking establishments. Not surprisingly, Deauville was transformed into a chic resort that became immensely popular.

At the time Deauville was three hours by train from Paris and two hours ten minutes by fast car. The Deauville 'season' opened at Easter and the casino and the Normandy Hotel remained open until the end of September, but the social elite gathered for only three weeks from 1 August. Fashionable London would no more dream of missing this social gathering than it would forget Nice and Monte Carlo in the winter. 'Deauville is a true butterfly, a phenomenon of whirling colour, social high lights and unparalleled gaiety for a brief breathless period out of the heart of the summertime,' explained Basil Woon. Horse racing on the first Sunday marked the opening of the festivities, which ended with the grand prix held on the last Saturday in August, which rivalled the scale of Longchamps in Paris. Each day the blue train brought people from Paris, and a ferry carried people from London via Southampton and Le Havre.

The casino was fronted on the seaside by a wide formal park, green lawns and flower-patterned terraces. Billy Arnold's American band furnished the music every afternoon and evening, and the Ambassadeurs restaurant within the casino was, besides Ciro's, the only smart place to eat. The Normandy had a marvellous courtyard full of apple trees, but there were other good hotels to stay in, such as the Royal and the Splendide. However, by 1928 Deauville had apparently 'become more and more a resort for gamblers, actresses, professional beauties, dress buyers, tourists and business men and less and less a resort patronised by the social elite'.[37]

Life revolved around the casino, the race track, polo matches and the beach. An average day began at 10 a.m., but for many it was much later. The Dollies would have woken up to the sound of the surf pounding on a clean white beach and the smell of a brisk salt breeze perfumed with flowers in full bloom. The fashionable hour for a dip in the sea was 11 a.m., and the Dollies followed the accepted custom for ladies to set new fashion trends with their bathing attire. Just before noon they dressed and made themselves presentable for the vital function that always preceded lunch – an hour at La Potinière. This small café, with its terrace in the cool shade of a tiny grove of trees just behind the casino at the foot of the rue Désiré le Hoc, was unique. 'There is nothing like it anywhere,' said Basil Woon, and it was so popular that it spread out over the street. Everyone, including the Dollies, whetted their appetite by gossiping about the activities of the previous night and what might be expected that day; needless to say the Dollies were also frequently the subject of gossip themselves. Then by 1.30 p.m. the place was abandoned. The distinctive characteristic of the Deauville crowd was 'the instantaneous migratory flight swooping like a huge host of gay-hued care free birds from one pleasure pasturage to another'. Luncheon on the open terrace of the Normandy was next, then a stream of cars and carriages departed for the races, while the more energetic enjoyed golf and tennis. A brief siesta followed in the late afternoon before the evening festivities at the casino. Here the Dollies would dine, entertain and socialise before their performance. Throughout August their gorgeous garments and amazingly skilful dancing drew larger crowds to the casino restaurant than had ever been seen before.[38] Finally, after midnight, they would join the steady stream departing for the casino, where they drew large crowds observing their uncanny nerve for a flutter. Just like their competitive behaviour with their admirers, their gambling antics showed their rivalry, as they tried to outdo each other at baccarat and chemin de fer. Interestingly, their admirers and gambling were often inextricably linked: the more wealthy the admirers, the more extravagant was the performance of the Dollies at the gambling tables.[39]

The Dollies also met many old friends from London, including the Duke and Duchess of Sutherland and Lord Beaverbrook, who regarded Deauville as his favourite resort. At the time Beaverbrook was engaged in discussions with the Aga Khan about Great Britain's relationship with Turkey,[40] but must have had time for some diversions with the Dollies. They also met new friends, among whom was the mayor, Henri Letellier, who was later to take a great interest in Jenny.

However, their most notable admirer became King Alfonso of Spain, under the incognito of the Duc de Toledo, who arrived as the guest of the Marquis de Viana and his son Fausto. After seeing the Dollies dance, King Alfonso decided to call on them one afternoon. He complimented them in English on their dancing and then sat down for a chat. Jenny recalled: 'Whether he arrived from the polo field in white breeches or in his flannels, King Alfonso was always the same debonair, joking companion. We became greatly attached to him and learned to admire his even disposition and his absolute fearlessness.' His visits became such a regular event that he was often smuggled into their apartment through other entrances to avoid the crowds of onlookers.[41] And so they all dined together, danced together, swam together, played together on the beach and met in their apartment day after day. One must wonder whether this liaison was innocent or a double adventure: Jenny with Fausto and Rosie with King Alfonso.

Alfonso was extraordinarily popular, because of his great charm, his simplicity of manner and his kindness. On occasion in the casino he disappeared into the men's room to escape the interest of his female admirers – in this respect he was described as being good tempered and long suffering.[42] However, he certainly did not appear to avoid the attention of the Dolly Sisters.

Despite the formality of these gatherings, they laughed and joked together with apparent naturalness. One afternoon King Alfonso said:

'Miss Dolly, I command you to kiss Fausto.'

To which Jenny replied: 'Your Majesty forgets that I am an American and that you are on French soil.'

'Bravo for you,' exclaimed the King. 'But I've got the better of you. Fausto, I command you to kiss Miss Dolly.'

Fausto rose to his feet, saluted the King and made for Jenny.

'I've got to obey my King,' he explained, desperately seizing her by both arms and trying to kiss her as she tried to escape.

His Majesty convulsed with laughter and, trying to be serious, said:

'Fausto, I command you to kiss that girl.'

This time there was no escape. Fausto pinned Jenny to the wall and kissed her full on the lips.

'My commands must be obeyed,' King Alfonso announced. 'You thought you could defy me by waving the American flag, but you see I am still King of Spain.'

Later that night at dinner he shook his finger warningly at Jenny and said: 'I'll show you who is King.'

At the end of the season, after their last performance in the casino when things were quieter, the Dolly Sisters were enjoying a late supper in the restaurant with two male American friends when M. Cornuche came over to them and said that King Alfonso had expressed the wish that they should dance for him privately.

'But our costumes are all packed up. We just can't,' protested Rosie.

'But it is His Majesty's command,' said M. Cornuche.

'His Majesty can't command us,' Jenny retorted.

The discussion and M. Cornuche's pleadings continued until the Dollies finally consented, excused themselves from their dinner guests, returned to their apartment, unpacked their dance frocks, returned to the casino and began their private performance for the King. They bowed to him before they began and at the conclusion of the number.

His Majesty went over to them, thanked them and asked, with a twinkle in his eye, if they knew why he had requested that they should dance for him.

'The whim of a King,' Jenny replied facetiously.

'Only half of it,' he replied. 'I saw you were so interested in those young men at your table that I decided I would separate you from them – for a while at least,' he laughed. 'Besides I have never forgiven you for refusing to obey my command. What's the use of being a King if I am not obeyed?' And with this he said farewell.

Since the Dollies had allowed the work offers from London to evaporate by accepting the Deauville offer, they returned to New York for another vaudeville tour. Leaving Cherbourg on 27 September aboard the *Majestic*, they arrived in New York on 3 October 1922 with their trunks full of more new frocks.[43] They proudly announced that the nice thing about their sixteen trunks loaded with 'things of fluff and fashion' was that they had paid the bills themselves. 'No husbands to sign the cheques you know.'[44] In an interview they explained why all the new frocks were so necessary. From years of experience they concluded that 'every dance has its own atmosphere, its own colour, its own contour' and so each new dance had to have a complete ensemble to reflect it. They asked their designers to watch their steps and then interpret the costume based on their initial ideas.

While in Paris they had come across 'that brilliant young artist Erté', who 'designs very bizarre and exotic frocks for the most famous beauties of Europe'. Russian-born Erté had established his name as one of the leading stage designers in Paris and was on the verge of international recognition. After seeing the Dollies perform, Erté introduced himself and gave them some fascinating suggestions. 'He told us that our complexions and figures appealed to him. Quite a compliment, since he refuses to create clothes for those who don't. He liked our style . . . almost immediately he did each of us a frock.' This incident provoked them to go on a shopping spree in Paris and in ten days they added forty gowns to their existing wardrobe, many of them, they claimed, designed by Erté, although they also bought more costumes on their arrival in New York.[45]

According to Erté's notebooks,[46] which provide a definitive list of his costume sketches, numbered and dated and annotated with production details and names of key performers, it can be confirmed that he did not design costumes for the Dolly Sisters at any time. One can only think that their claim was some sort of publicity stunt to attract attention, since Erté was at

Above left: Margarethe Deutsch with her twin daughters Roszika and Yansci, Budapest, Hungary, *c.* 1900. *(Author's collection)*
Right: The Dolly Sisters in negligées from *His Bridal Night*, Republic Theatre, New York, 1916. *(Author's collection)*

Below left: Dolly Sisters in *His Bridal Night*, Republic Theatre, New York, 1916. *(Author's collection)*
Centre: Dolly Sisters in *His Bridal Night*, Republic Theatre, New York, 1916. *(Author's collection, from Andrew Orr)*
Right: Dolly Sisters in *Oh Look!* regional tour of USA, 1918–19. *(Author's collection)*

Above: Dolly Sisters dur
one of their vaudeville
tours of the USA, 1922
(Author's collection)

Far left: Dolly Sisters in
Oh Look!, regional tour
USA, 1918–19. *(Author
collection)*

Left: Dolly Sisters durin
the run of *Paris en fleurs*
Casino de Paris, Paris,
1925. *(Mike Everson
collection)*

Right: Dolly Sisters in 'The Dollies and the Collies' number from *Paris–New York*, Casino de Paris, Paris, 1927. *(Author's collection)*

Far right: Dolly Sisters in *Babes in the Wood*, New Oxford Theatre, London, 1921–22 *(Author's collection, from Andrew Orr)*

Left: Dolly Sisters in their bridal attire from *League of Notions*, New Oxford Theatre, London, 1921. *(Author's collection)*

Right: Dolly Sisters being 'led' by Clifton Webb in the 'Pony Trot', *Fun of the Fayre*, Pavilion Theatre, London, 1922. *(General Photographic Agency/Hutton Archive/Getty Images)*

Above: Dolly Sisters in *Paris en fleurs*, Casino de Paris, Paris, 1925. *(R. Sobel/Henry Guttmann/Hutton Archive/Getty Images)*

Far left: Dolly Sisters arrive in New York aboard the *Aquitania*, 4 October 1922. *(Author's collection)*

Left: Dolly Sisters and Maurice Chevalier rehearsing *Paris en fleurs*, Casino de Paris, Paris, 1925. *(Author's collection, from Andrew Orr)*

Above left: Dolly Sisters in the *Greenwich Village Follies*, Shubert Theatre, New York, 1924. *(Author's collection)*
Right: Dolly Sisters in *Paris en fleurs*, Casino de Paris, Paris, 1925. *(Author's collection)*

Below left: Dolly Sisters in *La Valse lumineuse* from *Paris en fleurs*, Casino de Paris, Paris, 1925.
Right: Dolly Sisters wearing the 'Mazurka' costumes in *Paris sans voiles*, Ambassadeurs Theatre, Paris, 1923. *(All author's collection)*

Left: Dolly Sisters with Gordon Selfridge and his daughter in Le Touquet, 1926. *(Courtesy Selfridge's Archive at the History of Advertising Trust)*

Below: Dolly Sisters on the beach at Deauville, mid-1920s. *(Eric Concklin collection)*

Bottom left: Rosie with Mortimer Davis Junior, 1928. *(Courtesy of University of Southern California, on behalf of the USC Specialized Libraries and Archival Collections)*

Bottom right: Dolly Sisters with their mother and father, 1922. *(Courtesy of University of Southern California, on behalf of the USC Specialized Libraries and Archival Collections)*

Dolly Sisters appearing in the Battle of the Flowers, Cannes, spring 1927. *(Eric Concklin collection)*

Below left: Dolly Sisters in gypsy costume in the late 1920s. *(Author's collection from the Towyna Thomas Collection, originally owned by Max Pierce)*

Right: Jenny showing one of her models at her couture establishment, Paris, 1930. *(Courtesy of University of Southern California, on behalf of the USC Specialized Libraries and Archival Collections)*

Above left: Edward Dolly in 1927. *(Author's collection)*
Right: The wedding of Jenny to Bernard Vinissky, 1935. Left to right: Irving Netcher, Rosie, Jenny and Bernard Vissinsky. *(Courtesy Film and Photo Archive, Wisconsin Center for Film and Theater Research)*

Below left: Rosie and Jenny in Chicago, c. 1935. *(Courtesy Film and Photo Archive, Wisconsin Center for Film and Theater Research)*
Right: Jenny with her two adopted daughters shortly before her suicide, Los Angeles, 1941. *(Courtesy of University of Southern California, on behalf of the USC Specialized Libraries and Archival Collections)*

the time becoming very famous for his artwork in such magazines as *Harper's Bazaar* and his creations would soon be seen on Broadway.

With this mass of frocks at their disposal, they starred in a new show staged by Lew Leslie, of Plantation Club fame, at the Club Maurice on Broadway and 51 Street, a basement venue that reopened as the Monte Carlo in early November.[47] They received the vast sum of $2,000 a week, but they apparently failed to draw in the audience and retired early after a month.[48]

They slipped into another new club, but this time as paying customers in support of the comedian Jimmy Durante, a performer of manic intensity, and his team at the Club Durant. Although the club 'officially' opened in January 1923, it in fact opened its doors to the cream of the theatre world on 18 November 1922 and was swinging after other clubs had closed at about 3 a.m. News of Durante's club travelled fast, and it was immediately raided under the Prohibition law by the police armed with axes and sledge hammers. They were horrified to find the 'aristocracy' of the New York night crowd, including George M. Cohan, Al Jolson, the columnists Bugs Baeer and Damon Runyan and, of course, the Dolly Sisters – all drinking merrily. The police beat a discreet retreat, clearly aware of the adverse publicity that would follow if they arrested such famous people.

Nightclubs aside, the main purpose of the Dollies' visit was their eight-week run in the Keith vaudeville houses opening in Washington, DC on 4 December in a dazzling dancing divertissement together with the singer and dancer Harry Richman and their brother Eddie.

For this new act the Dolly Sisters did a jazz dance, a waltz creation, a torture dance in the slums of Paris, the pony trot and the tom-tom dance. After the pony trot, the curtain came down and a piano was pushed out in front. The Dollies would climb onto it and, with their knees crossed, sing 'The Old Man's Whiskers'. *Theatre* thought that they were 'a pictorial delight as usual' but was not impressed with the act. It described the Apache dance number entitled 'The Torture Dance': torture to watch, the song and dance number stupid, and Richman's comedy banal. 'The Dollies as an attraction for vaudeville are too dainty and rare a phenomenon to be wasted in an exhibition so crude and unpolished as this one . . . more is to be expected of them.'[49]

Despite criticism of the show, Harry Richman was effusive about his time with the Dolly Sisters, saying that they had 'one of the greatest acts I ever saw in my life'. 'They were warm, gracious girls and for a time they were like my family. I couldn't spend money when I was out with them. There was always a late snack after each show and one or the other of them or Eddie picked up the check every time.' He was well aware of their allure and mentioned that practically every millionaire he knew was after them. One night in Pittsburgh, a wealthy man arrived in town and gave the Dolly Sisters supper after the show. They did not stay out late and came back to their lodgings early. The next day, two large packages arrived from Pittsburgh's biggest store. Each contained a mink coat. The note from the gentleman said: 'This is just in appreciation for the wonderful times you showed me when we were in Paris.'

As far as I knew, they got their fabulously expensive fur coats and evening dresses solely because they were so beautiful, not because of bestowing their favours. Whenever anybody asked 'where did you get that coat?' the sister who was asked would only give a sly, secret smile. They were highly moral as a matter of fact . . . a good many girls I knew got mink coats in the traditional manner. The Dollies had such class and were so sweet and gracious they never had to sleep with men.[50]

Richman paints a picture of them being totally sweet and innocent, but is he to be believed? Could he have been mistaken? They were, after all, newly divorced, affluent, intelligent, good company, unusually beautiful and 30 years of age. Could they really be as virtuous as Richman believed? More likely, given the time and the prevailing morality, they were extraordinarily discreet about their relationships.

Many years later Ashton Stevens of the *Chicago Herald* related a story about the Dolly Sisters and a well-known French financier, who had been a distinguished French air-force pilot and had taken down many German planes during the First World War. The financier was an ardent admirer of the Dolly Sisters, and they had introduced him to Ashton Stevens in their extensive suite in the Congress Hotel in Chicago. Many years later Jenny told Stevens 'a wonderful story that involved the financier slightly and her father greatly'. During the run of a show in Chicago (more than likely *Sitting Pretty* in autumn 1924) the Dollies invited their father to come to stay for a week and named the day of his arrival. But he decided to surprise them and arrived three days early.

> Without announcement the old gentleman found his way to the extensive suite which was for the moment occupied only by a pair of chambermaids who took no account of his entrance by one of the several open doors. Papa Dolly started to look around. He recognised Jenny's silvered toilet articles on a dresser – and in a nearby bathroom he encountered toilet articles that certainly did not belong to Jenny. Among them were a straight blade razor, a shaving mug and a bottle of definitely masculine lotion. Papa Dolly swiftly beat it. He did not visit his daughters that night, nor the next, nor the next. He was, Jenny said, a man of tact. For three nights he saw his daughters only from the balcony of the theatre in which they appeared.

By the time he did greet them in their suite, there was no sign of straight razor blades among the suite's appointments.[51] Needless to say Jenny found out about her father's early arrival. Who was the distinguished financier? As it happens, a certain French financier by the name of François Dupré, aged 36 and a known admirer of the Dollies, arrived in New York aboard the *Paris* from Le Havre on 6 December 1924,[52] just about the same time that the Dollies were enjoying a good run in their show in Chicago. But, strangely, Dupré was believed to be under Rosie's influence rather than Jenny's. Had there been another case of mistaken identity, with Mr Dolly getting his daughters confused, or had M. Dupré initially been in love with Jenny? More to the point, this story contradicts Harry Richman's view, but discretion was clearly the thing.

9

The Paris Debut

On 30 January 1923, serenaded by Mal Hallett's band, the Dollies and their brother Eddie boarded the *Berengaria*, regarded as the most fashionable of all the liners, and returned to Europe, and in early February left Paris for their first excursion to the French Riviera. Eugene Cornuche, who ran the Deauville casino, also owned the Cannes casino and had secured the Dollies for Cannes after their success at Deauville the previous summer. They would have travelled on the Blue Train, the most beautiful and culturally significant train of its time, which had only just begun its service to the Riviera on 8 December 1922 and had connecting luxury compartments for eighty first-class passengers and a first-class dining car. Leaving the Gare Maritime at 1 p.m. sharp, the train stopped at the Gare du Nord and Gare de Lyon before beginning the long journey south to Dijon, Chalons and Lyons with cocktails and a superb dinner. The train reached the coast the following morning at Marseilles and then called at Saint-Raphael, Cannes, Juan-les-Pins, Antibes, Nice and Monaco before terminating at Menton.[1] How chic it must have felt to leave a cold and grey Paris one afternoon and wake up the next morning to the sight of mimosa and

orange trees and the blue waters of the Mediterranean glittering in the sun.

After the First World War English society returned to its old habits with the seasonal migrations of the past – travelling south in winter in search of a warmer climate. Cultured people went to Florence, Rome, Naples and Egypt. Smart people went to Nice, Monte Carlo and Cannes, where the hotels were luxurious and very exclusive. The Negresco in Nice and the Carlton in Cannes were both considered the smartest on the Riviera. But to the old guard, returning to their usual pastures, something was decidedly different. They observed that the exclusivity of the Riviera had become tarnished. When the Dolly Sisters arrived, some thought that their ostentatious display of jewellery and their frivolous behaviour were vulgar and struck a rather discordant note. It was a commonly held view that many ex-actressess and dancers had succeeded in overcoming their lack of breeding, but the Dolly Sisters were regarded as quite a different story. 'They were brash in a new and disconcerting way – very modern and indiscreet and quite unbearably nouveau riche.' The well-bred English visitors returning home began to wonder whether the Riviera was becoming overrun with undesirables.[2]

The Dollies were part and parcel of a new type of visitor to the Riviera, one that the old guard clearly despised – Americans! Many of the old breed of gamblers had vanished. The Russian aristocracy, once the heaviest gamblers in Europe, and the rich noble families of the German and Austro-Hungarian empires had been largely wiped out. Their places were taken by the growing numbers of freshly minted American millionaires, although they tended to avoid Monte Carlo, with its more exotic atmosphere and its eccentric inhabitants dedicated to gambling, and gravitated to the newer casinos at Nice and Cannes.[3]

The Dollies settled into the glamorous Carlton Hotel and would have loved the opulence of the nearby casino complex, surrounded by wonderful gardens that included an opera house and the Ambassadeurs restaurant. Cornuche had transformed the ambience of the restaurant by employing the talented artist

Jean-Gabriel Domergue to stage elaborate themed gala fêtes that became legendary for their amazing decor and style.[4] Domergue was a French artist who had first attracted attention after the First World War with his colourful and vibrant paintings of dancing girls. He then became famous for painting numerous portraits of leading French celebrities, including the famous picture of a nude Josephine Baker. Branching out into costume and set designs, he worked for various French music halls and became artistic adviser to the Comédie Française. Later he was engaged by the British film producer Herbert Wilcox to design the costumes and sets for the film *Madame Pompadour* (1927). He became a friend of the Dollies and later painted the Dolly Sisters individually and acted as stylist for Jenny's properties. Domergue was an odd little man in appearance, with a goat-like beard and long straggling mutton chops, but he was very much *à la mode* and leapt into the limelight during the 1927 season, when he was cautioned by the Prefect of the Alpes-Maritimes for his extremely brief bathing costume.[5]

The seasonal festivities in Cannes were already in full swing when the Dollies arrived. Each Saturday night from the start of the season there had been a gala evening dinner at the casino with a themed fête. A Moroccan night featured Harry Pilcer and his dancing partner Wynn Richmond; the following Saturday saw the courtyard of an old inn in Seville with musicians playing popular Spanish songs of the eighteenth century as a background for the dancer Argentinita. In a neat little invitation booklet, Domergue implored all the diners to wear appropriate dress for each occasion, but alas 'who could ever get self-conscious British aristocrats to wear anything but ultramodern raiment?'[6]

Then came the Dollies in a wintery-themed gala evening. The huge chandeliers were half covered in cotton wool cut in the shape of large holly leaves. There was a giant snowman in one corner and little leafless trees covered in crystallised imitation snow. The lights were turned down for the entry of the Dollies, who appeared in white tulle frocks. At the same time waiters handed out paper bags filled with imitation snowballs and everyone pelted each other while the Dollies skipped daintily out. They returned dressed as jet black ponies with high head-plumes and other jingling equine paraphernalia driven by Billy Arnold with a cracking whip and hard bowler hat as he directed them at a gallop round and round until the entry of a reindeer and a walking snowman was the signal for a renewed 'fake' snowball fight.[7]

The Venice of Casanova was the next themed gala, and the Dollies, dressed identically in Venetian gowns escorted by their brother Eddie, gave another performance.[8] Immensely popular, they continued dancing for the next few weeks,[9] before they moved on to Cap d'Antibes. Their fascination with the Riviera had begun, and, despite some resentment from the old guard, they became permanent fixtures for the next decade.

Hotels on the Côte d'Azur usually closed from late spring all through the summer. But in the summer of 1922 two Americans, Gerald and Sara Murphy, rented a whole floor in the Grand Hotel at Cap d'Antibes. Outside they created a beach by removing the seaweed to reveal the sand and dowsed themselves in banana oil and sunbathed. The locals considered this behaviour very strange. The Murphys enjoyed themselves so much they bought a villa at Antibes, and numerous visitors dropped by; in 1925, for example, guests included Scott and Zelda Fitzgerald, Rudolf Valentino and Mistinguett. Within a few years the whole character of the Riviera had changed. Sunbathing in the summer and dining al fresco amid the orange and lemon trees became fashionable.

While the Murphys put down roots at the Cap d'Antibes, a local businessman also became aware that the area had potential. Édouard Baudoin, a well-known restaurateur from Nice, saw a film that depicted a beach-party scene in Miami. He had already assessed the potential of Juan-les-Pins, which at the time was just a collection of pine trees and sand. He purchased a dilapidated and almost bankrupt casino there and rebuilt it. On opening night, sometime in March 1923, he staged a cabaret and, having seen the success that the Dolly Sisters were having in the Cannes casino, persuaded them to star in his opening-night gala in an attempt to put his casino and Juan-les-Pins on the map. Baudoin was rewarded handsomely and the casino became fashionable because it was well placed between Cap d'Antibes and Cannes, and with the new summer season the beautiful sandy beach also became a draw. By 1928, besides a casino, Juan-les-Pins had numerous charming villas, two excellent hotels and the renowned Restaurant de la Frégate.[10] It also became another home from home for the Dolly Sisters during their well-earned holidays.

Before returning to Paris, the Dollies would also have made a short trip to Nice, described as the smartest resort on the 'diamond coast', staying at the Negresco Hotel. Here, nightlife focused on the seafront municipal casino on the Promenade des Anglais, the New York Bar favoured by Americans and the two fashionable cabaret clubs: Le Perroquet and Maxime's. Nice also had the famous carnival, which still endures to this day – two weeks of festivities in February. The carnival had a very old tradition going back to at least the thirteenth century, but in the late nineteenth century it was made into one of the most fashionable in the world.

One of the major events was the famous battle of the flowers. The first flower parade was organised along the Promenade des Anglais in 1876 and had by the 1920s become a huge event. Every species of wheeled vehicle decorated as flower floats slowly appeared from the casino gardens, and a prize for the best decorated was awarded. They were overflowing with pretty young girls, who threw flowers into the crowd of spectators, although the original idea was to throw flowers at those they desired.[11]

After the pleasures of the Côte d'Azur, Jenny travelled to London to help her brother Eddie arrange the dances for the Cochran show *Dover Street to Dixie*, launched at the London Pavilion at the end of May. On her return to Paris she began rehearsals with Rosie for their debut in the French capital. Impresario Oscar Dufrenne presented the Dollies modestly at the Ambassadeurs theatre off the Champs-Elysées in early June 1923 in a show entitled *Paris sans voiles*,[12] or *Brighter Paris*, a title that may have been used to evoke the success of *Brighter London* at the London Hippodrome. The show included the home-grown talents of Edmonde Guy and her partner

Van Duren, and became a showcase for Eddie Dolly, fresh from his London triumphs for Cochran, who had arranged all the dances for a troupe of eight 'London Boys'. By all accounts it was admirably mounted for such a small stage and was worthy of Dufrenne's much larger venue the Palace Theatre, where they would ultimately perform.

The Dollies first appeared as American roses in 'Let us Make a Pretty Bouquet' and then danced a rollicking Mazurka in a scene depicting the Grand Derby in 1883, contrasted with the Grand Derby of 1923. They blacked up for 'Plantation Days', where, surrounded by growers and planting machines, they danced and sang plantation songs. By far their most important scene was 'Destiny', a sketch in four acts, in which the Dollies, dressed by Jeanne Lanvin, performed a melodramatic depiction of the life of an actress, terminating in an acrobatic dance in a seedy nightclub. This apparently had been a big success in New York.[13]

'Destiny' was an extraordinary sketch in more ways than one. It was almost like a typical silent film of the time – overstated and full of melodrama. It did, however, showcase the talents of the Dollies, not just as dancers but also as accomplished 'emotional' actresses. It relied heavily on the concept of deception and mirror images, which was a perfect frame for their duality as performers. Especially poignant was the irony of the story itself: the portrayal of an actress overcome by the trappings of fame – in some ways a rather prophetic view of their own destiny that was beginning to unfold.

The French press was effusive about their performances, saying the Dollies were enchanting, had a formidable triumph on their hands and were destined to become the idols of Paris, just as they had in London and New York.[14] *The Stage* thought they had an exuberant grace and a 'light fantastic touch and the girlishness that one seldom finds among French revue artists'.[15]

However, the joy of their Parisian debut was marred by the tragic news from America that their mother had died. Margarethe had gone to California in 1921 (possibly because her sister or sister-in-law lived there) and had planned to establish a dress-designing business, but poor health and her dislike of the climate defeated her and she had returned to New York, where her health deteriorated further.[16] Jenny described the evening that they were given the news.

> It was in Paris that my sister and I had the worse experience of our lives. It was just before our first show was ready to start. We could hear the excited Parisian audience filling the theatre talking and gossiping when we opened a cable from America. It was a short one. It just said that our mother, whom we were expecting to join us, had died. We looked at each other helplessly. It was too horrible and unexpected. Yet we had to do the show. They would never have understood. So without saying a word to anyone but the manager we just struggled through the evening and no one guessed, not even the critics. Neither of us . . . remembers a single detail of that night – except one, when we came to our senses and broke down. It was when we were singing a sad darky song about being homesick for the plantation and the things we loved. The word mother came into it and we were longing to see and kiss her again. We just could not sing those words. They stuck in our throats. My sister was the first to stop and I soon followed. The manager cleverly saw what was happening and ordered the girls to begin dancing. We got off the stage all right. As I said no one really guessed what had happened.[17]

The critic for *The Stage* saw one of the early performances and afterwards went backstage to congratulate them, only to learn what had happened earlier. 'You know how it is,' they said with pitiful bravery; 'we had to dance and smile just the same.' He was amazed by their resolve. 'It was one of the most moving things I have encountered in the theatre. Like true artists they had given a faultless performance and while the building still echoed with their success they sat weeping in their dressing room.'[18] Despite their obvious distress, the Dollies continued to fulfil their obligations, and, since they could not leave Paris, their father made the trip to see them.[19] Their commitment and sense of obligation were valiant, in strong contrast to a very close friend. Sophie Tucker was booked by Julian Wylie to star in his spectacular revue at the London Hippodrome in spring 1925, but, when she received the news of the death of her mother, she abandoned her contract and returned to New York. Wylie brought a court case against her, and she was later fined $500 with additional costs, which certainly did not aid her reputation in Europe.

After their delightful social life in London, with weekend parties at country homes and luncheons and dinners with London's elite, the Dollies were disillusioned with theatrical life in Paris. Although they found their French co-artists to be extremely cordial and were met with the greatest courtesy and consideration, they felt that initially they were not making new friends, as they had done in London. At first they were so busy with rehearsals, fittings and sightseeing that they did not mind being left on their own. Then came the distress of their bereavement. Gradually, however, they established a routine and started to socialise more.

After their opening at the Ambassadeurs one of their first outings was to the annual Quat'z Arts Ball. This event was supposed to be the famous gathering of art students in Paris, all wearing exotic fancy dress. The Dollies decided to go and dressed up. They were quite surprised to discover that the majority of the men were not young Parisians but New Yorkers as they bumped into the theatrical managers Gilbert Miller and Arch Selwyn, numerous Fifth Avenue couturiers, buyers from New York department stores and hoards of general tourists. They began to realise that, after midnight, the pleasures of Paris were primarily manufactured for American and British tourists.[20]

A month went by, and, despite being bathed in glorious adulation, the Dollies felt it strange that they had yet to receive a single invitation to a social event. They realised that there was a vast gulf separating the stage from French society and that Paris was yet again different from New York and London. In conversation they discovered that in Paris performers were rarely invited to the best homes. They were told that the theatre was often conducted on a different basis, with productions financed to showcase the mistresses of wealthy men, who were not ideal candidates for society gatherings. The Dollies soon came to believe the saying that women in America were objects of devotion, women in England objects of dalliance, while women in France were the objects of passion.[21]

So initially they socialised with long-time American friends such as Harry Pilcer. At the end of June he arranged an Independence Day fête, with the proceeds to go to blinded war veterans. An array of French and American stars, including the Dollies, appeared as part of an entertainment at the new Champs-Elysées restaurant. This had just been opened at 63 avenue des Champs-Elysées by Jules Ansaldi, who was well known in New York and considered to be one of the originators of cabaret on Broadway.

The disillusionment Rosie and Jenny felt at not being accepted in Parisian society soon came to an end. Luckily for the Dolly Sisters, in every capital city there was a group of prominent men who made a speciality of meeting all the new stage performers, especially if they were female. As the weeks rolled by they met all of them: M. Coty the multimillionaire perfumer, Gaston Menier the chocolate king, the witty, bohemian and ultra-Parisian André de Fouquiérès and the Duc de Vallombrosa, plus Count Boni de Castellane, the former husband of Anna Gould. There was also the charming Henri Letellier, the businessman and newspaper proprietor whom they had met at Deauville the previous summer in his capacity of mayor, who clearly had his eye on one of them.

Finally, their first glimpse of society life in Paris came with an invitation to luncheon with Mrs William K. Vanderbilt Senior (Anne Harriman Rutherford Sands), whose husband, the great-grandson of the famous multimillionaire Cornelius Vanderbilt, had died in 1920. The Dolly Sisters met her and her daughter in her beautiful house near the place de l'Étoile. Mrs Vanderbilt was particularly interested in helping aristocratic Russian refugees, and through her they met the leaders of the Russian colony, including Grand Duke Cyril, the pretender to the Russian throne, Prince Felix Youssoupoff, the slayer of Rasputin, and the Princess Yousoupoff, a niece of the late Czar. Later the

Dollies would recognise that it was only when Mrs Vanderbilt had taken them up that the conservative Parisian hostesses followed suit.[22]

Shortly afterwards Baroness Rothschild, the wife of Baron Henri, head of the French house of Rothschild, invited the Dollies to dance at a charity fête at her house. They employed the same tactics that they had with Philip Sassoon in London and politely declined, saying that they would be glad to dance for charity, but they would not appear unless they were received as guests.

Later, they received another invitation from the Baroness, asking them to take charge of another charity affair at her home, which they gladly accepted. Since they were still performing at the Ambassadeurs, they could not make the dinner, but they did make the late supper and met some of the most influential leaders of the French capital, and they were told that it was the first time in history that two music-hall stars had ever been received in the highest French society.[23] At last they had been accepted.

One of the Dolly Sisters' grandest dinner deceptions occurred shortly after their debut at the Ambassadeurs, where they pulled the wool over the eyes of Count André d'Aubigny.[24] The 50-year-old Count was reputed to be able to judge a woman merely by a casual glance and in that instant to be able to gauge her character, her habits and everything worth knowing about her. After the Dollies' performance, the Count managed to get a friend to arrange an introduction, and he fell head over heels for Rosie, or, at least, he was convinced it was Rosie and swore on the faith of his ancestors that he could pick Rosie from the two in any circumstance. 'But even if my eye should deceive me Mademoiselle,' he gurgled, 'I know my heart would tell me it is you.'

Rosie and Jenny were quite used to such comments and so decided to use their usual mischief to disturb the Count's confidence. Rosie accepted the Count's invitation to dinner the next evening. They met at a famous restaurant in the rue Saint-Honoré, probably Le Voisin, regarded as one of the best restaurants in Paris at the time. According to one gourmet, it was 'no place for the philistine' and was designed for those who really understood the art of eating and drinking and could settle the stiff bill without turning a hair[25] — the perfect dining establishment for a man in the Count's eminent position.

They had a discreet little table all to themselves in a far-off corner. 'I am sorry I haven't the least bit of an appetite,' said Rosie the moment they were seated. 'I've just had tea with some friends and must have eaten at least a half-a-dozen chocolate eclairs.' The Count was heartbroken. 'But if you insist my dear Count and if it pleases you,' Rosie continued, 'I shall try to eat a little omelette.'

That soothed the Count temporarily. He ordered an omelette 'à la Grande Duchesse' sprinkled with truffles, and a bottle of Chateau Margaux 1911. The omelette was a *chef d'œuvre* of the culinary arts, one of those things that melts in the mouth and causes a craving for more. And Rosie liked it. As a matter of a fact she ate nearly all of it. For a girl who had just eaten half a dozen éclairs, she showed a surprising appetite.

'It is this excellent cuisine,' smiled the Count, trying to comprehend; 'it develops the appetite'.

'Quite so,' Rosie agreed. 'But I can't eat another thing.'

At that moment one of the porters came and told Rosie that someone wanted to speak to her on the telephone urgently. Excusing herself, Rosie followed the chasseur to the telephone booth, but made a detour and met Jenny, who was waiting in a nearby room. They were dressed alike, even down to the rings on their fingers. Quickly Rosie told Jenny what she had eaten and what the conversation had been. Then Jenny took Rosie's place at the table with the Count.

'It was that wonderful man Georges Baud offering us a £1,500-a-week contract in South America,' she said in great excitement; 'most wonderful news isn't it Count? It's really given me an appetite.' Whereupon the Count proceeded to order something adequately to commemorate the happy occasion — a tender young partridge, one of the first six to arrive in Paris that season. It was so well carved and laid out that 'Rosie' consumed the greater portion of it, much to the perplexity of her host, who was beginning to wonder what on earth these foreign girls were made of.

'It's amazing really, how a bit of good news stimulates one's appetite,' said 'Rosie'. Just then there was another telephone call. Wondering who this could be, 'Rosie' hurriedly left the table and changed places with her sister again. Rosie returned to the table with a face beaming with joy. The Count saw her coming and instinctively must have hoped there was no more good news, but her smile and shining eyes told him there was.

'Think of it,' Rosie laughed, 'think of it Count, that good Georges telephones me again. He has got a £10,000 guarantee and all travelling expenses paid in advance. Isn't it great news? Ah now I must eat something really. That partridge was so perfectly exquisite that I wouldn't mind having some more.'

What the Count thought at this moment is not recorded, but he looked strangely embarrassed and mumbled something about the most marvellous appetite he had ever witnessed. His amazement grew into bewilderment in the course of the next hour when three more telephone calls resulted in a continued exhibition of appetite. There came two plates of delicious asparagus, some mushrooms cooked in champagne right before their eyes, a large dish of wild strawberries in cream, various kinds of pastry and ices, some cheese, and then more pastries and more cheese. The Count's face had ceased to be red. It was turning blue when Rosie suddenly remembered her car was waiting, since it was time to go to the theatre and dress for her performance.

'That was a delicious dinner,' she said in parting, 'and we might sup together after the performance, but I am never hungry after the show.'

'But you might get some more good news,' the Count said a little maliciously, before wishing her a fond goodbye.

The next day the Count received a little note: 'Dear Count — we thank you very much indeed for the splendid dinner you gave us yesterday. Rosie and Jenny.' The Count, obviously humiliated and in bad humour, immediately left for Deauville and vowed not to return to Paris before the Dollies had gone somewhere else. The comedy of the Dollies' dinner and the gay old count who 'fell in love' set all Paris chuckling over his misadventure and the cost of such a huge and unexpected meal at one of the most exclusive restaurants in Paris.

At this early stage in their Parisian career their growing obsession with gambling became more and more evident. It was noted that, on occasion, they would give their performance in Paris and then whirl off to Deauville (no doubt trying to avoid the Count) or Le Touquet for the later hours at the casino. After snatching some sleep at one of the hotels, they would return to Paris in their car the next afternoon ready for their nightly show.[26] In between these jolly jaunts there was more than enough to keep them entertained as the regular nightclubs began to reopen for the autumn. One of the first was the Club Danou atop Jane Renouardt's theatre opposite the famous Ciro's restaurant. This cosy venue featured the dancing of Peggy Marsh, who had been a hit at the Deauville Casino in August, plus the Tomson Twins, who had served in the British air force during the First World War and had just returned from a visit to America.[27]

But nightclubs were not the only thing on their minds. Jenny had fallen in love with the Vicomte de La Rochefoucauld (Tenny) and had become engaged. Not surprisingly, his parents, the Duc and Duchesse de Deauville, simply did not approve of the engagement and hoped that he would marry a titled lady. Jenny sent for his father and they had a long talk. 'I knew our proposed marriage would displease him and possibly ruin Tenny's career – especially as he was dependent upon his father's generosity.' Jenny acknowledged that, although she loved him, she had his best interest at heart. She suggested that, while she was busy appearing at the Ambassadeurs theatre, they should spend some time apart. Although Jenny's motives sound admirable, they should be taken with a pinch of salt, since she was undoubtedly in the middle of another love affair with someone else.

In early September 1923, as *Paris sans voiles* came to an end, Jenny wrote to Tenny and broke off the engagement; she told him not to try to see her again. On completion of their contract, the Dollies had decided to go to Biarritz, to stay at Pearl White's Hotel du Palais. This had once been the chateau of an empress, but Pearl had turned the drawing room into a successful casino and the imperial boudoir into her private apartment.

A former fishing village, Biarritz was the most attractive and romantic of French resorts, lying in a narrow strip of land between the Pyrenees and the sea. According to legend, Queen Hortense-Eugenie, wife of King Louis-Napoleon of Holland, inherited some land and built a chateau in this unheard-of spot. One day in 1807 it was so hot she bathed in the sea and set a trend. Thereafter the location became a firm favourite of royalty and the world's first fashionable beach, with increasing numbers of new devotees, such as King Edward VII, King Alfonso XIII of Spain and the Prince of Wales.

There were two train services: one at night via the Pyrenees, the Côte-d'argent express, and the daily Sud Express, but, unlike other resorts, Biarritz demanded a sojourn of several weeks rather than a fleeting visit. September was socially the best time to go, when the resort was at its busiest following on from Deauville. Deauville was seen as act one and Biarritz as act two in a 'comedy of extravagant pleasure'.[28] With three beaches, eleven de luxe hotels and a host of excellent restaurants, including La Chaumière and the Bar Basque, and numerous nightspots such as the Casanova, Casino du Palais-Royal and the Blue Room, there was no shortage of social activities.

However, on this occasion, Jenny knew that Tenny would follow her there, so, after ensuring Rosie was on her way to Biarritz, Jenny took the train to Marseilles, thinking she would eventually end up on the Riviera. Once in her berth she heard a knock at the door and there was Tenny. On receipt of her letter, Tenny had raced back to Paris and had been told of Jenny's trip by one of her staff. Hot in pursuit, he had managed to get on the train at the last minute. He refused to accept defeat, and, when his luggage arrived, he convinced her to take a trip by boat to Ajaccio, the capital of Corsica. By chance, when they arrived, they met Tenny's aunt, who was also on holiday, and she acted as a chaperone. As they toured the island by car, they expressed interest in meeting the famous bandit Romanetti. This was arranged in his secluded mountain home, which Jenny found more comfortable than their hotel. Afterwards they boarded a hydroplane for Nice and within a few hours were having lunch at the Negresco Hotel before returning to Paris.[29]

In the end Jenny abandoned Tenny, and within two months she was entertaining a new proposal of marriage. Can we really believe Jenny's view of her decision to terminate the engagement simply because she did not wish to displease his family? I suspect that, once again, despite the fact that she may have been in love, as she asserted, Jenny got cold feet. How could she run off and get married and abandon Rosie and their stage contracts just as they were poised for even greater triumphs? The allure of the Parisian footlights proved to be too overwhelming and the resistance from Tenny's family became a convenient excuse for Jenny to leave him behind and move on.

Tenny, in the meantime, relentlessly pursued other actresses and became the subject of much gossip when he fought a duel in the bois de Boulogne with Prince de Ligne over the affections of the American dancer Marion Forde, who, with her sister Ethel, had starred in *La Revue Mistinguett* in 1925. In the late 1920s Tenny married the pretty and sprightly 'créatice' of the musical show *Phi-Phi*, the actress Alice Cocea. By this time the rigid restrictions of old French family traditions were rapidly being eroded. For example, Comte Guillaume de Ségur had courted scandal by marrying the much older Cécile Sorel, the former star of the Comédie Française in 1926. At the time, no one believed that Ségur would have the courage or the audacity to defy his family wishes, but he did. His actions were followed by the equally scandalous marriage, at about the same time, of the Marquis de la Falaise to Gloria Swanson.[30]

By early October, and back in Paris, the Dollies would have attended the reopening of the famous nightclub Le Perroquet, above the Casino de Paris on the rue Clichy, for the winter season. But the blaze of popularity and publicity was left to Le Jardin de ma Sœur in the rue de Caumartin, which opened for a second season run by Oscar Mouvet, Elsa Maxwell's interest having waned. The Spanish dancer Argentinita, who had been a hit the previous year, had been engaged again, and at the gala opening night the Dolly Sisters were celebrity guests, along with the Tomson Twins, the couturier Patou, Peggy Marsh, Nina Payne, Harry Pilcer and Henri Letellier.[31] A few weeks later Peggy Marsh moved to Le Jardin de ma Sœur from the Club Danou to dance with Ben Barette. Seated in the front tables for this new show were Eddie Dolly and his wife Velma Deane,[32] an actress who had been appearing in Eddie's new cabaret show at the Café de Paris in London, the dress designer Dolly Tree, who had been creating new costumes for the Dollies to wear in their next show, and the Broadway actress and silent film star Rubye de Remer.[33]

Before embarking on their next stage project, the Dollies appear to have been waylaid by the silver screen: it was announced that they were going to appear in some French two-reelers.[34] Whether these films were made and released remains a mystery. With or without film work, the Dolly Sisters were already very busy, and by the middle of November they were back on the stage in Oscar Dufrenne's spectacular *Oh! Les Belles Filles* (*Oh What Pretty Girls*) at the Palace Theatre.[35] The Dollies once again 'carried the Parisian theatre-goers off their feet by sheer grace and merriment . . . they have surpassed themselves . . . whatever they do is effortless, elegant and enchanting'.[36]

Their first entrance was in a scene set in the bois de Boulogne, in which they wore black riding habits and rode on white horses in a black and white woodland set. Next they became Brazilians in 'Sur les rives de l'or' (On Golden River Banks), wearing big dark hats and fringed gowns. In 'La Bourse de l'amour' (The Stock Exchange of Love) they wore extravagant white gowns by Patou, embroidered throughout with diamonds and with massive fringes of white ostrich feathers, and huge feathered fans. In 'Arabesques' they appeared as Hindu women whirling barefoot in bright costumes of gold, crimson and lacquer. In 'Le Chale espagnol' (Spanish Shawl) they were draped in beautiful shawls with large black sombreros. There was also a repeat of 'Destiny', their most successful scene from the Ambassadeurs show.

Described as the 'most seductive little creatures',[37] they once again enchanted Paris together with a new leading man, Billy Reynolds, who had worked with them in the Cochran show *League of Notions* in London. 'The Dollys cannot afford to be without a partner and he has excellent stage presence. He is to them what Harry Pilcer was for Gaby Deslys and Earl Leslie is to Mistinguett.'[38]

Towards the end of 1923, during their huge success with *Oh! Les Belles Filles*, a wild rumour swept London, New York and Paris that one of the Dollies had been kidnapped by a wealthy suitor, whom she had been forced to marry. Eventually the truth emerged that Jenny's prospective bridegroom had made some joking remarks at a dinner in her honour, which were taken out of context. Jenny indicated to the press that there might be an announcement of engagement. 'I cannot consider myself alone,' she said, 'I must think of my sister, for whatever success we have attained we have accomplished it together. . . . If I marry I must give up the stage. The marriage proposal I am considering stipulates that if I accept I must quit the footlights forever when my contract at the Palace expires next May.' Jenny refused to name the suitor but said he was one of the wealthiest men in Paris, who had amassed his fortune in South America.[39] The only person who could possibly fit the bill was the mature and debonair, yet still eligible, Henri Letellier, 'the richest figure in Parisian life', with a palatial house at 3 rue Spontini.[40]

The Dolly Sisters had already met him in his capacity of mayor of Deauville during their first visit to the seaside resort in July 1922 and renewed their acquaintance during their late-night jaunts to Deauville in the summer of 1923, which is where this new romance had blossomed. Henri was about 55 years old, but looked, and liked everyone to believe, that he was 40. Spare, slim waisted, of middle height, with very engaging dark-brown eyes, black hair curving on either side of his forehead, and a distinctive and enormous nose, he was always faultlessly dressed in one of his 1,260 suits and took five hours to dress, ninety minutes of which was devoted to choosing his neck-tie.

Henri's father, Eugene Letellier, had started as an architect in Trouville where he was born and went on to design and build the first Trouville casino and eventually became mayor. Later, Eugene got involved with the building of the Panama Canal and made a fortune out of projects in South America. Henri continued in his father's footsteps and expanded the family business to include a coal mine on the northern frontier, oil wells in Mexico and Romania, rubber plantations in Honduras, railroads in North Africa, a restaurant in Sofia, hotels in France, Spain, Italy and Belgium, several theatres, including a share in the Moulin Rouge, the largest factory for the manufacture of bathroom porcelain in France, and an interest in almost every gambling concern in Europe. However, Henri's pride and joy was his newspaper, *Le Journal*, which by 1925 had the third largest circulation in the world at 1,280,000 daily. It was also Henri's vision and money that originally backed Eugene Cornuche to develop Deauville as a resort to rival Le Touquet.

According to Constance Rosenblum,[41] Letellier had 'a richly deserved reputation as a world class playboy' and had a passion for racehorses, food, art and gambling – all of which would have endeared him to Jenny, without mentioning his fabulous wealth. However, his greatest passion was women, and, although he married three times, his collection of mistresses was legendary.

Jenny was obviously aware of Letellier's notoriety as a womaniser. She certainly could not have missed the incredible publicity that surrounded him when he was named in the divorce proceedings against the infamous gold-digging femme fatale Peggy Hopkins Joyce in 1921. Despite his reputation, she had seemingly followed obliviously in Peggy's footsteps.

At the same time as Jenny's love affair – and if Jenny was busy, Rosie must have been too – and their obligatory performances at the Palace Theatre, the Dolly Sisters continued to make the time to give valuable support to a range of worthy causes. In January 1924 they provided a 'divertissement' after midnight with the dancer Nina Payne and the singer William Martin for a Franco-American ball at the Hôtel des Invalides in aid of funds for war veterans hosted by the French president Millerand and the American Ambassador.[42] Then in March Eddie Dolly became the horse trainer taking his sisters through the ever-popular pony trot as part of a charity entertainment at the Gala de l'Union des Artistes at the Nouveau Cirque for retired theatrical folk.[43] Finally in April, they performed at a matinée dansante given by the Bernheims at their beautiful house in the avenue Henri Martin accompanied by the Cricket dance band and Billy Reynolds.[44]

Never missing a neat trick, the Dollies then embarked on a wonderful publicity exercise as they sprung a new fashion fad on the Parisian public – the *Bouledogue* (bulldog) collar invented by Marthe Regnier, the famous French actress and couturier who was believed to be engaged to Harry Pilcer.[45] Nicknamed the 'Dolly Dog Collar', it was made of black and white leather with a double fringe of stiff badger hairs, a solid gold name-plate and a golden padlock – in short, exactly the type of thing that French bulldogs wore. To launch the new apparel they appeared together on the rue de la Paix leading twin bulldogs. The dogs wore ropes of pearls, while the Dollies wore their shiny dog collars. Rumour had it that the Dollies were as uncomfortable as the dogs.[46]

In the spring of 1924. old friends of the Dollies arrived back in Paris. The dancers Maurice Mouvet and Leonora Hughes appeared at Le Jardin de ma Sœur, renamed the Embassy Club, before going to Saint-Moritz for the winter season.[47] And Florence Walton and her dancing partner, Leon Leitrim, were also booked for a variety of performances.[48] However, the most important social event in Paris at this time was the marriage of the movie star and beauty Rubye de Remer to Benjamin Throop, the Pittsburgh coal magnate and heir to $25 million. Rubye was an old friend of the Dolly Sisters from her dancing days for Ziegfeld, and they were her attendants at the wedding on Monday 7 April at 11 a.m. followed by an elaborate breakfast at Ciro's, with guests including travel writer Basil Woon, Constance Talmadge with her latest beau Chicago department-store heir Townsend Netcher, and Leonora Hughes and Maurice Mouvet. After a short honeymoon, the happy couple sailed back to America, and Rubye faded from the limelight.[49]

During all these social activities and performances Rosie was suffering from periodic bouts of appendicitis. She had been ill in March and had taken a few days' leave from *Oh! Les Belles Filles*, but went back to work too soon and shortly after Rubye's wedding had become so run down that a new attack of appendicitis was complicated by grippe, bronchial trouble and a high fever. Once again Rosie was out of the show, leaving Jenny to manage on her own. At one supper party, Jenny popped in for a few minutes before rushing back to look after Rosie. Both sisters would be plagued by appendicitis, but studiously avoided surgery until a few years later, when it became imperative.[50] However, it was not long before Rosie was back in *Oh! Les Belles Filles*, and by the end of May they doubled in a late-night cabaret show at Le Seymour, supported by the Sonore Band with Bobbie Hind and dressed in exquisite costumes by Patou.[51]

At the end of June 1924 *Oh! Les Belles Filles* closed and, after an extensive round of social activities, the plage of Deauville beckoned. Both sisters were enjoying life, reaping the rewards of professional success and trying to keep emotional entanglements at a distance. Jenny's relationship with Henri Letellier may well have fizzled out because she was reluctant to give up her career, but they would have still seen each other socially. At the same time, gossip began to circulate that she was now being chased by the most eligible bachelor in the world.

THE PRINCE OF WALES AND NEW YORK ANTICS

On 6 July 1924, Henri Letellier, as mayor of Deauville, arranged a publicity exercise to open the season and announce new bathing facilities. The Blue Train arrived one afternoon less than three hours after leaving the Gare Saint-Lazare loaded with celebrities including the Dolly Sisters, who were guests of M. Cornuche at the Hotel Royal. A dinner was given at the casino, and the next morning, prior to lunch at the Normandy Hotel, the mayor showed his guests the new bathing structures.[1] Bathing had become Roman in its sumptuousness, with a hundred, new luxury compartments decorated in Pompeian style stretching along the ridge of the beach. Corridors of blue-and-white tile connected all the dressing rooms, each provided with running water and the last detail of luxury. The corridors were broken at intervals with loggias spreading in a colonnade of marble columns around a circular pool of water fed by ornamental fountains into a basin of azure tiles.[2]

In the weeks following, the Dollies, accompanied by their friend Pearl White, enjoyed the beach during the day and gambled the night away. They had their own appointed places at the casino and were seen dealing out bundles of thousand-franc notes without turning a hair, and soon struck gold, reputedly winning half a million francs.[3] As well as winning at the gambling tables, they were also the subject of considerable talk at the Café La Polinaire, the centre of society life in Deauville. The gossip had begun at the beginning of 1924 and carried on throughout the year and focused on their relationship with David, Prince of Wales, and a mystery friend. In later years it was recognised that the Prince of Wales was one of their semi-permanent companions, trailing them to the Riviera or Normandy coast,[4] and many regarded him as one of their 'favourite escorts'.[5]

A carefully worded press story[6] indicated that they were being collectively called the new Gaby Deslys, a thinly disguised connection between the Dollies' antics with the Prince of Wales and the alleged affair that Deslys had with King Manuel II of Portugal, which gossip claimed had cost him his throne.[7] David, referred to as Prince Charming, seemed set to make the Parisian glory of his grandfather Edward VII pale into insignificance with his attentions to Jenny. Equally disturbing to some was the fact that one of his close friends had become enamoured with Rosie.

This friend was probably Captain Edward Dudley (Fruity) Metcalfe, who accompanied the Prince on his trips at this time. 'Fruity', a superb horseman, was a tall and good-looking Irishman with reddish hair and blue eyes who became responsible for the Prince's polo and equine diversions in 1922. He was one of the Prince's favourite companions because, although perfectly respectful and efficient, he treated him as an ordinary person. He swiftly became an integral part of the Prince's life and circle and accompanied him on his nocturnal activities. Charming, high-spirited, full of fun but with little money, Fruity was also viewed by some as being irresponsible and 'a pernicious influence' on the Prince. In 1923, when he was in his late thirties, he had fallen in love with Alexandra (Baba) Curzon, daughter of Lord Curzon. They married in 1925, though Fruity was far from loyal, and during the trip to New York in late 1924 he became the centre of a minor scandal. Visiting a

prostitute and finding himself unable to pay, Fruity was chased by the whore –
minus his trousers, which she had stolen, and his wallet, which contained
several letters from the Prince.[8]

Fruity fits the bill nicely as the other man in the 'double adventure' which
had come to people's notice in the first part of the year, when the Dolly Sisters
were guests at a Parisian dinner party. Here they had renewed their
acquaintance with his Royal Highness after spending some time with him in
London in previous years.

During 1924 David, Prince of Wales made numerous trips to Paris. His
first visit took place in early January. Arriving incognito as the Count of
Chester, he spent his first night at the Hotel Maurice on the rue Daunou and
invited friends to dinner followed by dancing until well past midnight. The
next evening he dined with six friends at Ciro's. Then, on Thursday
10 January, he was guest of honour at a ball given by the Marquise de
Polignac (Nina Crosby), in the Champs-Elysées, but afterwards went to one of
the theatres. On the Friday evening he attended a dinner given by the British
Ambassador and the Marchioness of Crewe, to which a number of his personal
friends were invited. Following this dinner the Prince and friends partied the
night away at the Embassy Club (Le Jardin de ma sœur) run by Oscar Mouvet.
Finally, on Saturday 12 January he dined with a party hosted by Mr and Mrs
Fred Bate at Henri's restaurant. He then went to their apartment before
returning to the Embassy Club to dance.[9] His busy social calendar as reported
in the press made no mention of who his friends were and who he was
entertaining nor which music hall he visited. And yet the implication was that
the Dolly Sisters, after their performance in *Oh! Les Belles Filles* (which was
perhaps the show the Prince of Wales went to see), were his guests at his
'gatherings', including his visits to the Embassy Club – which was also one of
the Dollies' regular haunts.

In April he was back again. Following a riding accident, he had been
recommended to rest by his physician, so, accompanied by Brigadier-General
Trotter, the Prince embarked on a ten-day holiday in Biarritz, staying at the villa

Hellafanthe.[10] En route he stopped over in Paris on Wednesday 2 April, but there were no reports of any social events, most probably because of his injury, so he may just have entertained in his hotel. Interestingly, one of the Dollies was allowed to leave *Oh! Les Belles Filles* for a short break in Biarritz at this time.[11]

The Prince of Wales returned to Paris on Monday 14 April for a forty-eight-hour incognito visit. That night, with Mr and Mrs Fred Bate and the Comte Gabriache, he went to the Embassy Club, where the entertainment was provided by the dancing of Maurice and Leonora Hughes. Afterwards they went on to Kiley's, the American dance cabaret in Montmartre. The following evening he dined at his hotel and spent a quiet evening with friends. On Wednesday 16 April he was the guest of Mrs and Mrs Charles A. Munn, well-known Americans in Paris, at their apartment with five other unidentified guests.[12] Once again the Dolly Sisters may have been present at some of these social gatherings.

From Paris the Prince went to Le Touquet, staying at the Hermitage Hotel,[13] and he made a further trip to Le Touquet between 7 and 10 June and perhaps a visit to Paris. There was another longer trip to Paris from 5 July 1924 with Prince Henry.[14] He stayed at the British Embassy, and there were various official functions during his visit, including a reception given by Lord and Lady Crewe at the Embassy, lunch with the new President M. Doumergue, followed by his attendance at the official opening of the Olympic Games. Later the Prince took a private apartment for a few days, but this time there were scant reports of his social activities, and, since the Dolly Sisters left for Deauville on 6 July, their time together may have been limited.[15] According to American *Vogue*, during one of these trips to Paris that summer the Prince 'slipped away from officialdom' and went with a party of friends to Seymour's nightclub in the rue Mogador. Here he was entertained by the famous black singer and performer Florence, who we are told had a 'diplomatic appreciation of the merits of her clientèle' and led other black performers to give the Prince 'one of the most delightful informal evening's amusement any young man could wish to have'.[16] But one must not forget that during June 1924 the star attraction at Seymour's was the Dolly Sisters. Perhaps this was the real reason why David went to Seymour's in the first place.

Besides the allure of golf, the Dollies were another reason why the Prince of Wales decided to visit Le Touquet again for the weekend of 11–13 July. The Prince was repeatedly told that the rumours of his attachment to Jenny would end by gaining him a bad reputation, but he continued to see her in Deauville, which he liked only in small doses, although he adored playing golf at the Paris Plage.[17]

During the summer indecision reigned over what the Dolly Sisters should do next in their career. C.B. Cochran was trying his best to secure the Dollies for another show in London. At first it was announced that they would leave Paris in the spring of 1924 for a novel attraction – an all-female revue – but the idea was shelved.[18] They then agreed to appear with Harry Pilcer and Little Tich in Edmund Sayag's summer show at the Ostend Kursaal to begin in August.[19] This engagement was also abandoned, and they then decided to perform for two weeks in London at the Piccadilly Hotel cabaret.[20] This was also cancelled in favour of a return to New York to appear in John Murray Anderson's *Greenwich Village Follies*.

Anderson had been trying to secure them for one of his shows for some time, ever since they had worked together in London in 1922. He had finally succeeded in luring them back to their hometown with a rather large offer. But it cannot have been the amount of this offer alone that swayed their decision: the Prince of Wales was also at this time planning a trip to North America.[21] It is more than likely that the Dollies were attempting to plan their itinerary to match the plans of the Prince of Wales. As they made preparations to leave for the USA, it was believed that they would actually join the Prince of Wales on the same boat. Someone clearly intervened, and travel plans were rearranged. Despite this intervention, it did not stop them seeing each other once again in New York amid even more controversy.

Knowing the Dolly Sisters were to return to New York for a prolonged visit, the French couturier Patou decided to launch an offensive against

America with the Dollies as his secret weapon. Despite the fact that his clothes were far more 'American' in style than Chanel's, her name and brand still predominated, and Patou need to break into this lucrative market. Patou had already dressed the Dollies in *Oh! Les Belles Filles*, went to the same nightclubs in Paris and shared their passion for gambling and Deauville in particular. Presumably with no charge, he created 200 outfits for the Dollies, including everything that went with them from lingerie and dressing gowns to slender lacquered canes. Daily two-hour fittings were required for two months to assemble the collection, although the advantage of the sisters being identical twins was that they could take it in turns. His plan became 'the best publicity stunt of his entire career and one which was to put him on the fashionable American map so firmly that the name Patou became synonymous in the minds of many American women with Paris Couture'.[22] When the Dollies arrived in America, they became Patou's 'Mannequins de Ville', and they ensured that everyone knew whose clothes they were wearing.

As the sisters embarked on their new American adventure, their views about dancing, which had certainly not changed over the years, were aired again in the press to coincide with their visit. Dressed in kimonos, they had been interviewed in their dressing room at the Palace Theatre, which was described as a charming boudoir with lacquered Japanese furniture in red and gold and black with Japanese prints on the walls. The interviewer thought it was an odd setting for two Hungarian-American girls, but he decided that he liked the contrast and concluded that 'the effervescent Dollies were Oriental with a large addition of "Western pep"'.

Jenny told him:

We think dancing that comes spontaneously is likely to be more beautiful, more natural and a greater pleasure to the public than steps that are drilled into one by a master . . . you must have dancing in you, you must feel it as well as love it, to get it across to the audience. The races that dance as naturally as they speak or walk are the ones that produce the best professionals. The Hungarians are such people . . . a Hungarian girl would laugh if she were told to go to a teacher for her national dances. They are in her blood. And she can acquire other rhythms merely by looking on and seeing how the stunt is accomplished. The moment she gets the feeling of joy from which the new form sprang, the difficulties vanish in a wave of intuition. Joy! That's the other word for dancing. I don't mean to say that everyone can perform with distinction: genius must be taken into account. But everyone of a dancing race who inherits the bent can swing into the steps without a teacher's aid just as everyone gets pleasure from watching them on the stage.

Jenny paused: 'Let's go and be natural. There's my formula. . . . You're sure to benefit from the poetry of motion.'[23]

The Dollies left Cherbourg on 26 July for New York aboard the *Aquitania*, arriving on 1 August 1924.[24] They stayed at the Ritz Hotel for a few days and spent some time with their father in Bensonhurst before beginning rehearsals for the *Greenwich Village Follies*. According to the reporter from *Dance Lover's*, both sisters created a sensation with their latest Parisian fashions, but an even bigger impression was created by the fact that both sported twenty-eight-carat engagement rings.[25] During rehearsals they were interviewed by a reporter from the *New York Tribune*, who described them as being 'not very grown up nor a bit spoiled'. They were both bubbling over with enthusiasm about life in general and the Prince of Wales in particular, and they would rather sing his praises than talk of their own success. With a touch of a foreign accent, they answered questions with the words tumbling out of their mouths, as they good-naturedly interrupted each other. At the same time, their hands flew up and down and they threw their heads back as they giggled like schoolgirls.

'If the Prince of Wales ever kissed the Dolly Sisters,' the reporter made clear, 'they're not telling on him. Doubtless it is this ability to keep a secret which has made them the favourites of royalty and notables all over Europe. That and their effervescent spirits, youth and good sportsmanship.' They might not have been too grown up, but they knew one of the secrets of being popular: 'We try to be good sports and nice to everyone.' At the same time they realised the vital importance of discretion.

The sisters thought that the Prince was 'the most wonderful person ever'. Rosie went into sincere raptures with no conceit in the thought that she was a friend of the Prince. 'He's a wonderful dancer and wonderfully popular. Where is there such a good fellow and good sportsman in all the world? He throws Paris into a riot. He dances like an American and does all the dances well. He plays the drums exquisitely. Oh, he is terribly smart. He's the cutest trick.' She added: 'He never allows you to address him as your Highness or to bow. He has that unspoiled look, that boyish charm.'

Jenny commented: 'He's a great sport and doesn't make you bow down. He won't come round unless you drop the ceremonies. He reminds me of a jolly college boy. He is the most fascinating kid you ever met. He is a better dancer than the Spanish King because he knows more steps. We taught him a lot . . .'. When dancing, 'he talks about anything and makes you forget you are with the Prince of Wales. It is almost impossible to believe you are with him after you have met him for the first fifteen minutes. It is difficult to realise he's the idol of the world, he's so unassuming.'

Clearly noticing what others had thought to be engagement rings on their fingers, the reporter turned the discussion to a subject about which there was much speculation: the bride whom the Prince must eventually choose. Rosie merely observed: 'He has been reported engaged so often, I don't know, but I suppose it will be an English girl. I don't think he wants to marry at all.' The reporter pointed out that on Jenny's left hand there sparkled the biggest diamond solitaire imaginable, but the only confession that could be wrung from her was: 'No we are not engaged, because when people do ask us if we will marry them, we never say "yes" we never say "no" but always "maybe".'[26]

The Prince of Wales arrived in New York aboard the *Berengaria* a month after the Dollies had arrived on 30 August. It was a visit that proved to generate considerable controversy and criticism.[27] David's visit was ostensibly to spend time at his ranch in Canada, with a stop of only a few days in New York, but he ended up spending three weeks in New York and less than a week on the ranch. Accompanied by Fruity Metcalfe, Brigadier G. Trotter and Alan 'Tommy' Lascelles (his assistant private secretary), David took up residence in the palatial home of James Burden, the steel millionaire whose wife was the great-granddaughter of Cornelius Vanderbilt, at Syosset, Long Island, and settled down to watch the international polo and horse racing, although other diversions became manifest, as there was no shortage of people eager to oblige him. To the most influential members of American society his visit to Long Island was of immense importance, and any association with him was vital to their status. He went to a luncheon party given by Mrs Harold Irving Pratt, wife of the oil millionaire, at her Glen Cove estate, a dinner and dance at the home of Mrs William K. Vanderbilt in Jericho (she was, of course, known to the Dolly Sisters, since she had met them in Paris in 1923) and a ball given by the communications millionaire Clarence Mackay at his country home Harbor Hill, Roslyn, for 1,200 guests and a cost of $1.5 million.

Despite all his obligations, right from the outset the Prince of Wales began an interesting game of attending official sporting or social functions and then disappearing. On 31 August, after sporting activities, he vanished in the afternoon and then the evening. On 3 September he went to a dance and stayed out until 6 a.m. Once again on 5 September he was out all night. On 7 September after Clarence Mackay's ball he slid away early with two women and a man and did not return until after 5 a.m. This routine continued unabated, despite the Prince's assertion to his private secretary Godfrey Thomas by letter that he had been on his best behaviour 'and avoided the demi-monde like the plague till it became boring'.[28]

So where was the Prince going, who was he seeing and what was he doing? At the beginning of his holiday the Prince had met the comedian Will Rogers at the Piping Rock Club polo dinner, and Rogers had tried to organise a special Broadway entertainment, bringing selected entertainers to perform for him on Long Island. This idea was not viewed favourably, so another idea must have been hatched. On 18 September the Prince came into New York incognito and travelled on the subway to visit various sights. After dinner at the home of Harrison Williams, the utilities executive regarded as 'the richest man in America',[29] he went to see *Rain* at the Gaiety before going to the Lido-Venice Club at 53rd Street near Park Avenue, where he was a guest of Mrs Charles Cary Rumsey, the former Mary Harriman, daughter of the railroad magnate and wife of the sculptor. Here he was given a very special late-night performance by Will Rogers, the Dolly Sisters (who had just opened in *Greenwich Village Follies*) and ten girls from the *Ziegfeld Follies* and Earl Carroll's *Vanities*. The entire lower floor of the club was given over to the Prince and his guests, who included his close friends Dickie and Edwina Mountbatten, Lady Diana Cooper, a close friend of Edwina Mountbatten Mrs Richard Norton (within a year she was to become the mistress of Lord Beaverbrook), and Mrs Frederick Cruger, described as the Prince's favourite American dance partner. The Prince's table was placed right next to the dance floor so that he could have a front-row view of the proceedings, which was convenient for Rogers, who aimed all his jokes at the Prince.[30]

This was not the only nightclub that the Prince frequented, since he apparently became a regular at Texas Guinan's El Fay Club, which had opened in May 1924 and had become the hottest spot in town. The Dollies would have made a point of visiting the El Fay Club because of their friendship with Texas Guinan, but the Prince's excursions would have caused more than an eyebrow to be raised by those in royal circles both in America and back at home in London, because of the fact that the El Fay Club was run by the gangster Larry Fay and was not the sort of place a future king of England should visit.

New York nightlife had changed considerably since Prohibition had come into effect. After an initial slump, things had blossomed again in 1924 with the rise of the speakeasy, which had an uneasy and often tenuous existence. These clubs were often smaller, more informal and more intimate than pre-war cabarets with less extravagant décor, since they might be closed down at any time and were largely run by gangsters. Some, such as the Silver Slipper, the Parody and the Frivolity, stayed around for a number of years in the same location, but many came and went with each season. At the same time the fascination with the Afro-American world of Harlem led to the black vogue, creating a string of what were called black-and-tan clubs. Lew Leslie had started the ball rolling with the Plantation Club in 1922, but more followed, mainly in Harlem in a strip called the Jungle between 130th and 138th Streets, with Connie's Inn, the famous Cotton Club and many others. However, for many of the older, less adventurous night owls the danger of police raids and the unappetising trip up to Harlem forced them towards the safer ballrooms of hotels such as the Biltmore, the Pennsylvania, the Commodore and the New Yorker, which featured rippling waterfalls, starlit skies and the dance music of Vincent Lopez and other big bands.[31]

The Prince was definitely not in this latter category, and, according to Texas Guinan, he was in the El Fay Club the night Prohibition agents decided to stage a raid. When the alert was given, she rushed him into the kitchen, dressed him as a chef and told him to fry eggs. She put Mountbatten behind the drums and told him to pretend to be a musician. For her hospitality and quick-wittedness, 'Eddie' (as she called the Prince of Wales) gave Tex a gold, black and green enamel vanity case studded with diamonds.[32]

Considering the press coverage of the Prince's nocturnal antics, it is not surprising that criticism surfaced. The English businessman Frederick Cunliffe-Owen wrote to Downing Street to complain that Fruity Metcalfe had arranged for the Prince to be entertained by dubious people such as Cosden the oil speculator and Fleishman the yeast king. But most outrageous of all, he claimed, was that the Prince 'had insulted one eminent hostess by asking that the Dolly Sisters – notorious little Jewish actresses who have never been received anywhere – should be invited to a ball given in his honour'. The Prince apparently declined to attend when his request was refused. The anti-Semitic jibe was made even more poignant by the fact that there is no evidence that the sisters were Jewish. Cunliffe-Owen's comment must have been made either from hearsay or from the misguided assumption that, because of their exotic appearance, the twins were Jewish. The British Ambassador called Cunliffe 'a tiresome busy-body who cuts no ice' and added that the charges were grossly exaggerated, but nevertheless the Prince's hectic hedonism was a concern. The Prince's private secretary Godfrey Thomas was furious and claimed the content of the letter was 'a tissue of malicious and probably deliberate falsehoods' and went on to state that the Prince of Wales had not known the Dolly Sisters were in New York[33] – an infelicitous statement indeed given the facts. Perhaps because Godfrey Thomas was in London and not New York, he really did not know the full extent of what was happening or maybe his comments formed part of a cover-up to help shield the Prince.

Since the Prince's liaison with Jenny during the spring and summer in Paris and Deauville had already caused considerable consternation, could his disappearing acts and the denials prove his liaison with her? Did he continue to see her during the first part of his trip before he set off for Canada on 20 September? Was Fruity Metcalfe still 'flirting' with Rosie? Was something going on that no one, least of all the Prince of Wales, wanted to become public knowledge? Or was it merely a mutual fascination rather than a love affair?

Tommy Lascelles wrote that, for ten years before he met Wallis Simpson, the Prince of Wales 'was continuously in the throes of one shattering and absorbing love affair after another' and that this included two well-known relationships with Freda Dudley Ward and later with Thelma Lady Furness, with whom he began a known affair in the summer of 1929.[34] To add Jenny Dolly to this list is not difficult and, if they did have an absorbing interest in each other, they were both pragmatic enough to realise that it would be transitory. Indeed, it was not long before Jenny allegedly fell under the spell of someone else. And yet their 'friendship' continued throughout the rest of the decade, and, when Jenny bought her chateau in Fontainebleau in 1928, the Prince of Wales was a favoured guest.

During all this controversy the sixth edition of the *Greenwich Village Follies* opened on 16 September at the Shubert Theatre with a Cole Porter score. Firmly in the *Ziegfeld Follies* tradition, the show was an extravagant production with beautiful James Reynolds costumes and décor, which included dazzling effects in an adaptation of Oscar Wilde's fable *The Happy Prince*.[35] The Dollies' reappearance on the New York stage, earning the huge salary of $2,500 weekly,[36] used two scenes that had become popular in Europe – the 'Dollies and the Collies' number, with Jud Brady's collies, and 'Destiny', which *The World* thought was one of the best numbers in the show.[37] They also performed in 'Two Little Babes in the Wood', a reprise of what they had done for Cochran in his 1921/2 pantomime, and 'The Hall of Mirrors' ('Make Everyday a Holiday'), where they appeared with showgirls on each side of imaginary mirrors, creating the illusion of reflection.

Despite the elaborate production qualities, the show was plagued with problems from the outset, and for some reason failed to showcase the talents of the Dollies effectively. Some thought that they did not fit into this type of intellectual revue,[38] others that they were out of their depth and overshadowed by the comedy team of Moran and Mack.[39] In fact they had been allotted only a limited number of scenes and were not used to their best advantage – a situation that precipitated much disagreement between them and Anderson as they pressed for changes. Anderson had presented them as de Courville had done in London before and had underestimated their talent. Like de Courville, he clearly lacked the vision of C.B. Cochran, for example, who tested their ability and showed them to great effect in a variety of diverse numbers rather than a few selected ones.

After playing for six weeks, the show itself was also not performing successfully, drawing only $22,000–24,000 weekly, whereas the house was capable of earning $34,000. The previous edition had done much better and was currently on tour in Chicago, where it was still making money. Morris Green, one of the producers, decided to make changes. To save money and royalties he cut out Cole Porter's score and replaced it with less expensive music, and also decided to lay off the Dollies.[40] They immediately received offers to star in a musical comedy built around them and a cabaret engagement. But their twenty-week contract specified that they could not work for anyone else.[41] So they could do nothing but continue to receive their rather amazing pay cheques and party until the owners of their 'contract' could find them something else to do.

One big party involved a trip to meet the president on Friday 17 October.[42] Along with thirty or forty other Broadway stars, the Dolly Sisters were invited to have breakfast with President Calvin Coolidge and then to perform for him in a specially devised set. They left New York by train, and a line of Cadillacs met them at the station in Washington to take them to the White House. A gentleman called Edward Bernays was in charge of the Broadway party, and, as he gathered his troupe together, he could not find the Dollies. After an extensive and, one must presume, rather frantic search, he discovered them in the station restaurant having breakfast. 'Girls!' he exclaimed, 'do you realise you are keeping the President of the United States waiting?' 'Let him wait,' Jenny replied. 'What is he anyway? Only a Vermont farmer.' And they kept on eating.[43]

As the Prince of Wales departed for London,[44] it was announced that the Dollies had declined a lucrative offer from the Keith Circuit and were going to star in *Sitting Pretty* as it resumed its regional tour, starting in Chicago. The show had run on Broadway during the summer of 1924 and had just closed in Boston. The owners Comstock and Gest, who had worked with them on *Oh Look!* in 1918, came to an agreement with Jones and Green, who had the Dollies under contract.[45] *Sitting Pretty* was a two-act play with a story centred on the troubles of a small-time crook who robbed the homes of the rich, but on one mission his plans are thwarted when he falls in love and becomes a reformed character. This lively musical comedy by Guy Bolton, P.G. Wodehouse and Jerome Kern was very similar to *Oh Look!* and was a perfect vehicle for the Dollies, but they had to wait until the beginning of 1925 to appear in their finery, dressed this time by Madame Francis and Charles LeMaire.

In the meantime they continued their night-time excursions, highlighted by the sudden announcement in the press that Rosie was to marry the playwright Edgar Allan Woolf. *The World* had discovered that the Dollies had been spending the afternoons at Woolfe's sociable and companionable apartment and that an engagement would be announced by the dancer Florence Walton at the recently opened Club Ostend, where she was dancing with her husband, Leon Leitrim.[46] Although the Dollies, in the company of Florence Walton, were definitely out and about at Club Ostend and other nightspots, the marriage story was later denied. If indeed Rosie had become romantically involved with Woolf, she could not allow the rumours to persist, since she was already on the verge of an engagement to someone else.

Eventually the Dollies left New York for Chicago, where they opened to rapturous applause in *Sitting Pretty*. It was described as having one of the best musical scores and some of the best dancing in any of the season's new productions.[47] But, given the rather unpleasant events with the *Greenwich Village Follies*, they must have been delighted that the French producer Jacques-Charles had lured them back to Paris with a contract to appear in the second edition of *New York to Montmartre* at the Moulin Rouge.[48] After touring for a few months with *Sitting Pretty*, they were on their way back to Europe, but not at the same time. Love had once again reared its head, and both sisters were seemingly afflicted at the same time.

SELFRIDGE AND WITTOUCK

Rosie sailed back to France on her own aboard the *Olympic*, arriving on 9 May 1925. She immediately stepped into the excitement of the new Paris season, attending the opening of Le Jardin de ma Sœur with friends Maurice Mouvet and his new dancing partner Barbara Bennett, Mae Murray and the ex-Mrs Mouvet, Florence Walton.[1] They were also celebrating the fact that Murray's divorce from the MGM film producer Robert Leonard was imminent.[2] The reason for Rosie's return to Paris on her own and Jenny's delay in New York was soon made clear. A few weeks after all this revelry Rosie announced her engagement to François J. Dupré[3] – probably her mystery guest in Chicago during the run of *Sitting Pretty*.[4] When asked about her sister's news, Jenny, who was still in New York, said rather emphatically: 'Oh is that so? I'm engaged too but just say he's an American boy.' She could not be outdone by her sister and had to match her announcement with one of her own, although the identity of this new fiancé, if indeed there was one, is elusive.

At 37, François Dupré looked young for his years, was extremely kind and shy, and had inherited the qualities of carefulness and moderation from his father.[5] Born in 1888, François was the son of Jules Dupré and his grandfather was the famous painter of the same name.[6] His father had worked in the Ministry of Fine Arts and had been deputy chief of staff for a cabinet minister.[7] His mother, Berthe Gueydan, had achieved notoriety by becoming the mistress of one of France's more colourful political characters, Joseph Caillaux, in 1900. François looked after all the business dealings of the Duc de Decazes, a wealthy Parisian socialite.[8] These fiscal capabilities obviously proved to be a major attraction for Rosie.

Jenny soon followed Rosie and left New York for Paris aboard the *Majestic* on 23 May in the company of old friends Jack Pickford and his new wife, the celebrated tap-dancer Marilyn Miller, and Clifton Webb with his new dancing partner, Mary Hay.[9] She arrived back in time to join Rosie for the June racing season and trips to Deauville, where they met another friend, Alice Delysia, the leading lady in Cochran's new production *On with the Show*.[10] Thoughts of Jenny's mysterious American fiancé were ousted by the excitement of placing winning bets on the horses and new flirtations.

Throughout June there were numerous race meetings, which culminated in the Grand Steeplechase at Auteuil (21 June) and the Grand Prix at Longchamps (28 June). Both race courses were located within ten minutes of Paris in the bois de Boulogne about a mile from each other, and during the summer the races had become an institution, with practically every American in Paris attending. The races themselves were often eclipsed by the kaleidoscopic pictures of colourful fashions that paraded around the green lawns, giving a sneak preview of the autumn couture shows.[11] The Dollies were renowned for attending all the important racing events around Paris and sporting new frocks from their favourite designers Patou and Molyneux, while indulging in one of their passions: gambling. It was generally recognised that they had 'cleaned up small fortunes betting on the ponies'.[12] On one occasion Jenny won $100,000 at Longchamps.[13] They had obviously gained valuable lessons from Diamond Jim Brady earlier in New York and were now putting his advice to good use.

At these racing events Jenny met a new admirer, Jacques Wittouck, a successful Belgian businessman and owner of racing stables.[14] Wittouck was the sole surviving son of five children and, although no record exists of his date of birth, in 1925 he must have been in his forties. Wittouck's father, Felix, was an industrialist who had inherited the family business. Starting in 1910, Wittouck was the administrator of sugar refineries in Pontelongo in Romania, a position he kept until 1948. He was the administrator of an artificial silk factory in Tubize, and administrator then vice-president of iron works in Clabecq. He also worked for Bank Hainault, and in 1931 became the Belgian consul in Monte Carlo.[15] Previously Wittouck had been romantically linked with the beautiful French actress Jane Renouardt and had bought her the Daunou Theatre on the rue Daunou.[16]

After the races everyone trooped back to Paris, but many stopped for tea and dancing at one of the four hottest spots: the rustic atmosphere of l'Hermitage on the far fringe of the bois on the banks of the Seine; the favourite society place of the Chateau de Madrid in Neuilly just across from the bois; the Pré Catalan with its gardens and lights in the trees situated in the middle of the bois in its own grounds of several acres; or, finally, the small and confined but terribly Parisian Café d'Armenonville on the Paris side of the bois. During June each venue took it in turns to host a gala night, and it was important to be seen at each place on successive nights.[17] As the galas subsided, many went straight back to Paris ready for 'Cinq à Sept', pre-dinner cocktails from 5.30 to 7.30 p.m., with fashionable society gravitating to the Ritz and other large bars on the avenue des Champs-Elysées. This was followed by dinner at 9 p.m. at the smartest place in Paris, Ciro's on the rue Daunou, regarded as the most American of streets in Paris. Founded by an Italian-born Egyptian called Ciro in Monte Carlo before the First World War, it was then taken over by an English syndicate, which expanded and opened branches in Paris on the ground floor of the Hotel Daunou and then London, Deauville and Biarritz. Ciro's was regarded as 'more than a restaurant. It was the centre of fashionable Parisian life,' and it was a favourite haunt of the Dollies.[18]

Since their new contract for the autumn season at the Moulin Rouge specified that they could not appear before this in Paris, they accepted an offer to headline at the opening of what was to become the most important nightspot in London – the Kit Kat Club – situated in the Haymarket. When they arrived in London at the beginning of July, the Dollies were guests at a special welcome luncheon given at the Georgian Room in the Piccadilly Hotel, with an address from Sir Charles Ruthen (JP and Chairman of the Kit Kat Club), Sir Grattan Doyle (MP and sportsman) and C.B. Cochran, before the start of their performance on 6 July 1925. This ultra-chic members-only club was described as 'luxurious, but wonderfully comfy . . . a vastly patronised and fashionable resort'.[19] Members entered from the street into a fair-sized lobby, checked personal belongings into the cloakroom and made a grand entrance down a wide staircase into a huge room decorated in white and gold with luscious red wall hangings. Settees ran around all four sides, and the bandstand faced the staircase with a spacious balcony running around the room.[20]

During their run at the Kit Kat Club, which lasted until the end of August, the Dollies either rented or bought a house in Maidenhead. They would not have been able to visit Deauville for the season in August, but Pearl White, one of their closest friends and also a great lover of Deauville, visited them in July and spent some time with them in Maidenhead.[21] Pearl enjoyed a few weeks in Deauville before she arrived back in London on 14 August to take part in the rehearsals for Norman Lee's *The London Revue*. This was a spectacular affair at the Lyceum Theatre launched on 2 September 1925, but the show did not live up to expectations and closed at the end of October. However, Pearl was enjoying financial success elsewhere. Besides her casino and hotel in Biarritz, she also opened a nightclub in Paris and ran a stable of racehorses, as well as investing her money in trust funds.[22] During this period she also lost her admirer La Falaise. He was fascinated with movies and got a job on the set of the Paramount production of *Madame sans gêne*, where he met and then married Gloria Swanson. Despite her abandonment, Pearl quickly found happiness with a handsome young Greek millionaire called Theodore Cossika and travelled the world.[23]

For Jenny her appearance with Rosie at the Kit Kat Club in July 1925 was of major significance, because it was here that she met Gordon Selfridge,[24] the celebrated American millionaire and owner of the famous department store on Oxford Street bearing his name,[25] who came one night with his daughter Rosalie. Selfridge was then 69, Jenny half his age at 33. Considering the fact that Selfridge loved the theatre and knew people that the Dollies had become friendly with, such as Lord Beaverbrook and Sir Thomas Lipton, it is strange that they had not met before, during their earlier stay in London. If this was their first meeting, Lord Beaverbrook, who was a great friend of Selfridge, may well have introduced them after their performance. Beaverbrook's daughter Janet Aitken Kidd recalled that before long Gordon Selfridge and her father were batting Jenny and Rosie 'back and forth between them like a couple of ping-pong balls'.[26]

There was in fact another game of ping-pong going on. Selfridge had the same charitable heart, or, to be more precise, open wallet, as Wittouck when it came to Jenny's fondness for gambling, on the pretext that, like Wittouck, he never wanted to see Jenny's looks darken if she was forced to leave the casino too early.[27] The two men would be inextricably linked with her for the next ten years, with constant rumours of marriage as each took it in turn to be her escort, vying for her attention in a rather unusual *ménage à trois*. And yet, Jenny's most visible and widely acknowledged liaison was with Selfridge, to the extent that many subsequent writers appear to have had no knowledge about Wittouck.

Gordon Selfridge was born 1856 in Ripon, Wisconsin, and was abandoned when young by a father who went off to fight in the Civil War never to return. He was brought up by Lois, his strong-willed mother. Wading through a variety of jobs, he found he possessed a natural gift for commerce and so became general retail manager of Marshall Fields, the largest department store in Chicago. Made a junior partner in 1890, Selfridge introduced many innovations, including lifts, window displays and a restaurant, taking the store to even greater success. At the same time he also married the socialite Rosalie Amelia Buckingham, by whom he had four children, Rosalie, Violette, Harry Gordon and Beatrice. Eventually Selfridge left Marshall Fields to set up his own store in 1904 and then sold out for a big profit. After a period of reflection, Selfridge decided to begin a new life and build a new store in London, where he believed his expert marketing skills would reap wonderful profits. He was right, and Selfridge's department store finally opened on 15 March 1909.

During the years leading up to the First World War, there were rumours that Selfridge had met, courted and fallen for several beautiful women of the stage, including the dancer Isadora Duncan, who said of him: 'Selfridge had the most extraordinary, even cheerfulness I have ever met . . . this man found happiness in actual living.'[28] But by far the most poignant was his affair with Gaby Deslys.[29] The glamorous French music-hall star, who had already met and worked and socialised with the Dolly Sisters in New York, had opened at the Palace Theatre in *The Rajah's Ruby* in September 1914 and was shocking London with her French naughtiness and businesslike attitude. According to A.H. Williams, Selfridge became entranced by her because, 'beneath the theatrical froth . . . was a serious-minded and sympathetic woman'.[30] As her relationship with Harry Pilcer cooled, Deslys finally succumbed to Selfridge's persistent advances and moved into a house in Kensington Gore, which he bought, even though at the same time she was enjoying a close friendship with *Peter Pan* author Sir James Barrie, whom she had met a few years earlier.

The relationship between Deslys and Selfridge was a closely guarded, discreet affair, typical of the time, since he was still married. It continued for about three years, and he went to great lengths to please her. Showering her with thousands of pounds worth of jewellery, he also allowed her the complete run of his store and its contents. His attention and desire to please were beautifully captured in the story of her garden. One dreary day in early spring Deslys complained that the garden was an ugly mass of tangled weeds.

Selfridge immediately ordered the head of the floristry department to tidy everything as a surprise. They worked through the night so that, when she awoke the next day, there in her garden was a small green lawn, flanked by a profusion of spring flowers all in bloom.[31]

From 1915 the Selfridge family lived at 30 Portman Square, previously owned by Alice Keppel, the most favoured mistress of Edward VII, but the threat of air raids had precipitated the need for a safer country retreat, and in October 1916 Selfridge rented the furnished Highcliffe Castle near Christchurch, Dorset, at a cost of $25,000 a year. This neo-gothic building with a church atmosphere had been built in 1762 and had several reception rooms, over thirty bedrooms and expansive, neat lawns with wonderful views of the countryside. As Selfridge had to spend more time away from London, his meetings with Deslys became less frequent, and when she returned to Paris in 1917 the relationship drew to a close.

It was at Highcliffe that Rose Selfridge became very involved in her work caring for convalescent American soldiers until her death from pneumonia in May 1918. In February 1921 Selfridge moved from Portman Square to Lansdowne House on the south side of Berkeley Square, Mayfair (now the Lansdowne Club), paying a rent of $25,000 a year. The upkeep and rent of both properties, plus the increased level of lavish entertaining, must have taken up at least half of the $200,000 a year that Selfridge took out of the business as salary. Although he did not have the drain on his resources of a new mistress to replace Deslys, he continued his lavish spending, since he saw money 'in terms of spending rather than of making'.[32] He also bought a yacht and land at Hengistbury Head not far from Christchurch on which he planned to build a vast mansion.

By the time of his mother's death in February 1924, Selfridge's home circle had dissipated. Rosalie had married Serge de Bolotoff, Prince Wiasemsky, in 1918, Violette had married the Vicomte de Sibour in 1921 and Beatrice married Comte de Sibour in 1926. Gordon Selfridge Junior had also set up home with a girl from the toy department called Charlotte Dennis – a liaison that was to remain secret for thirty years. Thus his meeting with Jenny Dolly in 1925 was timely, since Selfridge was entering a new phase in his life. Although Rosalie and her husband lived with Selfridge at Lansdowne House, for the first time he felt truly alone and needed company. According to A.H. Williams, Selfridge's liaison with Jenny Dolly became the most serious of all his affairs.

It was also noted that, as his liaison with Jenny developed, his character went through a change, and he lost control of his emotions. Hitherto his attitude towards everyone had been detached, aloof and polite, but, after meeting Jenny, the excitement he found in her company carried over to his own demeanour and behaviour. It was also the one affair that has been depicted as being the most damaging to Selfridge in financial terms. A.H. Williams and Bill Bryson[33] believed that during this period he 'squandered' up to $20 million, the main beneficiary directly or indirectly being Jenny Dolly; as a result, he ultimately lost control of his department store. The commonly held view was that Selfridge was rich and Jenny liked spending his money. It was therefore not surprising that many referred to him merely as Jenny's 'sugar daddy'.[34]

Gordon Selfridge was a handsome man and had an easy manner, which, along with his natural confidence, was an appealing combination in business and social circumstances. Yet he was also emotional and at times sentimental, he lacked a balanced sense of humour and the ability to laugh at himself and was, if anything, somewhat too serious. In complete contrast, the dark, petite and dynamic Jenny Dolly had a magnificent sense of humour punctuated by continual laughter. So what on earth did a serious, elderly businessman and a younger, restless woman who lived life to the full have in common? Setting aside the attraction of Selfridge's wealth and Jenny's beauty and youthful countenance, A.H. Williams believed that their mutual attraction could be explained more fully by their love of gambling.

The Dolly Sisters were both seen as 'the most inveterate and nonchalant gamblers and most lavish money spenders' in Europe.[35] This obsession had clearly started with their excursions under the wing of Diamond Jim Brady to horse-racing events during their early years in New York. When they arrived in Paris, they had continual flutters on the horses and in no time at all discovered the delights of the casinos on the Normandy coast and the Riviera, with Gordon Selfridge frequently acting as their private bank. Here they especially favoured baccarat and 'quickly learned the importance of drawing two cards whose pips totalled 8 or 9'. Years later Jenny remarked: 'If I don't know anything else, I know huit and neuf in French.'[36]

A.H. Williams elaborated his view about the importance of gambling in the relationship of Selfridge and Jenny by saying: 'I should say that he saw at least part of his own daring and acquisitive image reflective in her tingling absorption in games of chance. She may have seen in him the father image, approving her daring.' He also believed that as Selfridge grew older his passion for gambling became more intense and was in fact a substitute sexual life.

At the gambling tables, Selfridge, the business genius with the coolest head and the strongest nerves, had a unique system of betting when he was with Jenny. Whether they won or lost made a great difference to him financially. He always covered the losses, while Jenny kept any winnings, and the stakes sometimes ran into four figures. At the same time he also hosted parties in France that surpassed anything he had ever staged in London; to some the lavishness verged on the vulgar, with too much food and too much champagne. No wonder, as the years rolled past, his debts increased.

On her rare trips to London, Selfridge ensured that the store and its contents, as well as his cheque book, were at Jenny's, and no doubt Rosie's, disposal. But his devotion did not end there. She also had a huge love of ice-cream, and supplies were sent to her in Paris daily by aeroplane, with her pet Pekinese dog receiving a chicken breast. Selfridge personally supervised the packing and transport arrangements. Besides lavishing expensive presents of jewellery, fur coats and other luxuries, Selfridge is believed to have helped Jenny financially in many other ways – assisting later in the funding of property and a business venture.

Immediately after their first meeting, Jenny was obliged to return to Paris, where she spent the rest of 1925 and the first half of 1926 performing at the Casino de Paris. During this period Selfridge regularly made the effort to visit her in Paris at weekends, and it was noted that his absences from the business became more frequent and if he was detained he would become irritable. Thereafter Selfridge, who travelled by plane because he loved flying and it saved time, frequently joined Jenny during her breaks from work on the Riviera and on the Normandy coast. When he was unavailable, she was never lonely, because Jacques Wittouck was at her side.

Does the generally held assumption that Jenny had a ten-year love affair with Selfridge hold up to scrutiny? And, more importantly, what was the basis of this relationship? Perhaps there is after all a different story, a much more complicated one. During their liaison Selfridge asked Jenny to marry him on several occasions, but she felt the age difference was too great and refused. When Jenny was not being escorted by Selfridge, she was attached to the arm of the much younger Jacques Wittouck. Wittouck also asked Jenny to marry him and was frequently described in the press as her major suitor, but they did not marry.

So what exactly was going on? Could it be that, just like Gaby Deslys, Jenny had been isolated as the object of affection by Selfridge, who pursued her relentlessly. In the end it was easier to take the path of least resistance and accept his persistent advances and his overwhelming attention and gifts, especially if it ran to the huge sum of £2 million! Jenny certainly was not at fault or to blame for Selfridge's financial decline – after all, what could a girl do faced with such circumstances? She had grown accustomed to being pampered and spoilt by many previous admirers, such as Diamond Jim Brady in New York or Henri Letellier in Paris. For her the situation was as natural as apple pie. Although she must have been attracted to Selfridge for the obvious things such as his money, influence, status and lifestyle, it is far too easy to assume that this was her only interest. Nor can their shared pleasure in gambling be the sole explanation for an alleged ten-year love affair. Besides these things they simply enjoyed each other's company, and there appeared to be a deep mutual bond of affection. But did they have a relationship in the conventional sense of the word? Was Jenny in love with him?

Significantly in August 1928 Jenny said that one of the most wonderful moments of her life was meeting 'the man I loved better than life'.[37] She refused to be specific about who this was and declared: 'That is my secret . . . I'm not saying.' It is really not surprising that she could not say, since she did have two suitors, and to name one would disappoint the other. Jenny's tangled emotional disposition and her true love remain mysterious. Interestingly, two months later it was announced in Paris, even if erroneously, that she had married Jacques Wittouck. And, when she was seriously ill in Paris in early 1929, it was Wittouck and not Selfridge who was at her bedside. One could argue that these clues hint at a closer attachment to Wittouck. And yet, overall, it was always Selfridge who was there for her and whom Jenny seemingly really relied on. It is more than likely that her comments do refer to Selfridge. As for marriage, she simply did not want to give up her independence by marrying anyone; it was better to keep both men guessing while ensuring that they continued their financial and material support

THE AMERICAN IDOLS OF PARIS

The impresario C.B. Cochran always maintained that Paris was the spiritual home of the Dolly Sisters,[1] and it is known that they preferred Paris to London, since they regarded London on occasion as 'stuffy'.[2] Because they came from the east side of New York, where life was less restrained, they never really felt comfortable or at home in London, even though they had made numerous friends and believed that they had become acceptable to London society. They preferred the more relaxed atmosphere of France and chose to buy houses in Paris. Yet, having spent most of their lives moving around, they would have found it impossible to remain in one place for long. Paris became their base rather than their home.

In the following years, when they took holidays from work and certainly after they had retired, they became migratory birds, following the social seasons, with a spell in Saint-Moritz during January, the Riviera and Cannes in particular during February and March, the horse racing and the opening of all the bright new nightclubs in Paris during June, Deauville in July and August, and then trips to Biarritz to fill in the gaps. They arrived back in Paris after a jolly time in London at the Kit Kat Club and most probably a short stop at

Deauville to catch the very end of the season. By late October 1925 they had begun preparations for the new Pierre Foucret and Jacques-Charles spectacular revue at the Moulin Rouge. But before long a public discord erupted over billing, as they discovered that Mistinguett was obsessive and ruthless about maintaining her profile and persona at their expense.

Jacques-Charles had left the Casino de Paris and had signed a three-year contract with the Moulin Rouge in August 1924. Negotiations to engage the Hoffman Girls, who had already scored a big hit for Julian Wylie in *Leap Year* at the London Hippodrome, had been conducted by Pierre Foucret, director of the Moulin Rouge, who was a better manager than diplomat and upset Gertrude Hoffman. So, to ease the situation, Jacques-Charles went to see her in New York and smoothed her ruffled feathers. During this visit he caught up with the Dollies, who were appearing in the *Greenwich Village Follies* and signed them for the second edition of *New York–Montmartre*, to be called *Mieux que nue* (Better than Nude). The contract stipulated that they would be the stars of the show, and also that, if either party broke the contract, the sum to be forfeited was six months' salary (about $22,000).[3]

For some reason it was decided not to star the Dollies in this show when it was launched on 27 August 1925, but for them to appear in the next production, due later in the year. During these negotiations Mistinguett went to see the première of *New York–Montmartre* (which opened 10 September 1924) and was so impressed that she believed that, if she was going to maintain her position as 'Queen of the Paris Music Hall', she had to appear at the Moulin Rouge and nowhere else. Although Jacques-Charles had been responsible for staging her earlier shows at the casino, Mistinguett had fallen out with him, and so she went direct to Foucret. After several persuasive meetings she came away with a contract stating that she would be the leading lady of the next show, would be a co-director of the Moulin Rouge and would have the privilege of her name in the title of the revue. The show was therefore titled *La Revue Mistinguett* and, although the Dolly Sisters were to get top billing, Mistinguett was the undoubted star. Thus they had found themselves in a rather invidious position. What room could there possibly be for the Dolly Sisters in this new arrangement?[4]

Before the Dollies arrived in Paris they must have been told about Mistinguett's negotiations with the Moulin Rouge, but nevertheless they continued to conform to their contract and duly arrived for rehearsals despite obvious disagreements. They claimed that it was at this point they realised that Mistinguett was going to be the real star and that they were to be relegated to secondary positions. They tried to rehearse, but Foucret gave them the material for only one number, which lasted a meagre fifteen minutes.[5] As a result they voiced their concern and stated that the situation was unacceptable. Jacques-Charles tried to save the situation by inserting a number called 'The Missdollytinguett Sisters'. Both Jacques-Charles and Mistinguett thought it was a harmless and quite amusing little scene, which made a joke of their supposed rivalries. When the Dollies had the text translated, they did not find it funny, and in the end decided to pull out of the revue. It would appear that at this stage Foucret offered to cancel their contract and pay them compensation of their agreed salary of $22,000, if they agreed not to perform in Paris in opposition to Mistinguett.[6]

The Dollies were not happy and saw the situation very clearly – they had been secured to appear at the Moulin Rouge as the headlining act and this had been overturned by the appearance of Mistinguett. They argued that their contract had been signed by all parties at the Moulin Rouge, including Foucret and Jacques-Charles, and said: 'We're not exactly so naive as to take chances on a contract with an agent . . . it was a binding obligation . . . it was stipulated in the contract that we were to be the sole stars.'[7] Besides the contract they also had the artwork for the initial poster showing them as the stars of the show and no one else. As they put it succinctly: 'There can't be two stars when only one is called for,' and continued by saying 'the Moulin Rouge has no case whatever for we know positively that they did not sign a contract with Mistinguett till six months after ours. She did not go to them until she had broken relations with M. Volterra at the Casino.'[8]

The Dollies pointed out that they had refused many other excellent opportunities to appear in Paris and elsewhere as headliners to fulfil this engagement[9] and estimated that they had lost in the region of $40,000. They had been offered a lucrative deal by the William Morris Agency to go to Palm Beach and Miami at $5,000 per week. And during the summer of 1925 they had been given a lucrative offer to play at the casino in Deauville by Eugene Cornuche. They gave up the latter offer because their contract specified that they should not appear anywhere else in France until the engagement at the Moulin Rouge had been fulfilled. Regarding Foucret's offer, they said: 'The long and short of it is that we are not wanted to appear in Paris at the same time as Mistinguett.' They made it clear that they disliked being blackmailed and would not leave Paris. 'The Moulin Rouge people thought they were dealing with some timid, easily bullied French chorus girls. They're finding out different. We're Americans and we know our business.'[10] They certainly did and took out a lawsuit against the Moulin Rouge for breach of contract and demanded compensation of the full $22,000.

Foucret was incensed by their comments and their lawsuit. He claimed that they had rehearsed the show for three weeks and had been given every consideration, and then he countersued for $22,000 plus the cost of costumes (the Dollies had insisted on having their own costumes made by a couturier of their choice, probably Patou) and publicity, on the basis that they had broken their contract. He denied that they had been deprived of being the headliners by Mistinguett by stating that she had very courteously made every concession to them. He added that they had been given five numbers totalling 30 minutes not the 15 minutes they claimed, and he referred to them as 'the temperamental pair'.[11] Although the slur was to be expected, it was quite inappropriate, since they had been totally misled by the devious antics of Mistinguett, who had wrapped Foucret around her nimble little fingers.

The whole of Paris was of course abuzz with the story, and, although Mistinguett was adored by the public, there were many who were clearly thrilled with the Dollies' tough stance against her and revelled in the ongoing saga. Because the Dollies pulled out of the Moulin Rouge four days before the launch, Mistinguett was faced with the task of completely restructuring the show and had to work twenty-four hours a day to get everything right.[12] The Dollies, on the other hand, skipped off to the Acacias nightclub to celebrate with Harry Pilcer, and, free of their contract, they danced all night to the admiration of the audience amid rumours that they had bought the club or had gone into partnership with him.[13] Equally infuriating for Mistinguett and Foucret was the news that the Dollies had been immediately snapped up by the management of the Casino de Paris and would appear as the stars of the new show with Maurice Chevalier that was due to open very shortly.

The court case continued through 1926, finally being resolved in their favour in the autumn. The Dollies then generated immense public respect when they donated the entire sum awarded to them to the Actors' Benevolent Fund. One could argue that the donation was a clever publicity stunt. It was. But the money was to some degree irrelevant. The issue all along had been one of principle. They would have been paid an equal, if not greater amount by the management of the Casino de Paris, so they could have doubled their earnings by keeping the money. Instead they had not lost anything, so they could reinforce their good nature by giving the awarded sum away. It was a wonderful gesture and a brilliant swipe at what was seen as the greediness of Mistinguett.

During the controversy over billing between the Dollies and Mistinguett, someone arrived in Paris who began to present an even bigger threat to Mistinguett as 'Queen of the Paris Music Hall'. The successful staging of *La Revue nègre*, which opened at the Théâtre des Champs-Elysées on 2 October 1925, catapulted Josephine Baker, the gorgeous black entertainer, to fame. She took Paris by storm and became Mistinguett's chief rival in the popularity stakes.

Another star in the making was the American black entertainer known simply as Bricktop (her real name was Ada Smith), who was in a short space of time to become one of the most celebrated nightclub hostesses of Paris. The red-headed Bricktop, or 'Bricky' as her friends called her, had a great personality and was a fabulous dancer. Fitzgerald, Hemingway and Waugh wrote about her and Cole Porter composed 'Miss Otis Regrets' for her. When Florence Jones, the resident singer of the Le Grand Duc on the rue Pigalle in Montmartre, left to open her own club, Florence's, Bricktop was brought over from New York, where she had been singing at Connie's Inn in Harlem, to step into her shoes, and she became an instant hit. 'Bricky' became friends with everybody who was anybody and she soon opened her own club called the Music Box in late 1926. This was followed by the club that bore her name in early 1927.

Bricktop met the Dollies through Cole Porter (he had written the score for *Greenwich Village Follies*, their last Broadway show), and they were regular visitors to her nightclub. Bricktop found it difficult to tell them apart and decided that 'it was easier to just think of them as the Dollys and not worry about who was who', adding: 'If you think the Gabor sisters were famous for their husbands and jewels you should have seen them in their prime.' She summed them up by saying: 'Everyone loved the Dollys . . . they were legends.'[14]

La Revue Mistinguett finally opened on 11 November 1925 with the American Forde Sisters (Marion and Ethel) replacing the Dollies. The Fordes had been engaged by C.B. Cochran for *Little Nellie Kelly* in mid-1923, where they had met Eddie Dolly, who had choreographed the show, and they then appeared in Eddie Dolly's *Dolly's Revels*, the first cabaret staged at London's Piccadilly Hotel in spring 1924. Although they were good dancers, one commentator observed that 'when they are dancing together one sees that, indeed, the Dolly Sisters are irreplaceable'.[15]

In joining the Casino de Paris and Maurice Chevalier, the Dollies held up the première of *Paris en fleurs* until 28 November 1925, as they rehearsed new numbers with their brother Eddie and waited for all their costumes created by Patou, although the rest of the show was costumed by Antoinette from designs by Jean Le Seyeaux and Zig.[16] Chevalier and the Dollies were supported by the singer and dancer Yvonne Vallée, whom Chevalier would marry in 1927, Madeleine Loys, Lily Scott, the dancing Rowe Sisters, the acrobatic dancers Roseray and Capella, the sixteen Lawrence Tiller girls and the solo dancer Dora Duby from San Francisco, who had already scored a big hit in London and on the Riviera.

Paris en fleurs was a triumphant hit, described as 'one of the best revues the Casino de Paris has ever had with the recognition that the pillars of the show were the Dolly Sisters and Chevalier'.[17] The Dollies appeared in a bewildering profusion of beautiful frocks,[18] as they became in turn shepherdesses, valseuses, Spanish danseuses, candied fruit and exotic diamonds in seven separate numbers. Their dancing was greatly admired: 'they are full of "go" in all they do, but of course their special attraction is the wonderful symmetry or parallelism of their movements'.[19]

The ingenious finale to the first act was inspired by French nursery songs entitled 'Rondes enfantines'. Madeleine Loys summoned the songs from the pages of a huge album and the songs personified by charming ladies appeared in a succession of exquisite little tableaux. One of these included the Dollies in a French version of Little Bo-Peep (Il Pleut, Bergère), dressed in quaint peasant dresses with voluminous short skirts and apple green bows in their bobbed hair.[20]

In Paris they also had several visitors to keep them entertained. Sophie Tucker, fresh from her appearance at the Kit Kat Club, took a break in Paris towards the end of 1925,[21] and John Murray Anderson also paid them a visit. Anderson observed that the Dollies had fabulous jewels, which they kept in an old shoe box under the dressing table. He was sitting with them between acts backstage when the Aga Khan called on them as well. Jenny was taking emeralds from the old shoe box to replace the diamonds she had been wearing, and the Aga Khan asked her whether she was afraid to leave such valuables in a tattered shoe box. Jenny said: 'No, Rosie and I figured out that it would be the last place in the world anybody would look for jewels.' The Aga Khan said: 'I must remember that.'[22] Various press reports indicate that the Aga Khan was another of their admirers, and yet it is no surprise that he does not mention them in his autobiography. After all, he was a devoutly religious man.

Another significant visitor was the greatest silent-screen star of the time, Rudolph Valentino, who was visiting Europe to attend the première of his latest film, *The Eagle*, in London and Paris in late 1925. He was also in the middle of divorce proceedings from his wife, Natacha Rambova, and was so upset that he tried to alleviate his misery by partying; for three weeks he slept only two hours a night. Accompanied by Mae Murray, who was also in Paris at the time, and the Dolly Sisters, after their own nightly performances at the Casino de Paris, he danced the night away at all the fashionable nightspots, including the Lido, the Ambassadeurs, Club Florida and Ciro's. After visiting Berlin, London and the Riviera, he returned to America early in 1926, and the world was stunned when eight months later he died on 23 August 1926.[23]

With Christmas the Dollies showed their generosity yet again with a special party for all the girls in *Paris en fleurs*. It was a supper affair in the hall of the Théâtre de Paris, which adjoined the casino. There were also a select number of other guests, including 'Priscilla', a columnist from the *Tatler*, and C.B. Cochran. Priscilla thought that they were 'perfect hostesses and the girls had the time of their young lives'.[24] At the time, the Dollies' father had also arrived in Paris to spend some time with his daughters over the festive season. In an interview he was asked for his view of the modern girl.

I am old fashioned . . . I don't care for the Jazz Age . . . and the way in which the young women conduct themselves in it. As an abstract thing, I don't even like my daughters dancing. But when I see them, all my objections vanish into thin air. I am ravished, carried out of myself, my breath is taken away. I can't speak. I can't find my voice to object. I think they are magnificent. Sometimes I feel like rushing out of my seat and stopping the show. I want to take my little girls home with me. Their dancing is so lovely.

The devoted father proudly added that he watched his 'two favourite performers' every night.[25]

During their lengthy stay at the casino, which continued well into the summer of 1926, the Dollies took a few short breaks from the arduous round of performances and escaped to Le Touquet to be pampered by Gordon Selfridge. At Easter, in the company of other showbiz celebrities, including Tallulah Bankhead, Phyllis Monkman and her husband Laddie Cliff (with whom they had danced in their first London show *Jigsaw*), their clothes and jewellery caused a stir at the casino, and one night everyone was intrigued by their violet wigs and matching frocks.[26] They aroused further interest at Whitsun, when Selfridge made sure they were invited to all his social events, including dinner with a party that numbered Lord Fitzwilliam, Lady Headfort and her daughter Lady Millicent.[27] It must have been at one of these visits that they were photographed with Gordon Selfridge and his daughter the Vicomtesse de Sibour.[28]

By the summer of 1926 the Dollies had left the cast of *Paris en fleurs* and were having a brief rest, although charity performances and social appearances were not ignored. They were acknowledged as having a generous spirit. 'Bless 'em, always to the fore in anything to do with charity,' exclaimed Priscilla in the *Tatler* earlier in the year at the *Bal des petits lits blancs* at the Opera House.[29] With the popular British actress Jenny Golder and the Rowe Sisters, they helped entertain at the inauguration fête of the extended premises for the Home for Theatre Girls. This hostel for dancers from the English dance troupes engaged in Paris was presided over by Lady Crewe, wife of the British Ambassador, who was patron.[30] They were also guests at an elaborate banquet for six hundred in honour of Oscar Dufrenne, the proprietor of the Palace and the Concert Mayol, when he was made a Chevalier of the Legion of Honour, France's highest civil award.[31]

One of the most important social events of the season in early June was the reopening of the newly renovated Ambassadeurs.[32] Edmund Sayag, the Algerian theatre and casino magnate, purchased from M. Dufrenne the lease on the Ambassadeurs theatre on the avenue Gabriel just off the place de

Concorde and the Champs-Elysées, where the Dollies had made their Paris debut.[33] The building was overhauled, with all the stalls and boxes swept away, as it was converted into a cool and airy mixture of extravagant nightclub and sophisticated restaurant, which had the advantage of being open air in the summer.[34]

For his first show Sayag imported Lew Leslie's all-black production of *Blackbirds of 1926* starring Florence Mills, direct from London and New York, which capitalised on the success of the *Revue nègre*. It was an instant hit, and the midnight launch was packed with all the smart Paris society along with American and French stage celebrities. Taking advantage of the champagne, foie-gras sandwiches and petits fours were, among many others, Josephine Baker, Dora Duby, Marion Forde, Sacha Guitry, Yvonne Printemps, Maurice Chevalier, Yvonne Vallée, Jane Marnac and, of course, the Dolly Sisters. Their support was not surprising, because shortly afterwards they appeared in *Dolly's Revels*, a mini-revue staged by their brother Eddie at the Kursaal, Ostend, owned and run by Edmund Sayag.

Ostend was a resort that, in the summer, combined all the elements of climate, comfort and pleasure with a beautiful promenade, sumptuous waterfront buildings, pretty parks, squares and avenues and numerous amusements. Most notable was the Kursaal, a pleasure palace without equal, the opening of which marked the annual summer season from 30 May to 30 September. Sayag's summer spectacle opened on 24 July 1926 with an extensive cast and an array of costumes designed by Dolly Tree.[35] The plan was to transfer the show to the Piccadilly Hotel in London after four weeks, but it is not clear if this in fact happened, and by mid-August the Dollies were firmly entrenched in the pleasures of Deauville with Gordon Selfridge and his daughter Rosalie, Princess Serge Wiasensky.[36] They caused a sensation one morning by wearing bathing costumes that incorporated a new fashion accessory – waterproof ostrich feathers. Rosie in a green bathing suit wore green feathers as a boutonnière; Jenny wore a white and blue suit with red feathers. When they emerged from the sea, the feathers fluffed up perfectly dry![37]

During this time Selfridge gave the Dollies a rather magnificent, if bizarre, present during a visit to Le Touquet. A girl's best friend is definitely diamonds, and millionaires have often said it with rocks, as lesser mortals say it with flowers, and wise girls have always accepted them. Gordon Selfridge took the banality out of such a glittering gift by choosing an original, if rather frivolous, setting. He gave the Dolly Sisters a pair of fine four-carat blue diamonds and got Cartier to set the stones in the shells of a well-matched pair of live tortoises. According to one press report, the Dollies used to take their new pets for walks on the front at le Touquet, to the delight of onlookers! If this is accurate, then the 'walks' must have taken all day.[38]

During 1926, David, Prince of Wales, made several trips to France. He spent the period 17–26 April in Biarritz, but either side of this holiday he spent a few days in Paris and perhaps managed to see the Dollies in *Paris en fleurs*. In early August he spent the weekend in Le Touquet, but, since the Dollies were in Ostend, it is unlikely their paths crossed. However, during 2–10 September he once again made a trip to Biarritz with stops in Paris.[39] Since September was the season to visit Biarritz, perhaps the Dollies, who were resting, also decided to take a holiday there at the same time. They were back in Paris by late October, when the Prince of Wales arrived for a three-day official visit. His duties comprised the inauguration of the Canadian Students' Dormitory at the Cité Universitaire, plus a dinner at the Embassy and lunch with M. Doumargue, the French president.[40]

However, he stayed at the Hotel Maurice rather than the Embassy, which enabled him to escape for some night-time fun. On the evening of 29 October, after his official duties, the Prince of Wales attended a private party given by the Boston millionaire Amos Lawrence, where he met Bricktop, who taught him how to dance the Black Bottom and the Charleston. He enjoyed himself so much that, at very short notice, he asked Bricktop to stage a party for him the following night at a Montmartre nightclub. The evening was such a success that it became Bricktop's Music

Box, one of the hottest nightspots in Paris.[41] Given the fact that the Dollies were friends of Bricktop and were regulars at her many venues, they were more than likely guests at this party.

At the time the Dollies were preparing for something unique. They had succumbed to the dream of many performers – staging and producing their own show and becoming managers in their own right. They rented the smart little red, white and gold Edouard VII Theatre from Alphonso Franck and staged a rather ingenious and exceptionally lavish revue, largely written by Sacha Guitry, entitled *À vol d'oiseau* or *As the Crow Flies*. The revue followed an aeroplane trip around the world, with the Dolly Sisters encountered in various corners of the globe, with the presentation aided by the extensive use of moving pictures. It opened on 12 November 1926. The Dollies, supported by an extensive cast of French performers, were dressed in an array of elaborate costumes by Jean Le Seyeaux, executed by Pascaud, and in gowns by their favourite designer, Patou.

À vol d'oiseau was regarded as the most fashionable theatre opening of the season,[42] since anything from Sacha Guitry's 'nimble brain' was 'quite an important function in Paris', and the Dollies were admired as 'the start, centre and finish of the show'.[43] The Dollies, now aged 34, were also observed to be in peak physical condition. 'Both are in marvellous training; their arms and their legs are hard as steel, their muscles as firm and their figures as flexible as any athlete could desire.'[44]

The Dolly Sisters were regarded as the life and soul of the piece: 'Not only do they dance well but they are so full of life and have so much the air of thoroughly enjoying it themselves that they carry everyone with them.'[45] In view of the recent court case against the Moulin Rouge, which they had just won, another critic decided that they had 'endeared themselves to the hearts of the Parisians for their simplicity and utter absence of side'. In short, they did not exhibit the common failing of many theatrical stars who believed that they were far superior to mere mortals: 'With the Dollys stardom does not mean an eternal station in the limelight and the front row.'[46]

Although the inclusion of moving pictures in the show was an ingenious idea, it did not go down well on the first night. A good third of the show consisted of what was apparently a travel film, while the Dollies' appearances were too few and too short. After protests the film portion was immediately cut, but even so it was still seen as inconsequential. Further alterations were made that had a positive effect,[47] and the management advertised the show as a great success, stating that it was a triumph, with takings of $4,500 in three days[48] and then $12,250 in ten days.[49] But at the beginning of December, Alphonse Franck, in a move followed by other theatre proprietors, decided to reduce the price of seats by 20 per cent, at the same time announcing that receipts had fallen and were not good.[50] There is confusion over what followed, with the reports at odds with each other. It would appear that Alphonse Franck decided to close the show, although no real reason for this decision appears to have been given.[51] Apparently the Dollies then decided to look for another theatre to restage their show but to no avail,[52] and so À vol d'oiseau closed on 3 January 1927 after a run of about eight weeks,[53] although for unknown reasons some press reports suggested that it closed after only three days[54] or fifteen days.[55]

Even though the author and the producers who doubled as the stars were incredibly popular and the production itself was lavish, the revue simply did not click with the audience and failed to make enough money. The Dollies expressed their disappointment with Guitry's script, which they felt had been responsible for the closure.[56] Indeed, this was seen by many as the real problem.

Despite the unpleasantness of the sisters being involved with what was perceived by some as a failure, their popularity was untarnished because they continued to express a generosity of spirit. It was reported that they had kept the show going long after it should have died a normal death from their 'sheer goodness and kindness of heart', because they were concerned that the less fortunate members of their company should not find themselves without a job at the festive time of year.[57]

This, of course, was not the end of the story. The Dollies had secured the use of the Edouard VII Theatre for a six-month period from 26 October 1926 to 31 March 1927. Franck's argument must have been that he was losing money and so was forced to suspend the contract and filed suit against the Dolly Sisters for a total of $2,000 for costumes, publicity and musicians, which he felt was due him. The Dollies contested the suit, which continued in the courts for several years until June 1931, when they were forced to concede and finally to settle.[58]

Despite these difficulties, Jenny must have been delighted when she received a thousand £1 Selfridge shares as a Christmas present from Selfridge,[59] following the formation of the Gordon Selfridge Trust and a share issue in September 1926.[60] At about the same time Jenny bought an old and somewhat dilapidated five-storey building that had been a hotel situated at 8 rue Pomereu, just off the place Victor Hugo in Paris.[61] By all accounts Selfridge assisted in the financing of both the property and the $500,000 that Jenny is reported to have spent on renovations, decoration and furnishing, which she personally directed. There was an ornate oriental roof garden, a drawing room with a vast carved fireplace, a coffee room in a setting like a modern Arabian Nights fairytale illuminated by coloured lights within columns and a Chinese salon where Jenny surrounded herself with her favourite companions, singing birds, which she kept to 'brighten dull moments'.[62] Not much except the actual walls remained of the original house, and, once completed, it had the air of having been lived in for years, so skilfully had the renovations been carried out. It became 'one of the show places of Paris',[63] although the description by the *Sketch* that it was a 'mansion' and had the bois de Boulogne as its background was quite misleading.[64] It certainly was not a mansion but a modest-sized terraced house that faced the bois, views of which could be seen only vaguely from the roof garden.[65] However, when brilliantly illuminated at night, it may well have had the appearance of a ruby-studded jewel box!

As work progressed on Jenny's new home, the sisters decided to take a well-earned rest before rehearsing what would be their last Parisian revue, *Paris–*

New York, due to be launched in the early summer at the Casino de Paris. These few months of rest and relaxation proved to be the most tumultuous period of their lives, as the real prospect of marriage reared its head.

Accompanied by Gordon Selfridge and their brother, Eddie, they spent most of January in the glorious winter snow of Switzerland.[66] Saint-Moritz was the seasonal stop for the rich and famous during the dreary months between Christmas and the Riviera season, and, when the Dollies arrived, the season was in full swing.[67] Social life centred round either the Carlton or the Palace, both of which offered nightlife as glittering and formal as that of Paris. After a long day of outdoor activities – skiing, skating, tobogganing and sleigh rides – teatime with hot chocolate, toast and honey followed by backgammon and bridge was a welcome relief, before dinner with the usual lavish display of evening gowns.[68]

And then, after snow and ice, it was time for a change of scenery and a little bit of sun. Like thousands of other exotic migratory birds, the Dollies headed south to the Riviera and made themselves at home in their favourite place – the luxurious Carlton Hotel, regarded as 'the most bohemian' of all the places of amusement in Cannes[69] and the exclusive enclave for the very richest and most famous of European society who did not own their own villas nearby. Here the Dolly Sisters would have been delighted to bump into many old London friends such as Lord Beaverbrook, C.B. Cochran, who had made them a great success in London, and Jenny's previous fiancé, Henri Letellier[70] with his new bride, the slender and wistful Yola Henriquet (who allegedly was later to have a 'liaison' with Lord Louis Mountbatten for over thirty years).[71]

A particular incident was vividly recalled. One evening Jenny swept into the Municipal Casino in Cannes, escorted by Gordon Selfridge. Her arrival made those enjoying the gaming tables stop, catch their breath, admire her beauty and wonder what excitement would now unfold; such was her reputation. She was wearing a black gown gleaming with sequins and a wonderful hat with ostrich feathers, while her arms were covered with jewels from elbow to fingertips – she looked a million dollars. Thelma Lady Furness recalled:

My eyes popped, I had never seen so many jewels on any one person in my life . . . every one of them was an emerald. The magnificent necklace she wore around her neck must have cost a king's ransom. Her bracelets reached almost to her elbows. The solitary ring she wore on her right hand must have been the size of a small ice cube.[72]

Jenny surveyed the room and, trailing Selfridge behind her, went like a homing pigeon to the *chemin de fer* table, where the gambling moguls of the time, the Aga Khan, ex-King Manuel of Portugal, Prince Esterhazy of Hungary and others, were playing for unlimited stakes. She swiftly cornered the big boys by playing a winning streak for all it was worth. The Aga Khan, King Manuel and the others soon dropped out, one by one, until only she and Esterhazy were left in the game. It was protocol in the casino to gamble with deadpan detachment, but she exulted with uncontrolled vehemence as she forced Esterhazy to the wall in what could clearly be seen as a rather personal duel. She had a stack of chips totalling at least ten million francs when she finally cleaned out the Hungarian prince. She stood up, looked at the crowd gathered around the table and laughed. 'I'm glad I whipped the great Prince Esterhazy. My grandfather was a serf on his estate in Hungary and was lashed by his overseer.' According to Elsa Maxwell, the society hostess who witnessed the entire event, this was democracy in action, since, although the woman was a commoner, she had been able to settle an old score with an aristocrat.[73]

Dressed exquisitely in matching outfits every day and for every occasion by their favourite Parisian couturier, Jean Patou, the Dollies were seen everywhere: at the races, the tennis courts, the gala evenings at the Ambassadeurs restaurant and the casino, not to mention starring roles in the annual 'Battle of the Flowers' parade. As Patou's 'mannequins de ville', the Dollies mirrored his official fashion shows staged at various functions throughout the Cannes season and were his special publicity tool. Their exuberance did not go unnoticed, and the commentator from the society magazine *Eve* observed: 'They always seem so pleased with life, so unspoiled and happy and gay, so full of fun. They are such a delightful contrast to some of the languid bored creatures one sees.'[74] They were adored for their clothes, their sense of fun, their lavish displays of jewellery and their heavy gambling in the baccarat rooms of the casino. Of equal delight to Riviera revellers was their decision to dance at one of the galas in the Municipal Casino,[75] where everyone turned out in force to see them.[76]

The themed galas, usually devised, staged and decorated by the artist Jean-Gabriel Domergue, were an orgy of sumptuous self-indulgence. In early March, for example, there had been a feast suggestive of picturesque pagan days or a lavish Roman banquet.[77] But the 'pièce de résistance' was a 'First Empire' (1804–14) gala held in mid-March with the big hall of the casino decorated in brilliant colours and laurel-crowned 'Victoires'. The gilt and purple chairs of the front row creaked and groaned with aristocratic dignitaries that included kings, queens, princes, princesses, dukes, duchesses and every other kind of European royalty imaginable.[78]

The aim of this particular gala was to re-create the spectacle conceived by Pauline Borghese in June 1810 at her palace in Neuilly in order to astonish her brother, the Emperor Napoleon, and the Imperial Court by its magnificence. Borghese had engaged the services of the ballet master of the Imperial Opera House, who employed a company of famous theatrical and operatic personages of the day to perform. In this re-creation, the Grand Maître des Cérémonies announced the celebrities as they appeared at the reception all dressed in gorgeous period costume. The enthralled correspondent of *Eve* said that the 'delightful anachronisms' of the Dolly Sisters, wearing white satin Directoire frocks and with huge aigrettes in their hair, danced their way through the evening 'in their usual inseparable way' and were the focal point for the entire event and enraptured the audience, securing round after round of enthusiastic applause.[79]

Significantly, not only did the Dolly Sisters perform for a massed audience of European royalty, but they also mingled with them socially. Given their humble origins, this was an amazing achievement, and Jenny's personal duel in the casino with Prince Esterhazy of Hungary takes on a different complexion with this in mind.

The official description of their relaxing spring break was of two glamorous women, both independent, successful and wealthy, who were able to socialise in society and were universally adored for the quality of their performances, for their characters and for their beauty. On the surface everything looked perfect and they were having a wonderful time. Beneath the superficiality of press reports, however, the reality was quite different. Usually the press enjoyed speculating about the love affairs of the Dollies, since they rarely gave anything away. The Dollies were discreet, unlike the darling of the tabloids, Peggy Hopkins Joyce, who made a point of discussing every nuance of her relationships with the press.[80] In this instance, the press had missed a trick and a very intriguing story indeed.

It had been widely reported that both sisters had hooked a big fish. Rosie was engaged to the Parisian socialite and businessman François Dupré and Jenny was involved with both Gordon Selfridge and Jacques Wittouck. At this point their rivalry rose to a new frantic height. Rosie, not wanting to be outdone by her sister's double act, two-timed Dupré with the Canadian multi-millionaire Mortimer Davis Junior, just as rumours of Jenny's impending marriage to Selfridge became more strident, and it was reported that he had purchased a half interest in the Casino de Paris and was to present it as an engagement present to Jenny, whom, he claimed, he was going to marry in June.[81] The implication was obvious: Jenny would marry, the Dolly Sisters would star in one last big show and then retire. Rosie was forced to confront reality and act fast.

It was noticed that both sisters left Cannes early on the pretext that Jenny was anxious to get settled into her new home before Easter. They departed on the same train as the King and Queen of Denmark but were unaware of this and had already made themselves comfortable in their compartment when their Majesties arrived on the platform escorted 'by the usual top-hatted municipal big wigs'. The Dollies did not see the royal couple and, since they had been greatly fêted by the authorities in Cannes, who were grateful to them for their many charitable acts, naturally thought that a farewell demonstration was being made in their honour. They bowed and smiled their thanks from their compartment. After a while they realised their error and retired to their seats in embarrassment. Naturally they were teased about it quite mercilessly afterwards. They were described as being so good tempered 'that they never mind a joke that goes a little against them'.[82]

ROSIE AND THE GOLD
AT THE END OF THE RAINBOW

After several engagements and false alarms Rosie finally succumbed to matrimony for the second time but in curious circumstances. After a pleasant time on the Riviera, she was observed without Jenny at the Embassy Club in London in the company of Gordon Selfridge and one of his daughters in mid-March 1927. She apparently looked thin and in ill health and it was believed that she may have slipped out of the French capital for a rest.[1] It transpired that Rosie could not have been too ill because she was in fact en route to America, where she married Mortimer Davis Junior, a Canadian business magnate and heir to a vast fortune, in Brewster, Connecticut, on 31 March 1927.[2] At the time, for very important financial reasons, everything was conducted in absolute secrecy, and Rosie claimed she was crossing the Atlantic to discuss a possible vaudeville tour and had not even told Jenny of her true intentions.[3]

Rosie and Davis Junior, affectionately called 'Morty' by Rosie and 'the fat boy' by others, had met either in Paris in the autumn of 1926 or in Saint-Moritz or Cannes. Rosie had hooked a big catch in more ways than one: Davis was described as being a pleasant young man 'somewhat too fat' and 'neither conspicuously handsome nor bright'.[4] He was a member of the international Riveria set, had a fondness for the gambling casinos of Deauville, Cannes and Monte Carlo and liked to spend money. According to one reporter, he had all the traits that would appeal to the Dolly Sisters and so was 'a most satisfactory husband for one of them'.[5] His appearance certainly did not seem to worry Rosie, since when Jenny first met him she commented: 'Ummm, he's pretty heavy', to which Rosie replied sweetly: 'Yes, but he's all pure gold.' It was the gold and the hostility from Rosie's new prospective in-laws that caused a major problem and hence the deception.

Sir Mortimer Davis Senior was regarded as the 'Rockefeller of Canada', a Canadian tobacco and whiskey magnate with a vast fortune estimated at the time at $150,000,000. He owned great estates in Canada, including the splendid country home of Saint-Agathe des Monts near Quebec and the palatial Villa les Glaieuls on the Riviera. The son of a Jewish cigar-maker in Montreal, he had taken his father's trade and advanced rapidly, taking control of the bulk of Canada's cigar, pipe, tobacco and cigarette markets. Turning to other industries, he merged several distilling companies to form Industrial Alcohols Ltd, one of the world's major distributors of liquors and allied products. Hard work and hard living in his youth broke his health, and he was forced in middle age to retire from active business and live in the balmy climate of the Riviera, although he kept in constant contact with his business interests back home. At the time of Rosie's marriage to his son, he was married to his second wife.

The career of the latest Lady Davis was as romantic and remarkable as that of the Dolly Sisters. Born Elly (Eleanor) Curran in New Orleans, she believed herself to be pretty and bright. She moved to New York and got a job as a telegraph operator then a manicurist in a hotel. One of her customers was a theatrical manager and offered her a try-out in the chorus of a show. In New Orleans, Count Guillermo Moroni, an attaché of the Italian Consulate, expressed an interest, and soon Miss Curran was the Countess Moroni and living the high life in Paris, Monte Carlo, Nice and Cannes, but the marriage did not survive. Divorced and with little money, she met Sir Mortimer Davis Senior, but he was married to the former Henriette Marie Mayer of California. This marriage was far from congenial, and he soon settled for divorce, with a $50,000 alimony, swiftly marrying the Countess.[6]

When the tale of Rosie's marriage became public knowledge in the spring of 1928, sympathetic friends explained her actions to the press. The wise and thrifty Rosie, who was regarded as being the 'business brains' of the Dolly Sisters, realised that she had come to a critical time in her career. It was believed by many that when dancers reached their 30s they must expect their footwork to slow, and it is a good idea for a dancer to retire into matrimony while she is still going strong.[7] It was widely recognised that Davis Senior was not in good health and that on his demise, which was believed to be imminent, his vast fortune would pass to his son. It was clear that anyone who married young Mortimer would, in a reasonable amount of time, be the wife of one of the richest men in the world.

Since Davis Junior was 'easy going and good natured like most fat boys', a wife with a strong character and business sagacity such as Rosie would eventually have access to the entire fortune. Equally she was eager to assume the title of 'Lady Davis', which she presumed, just like the fortune, would automatically pass to her. Alas for the poor bride who counts her chickens before they are hatched.

The reason for the secrecy about their marriage was quite simple – when Davis Senior and his wife Lady Eleanor Davis discovered that Davis Junior was expressing an interest in Rosie, they made it clear that they did not approve of her and really did not believe that she would make a suitable bride. They suggested that, if the relationship persisted, he would jeopardise his future financial security. As a result, what could they do but lie and hope for the best?

The happy couple returned to Paris separately, with Rosie arriving at Cherbourg aboard the *Olympic* on 22 April 1927.[8] She immediately purchased a residence at 16 Boulevard Maillot, opposite the bois de Bologne in the

Neuilly district of Paris, and a country house in the Île de France. Davis Junior must have joined Rosie in Paris at some point shortly afterwards.[9] Not a soul knew that they were newly married, and Rosie only took Jenny into her confidence to explain the deception and introduce her new husband.

At the time, Jenny was settling into her new house, although she spent some time around Easter (15–18 April) at Le Touquet with Gordon Selfridge. There were crowds ten deep watching her gamble in the casino. One night she was even obliged to use her chin to keep the top notes of her pile from fluttering away so high were they stacked in front of her![10] It would not have escaped Jenny's notice that David, Prince of Wales, arrived in Paris with Prince George on 13 April for a seven-day unofficial visit prior to a holiday in Biarritz and an official visit to Madrid and Seville. They were staying at the Hotel Maurice, and there were the usual reports of dancing into the small hours of the morning followed by riding in the bois de Boulogne, visits to the squash racquet association of Paris and the Auteuil horse-racing course during the day. After his trip to Spain, the Prince of Wales returned to Paris on 7 May for another week of nocturnal activities. It is certainly not inconceivable that their paths would have crossed once more during these trips to Paris.[11]

We are not told what Jenny thought of Rosie's actions and her plan to ensnare a new husband, a fortune and a title. Given that Jenny had always erred on the side of caution when it came to marriage proposals and continually thought about her sister and their career, one can only deduce that she must have been disappointed at Rosie's behaviour and lack of consideration. On the other hand, Rosie had a different point of view. It is likely that, despite a long engagement, Rosie felt that for whatever reason François Dupré was not right for her, even though initially she did not have the courtesy to tell him. During their holiday in Saint-Moritz and Cannes in the spring of 1927 things came to a head. Jenny was seriously entertaining two marriage proposals with rumours of an impending wedding to Selfridge, and Rosie may well have believed that very shortly she would be on her own. There was even gossip in Paris about a tiff between the two sisters.[12] It must have been these thoughts that precipitated Rosie's impulsive desire to sidestep Dupré and immediately to marry someone else who was a better financial bet and who had just conveniently entered her life.

The parallelism of the sisters' actions is quite astonishing and was made even more amazing by the fact that both were involved in a tangled web of deception and duplicity. The sisters were suspicious and wary of one another in terms of their matrimonial intentions. They were performing a subtle and complicated dance around each other – a dance of rivalry and bluff as they both tried to outwit and compete with the other while at the same time professing their sisterly devotion and love.

Rosie had to ensure that her marriage to Davis Junior remained a secret. And yet it must have been difficult to ignore his presence in her life. At first Rosie may have believed that she could emulate her sister's relationship with Gordon Selfridge and Jacques Wittouck by doing the same with François Dupré and Davis Junior. However, after a few months she may have cooled her relationship with Dupré, even if she did not actually tell him that their engagement was off. It was still believed by the press and the public that Jenny would marry Gordon Selfridge and Rosie would marry François Dupré. As they prepared for what was to become their last Parisian show, *Paris–New York*, talk of their impending marriages abounded. Regarding these rumours, Charles Odet in *Jazz* stated that they frequently denied everything and added: 'They laugh the same laugh. Shake their soft hair and sing a little ditty they made up with English words. English words that the French can never understand . . . they smile and remain mysterious.'[13]

Regardless of emotional entanglements they had a show to launch and they began rehearsing for their next show at the Casino de Paris. *Paris–New York* opened at the end of May. The *Sketch* announced that the Dollies were now established French 'institutions and as such may be said to rate with the Comédie Française, the Bank of France and the incomparable Mistinguett'.[14] Their importance and influence on the world of entertainment, and the Parisian music hall in particular, cannot be underestimated, and this is best illustrated by the fact that they were copied voraciously by such acts as the Dodge Twins, the Houston Twins, the Duncan Sisters, the Irwin Sisters, Les Sœurs Guy, Les Sœurs Broquin, the Brox Sisters and the Sisters 'G', to name but a few. In terms of novelty, the Moulin Rouge even went as far as employing the Mazza, the Poggis and the Boyer sisters to appear in the Mistinguett headlining show *Paris qui tourne* (1928). But even three sets of twins could not sparkle as brightly as the Dolly Sisters!

One critic said that, wherever the Dolly sisters appear, 'one finds the harmony and the happy comradeship behind the footlights that creates an atmosphere of pleasure and contentment which filters through the gold dust of the lights of the audience'.[15] Their generosity was widely acknowledged: 'their nice natures and the many quite unobtrusive little acts of kindness they have done to their fellow artistes' ensured their popularity with their fellow performers and the audience at large. With this show they were quite simply at the pinnacle of their professional lives.

The Dollies' ten appearances in *Paris–New York* were admired 'because their graceful numbers are spirited and because their burlesque is always sparkling, discriminating and free from vulgarity'.[16] The first was in a sequence about dances through the ages, where the Dollies introduced the Dirty Dig as the new dance for the future in 1930. In 'The Most Beautiful Gardens of the World' they portrayed 'The English Garden' with a reprise of one of their most popular numbers, 'The Dollies and their Collies'. The Ratoncheff Lilliputians appeared in the dressing room of the Dollies dressed as dolls on the gold, green and orange cushions of their divan, and the Dollies wearing enchanting Directoire frocks sang and danced with them. The Dollies sang 'Ain't He Sweet' and did a jazz dance with Snowball, and, as Hal Sherman gave an imitation of the Dollies and their Collies, the Dollies gave an impression of Hal Sherman, and then all three did a dance together followed by a finale full of feathers.

One of the more unusual scenes was 'A Question of Ships', a pantomime about naval disarmament, which was described as one of the best revue scenes ever witnessed. In a park, the Dollies, dressed as a little American girl and a little English girl, play with toy battleships. A little French boy arrives with an old sail boat. They invite him to play. Suddenly a little Chinese girl and a tough little Bolshevik appear. The little girls are frightened and fetch a big toy battleship for their French friend. But, when the dangerous Chinese and Bolshevik have gone, the little girls snatch the big battleship away from him and run away laughing, leaving him pensively playing with his old sail boat.[17]

Besides their debut, the most important launch of the season was the reopening on 1 June of Edmund Sayag's luxurious Ambassadeurs restaurant with an elaborate new floor show made up largely of American acts all dressed by Dolly Tree, who had relocated to New York from London in 1926.[18] As before, everyone who was anyone was at the première, including the royal princes George and Henry and many leading figures of French stage and public life such as Sacha Guitry, Yvonne Printemps, Jane Marnac, Jane Renouardt, Georges Carpenter, Josephine Baker, Mistinguett, Earl Leslie, Damia and, of course, the Dollies.[19]

According to Billy Milton, who was a friend of Billy Reynolds, the Dollies were canny if not rather devious; he observed their antics with their many rich suitors.

The dancing Dollies made a fortune and promptly lost it gambling. Luckily for them there was always a Gordon Selfridge waiting in the wings to come to the financial rescue. They had a neat trick that usually paid off handsomely. Whenever they saw one of their pet Rajahs or millionaire friends approaching they quickly removed whatever jewels they were wearing and gave them to Billy Reynolds to put into the tail pocket of his dress coat and then complained bitterly that times were so hard they had been forced to sell their jewellery. The boyfriend took compassion on them and generally obliged with a present of a new diamond bracelet or ring.[20]

Billy's observations should be taken with a pinch of salt. For example, they did not always lose at the gaming tables and often won vast sums with or without the assistance of others. They were clearly manipulative to a degree, and his story of subterfuge was undoubtedly based on fact. They were mischievous and loved playing games. This must have been another of their favourite tricks. But since their days on Broadway they had been showered with gifts from wealthy suitors without adopting any devious tactics – how else could they have accumulated so many glittering objects like magpies?

In complete contrast to Billy Milton's views about their acquisitive behaviour was another story about their magnanimity, calling them 'good fairies'. 'Everyone thinks of them in this way where ever they go,' announced Charles Odet in *Jazz*. He explained that the Dolly Sisters frequently gave their dresses to the chorus girls, jewellery to their dressers, and money to the stage fireman so he could take his girlfriend out for dinner and one of the stewards so he could buy a motorbike. As a result, everyone who came into contact with them adored them. Odet observed that their generosity was executed with simplicity, since they did things without attracting attention, and he added that money for the Dollies was simply a good thing to give away. 'Don't trouble about it. It's just nothing,' they said when he enquired about this facet of their personality.

Externally, with their lavish displays of jewellery, they looked brash and money conscious, but Charles Odet was convinced that this was a mask that carefully concealed 'their tenderness, generosity and sensitivity which would make them appear old fashioned'. In short, he believed that they went 'about their life with a simple heart, melancholic eyes, a gentle spirit and a long procession of gratitude and love trailing behind them'.[21]

This was indeed demonstrated at the end of June at the gala to raise funds for the unfortunates of the First World War. The Dollies, in their twin Patou frocks and magnificent jewels, along with many other stage celebrities, including Yvonne Printemps, Cécile Sorel and Spinelly, walked along the red carpet lined with crowds of sightseers on the Champs-Elysées into the brilliantly illuminated Claridge Hotel. During the evening there was an auction; among the notable bids, Sacha Guitry's donation was hotly contested, but he himself won it for $4,000. But the Dollies, 'without any theatrical display', had already given a cheque for $8,000. Even though they had made no fuss about their donation, it did not remain a secret, and once again they were praised for their generosity. 'They are very much loved and are warmly received because they have always been so unostentatiously generous whenever an appeal has been made to their hearts and purses and even without being asked they have come forward, times innumerable, to do all that they could for those who were in need of help.'[22]

It was an obvious disappointment to the Dollies that *Paris–New York* was running during the summer, which prevented them from spending their usual period of fun and frivolity at Deauville. The roof garden of Jenny's new home had become an essential haven and by some accounts had taken the place of the Deauville plage. Jenny was described as being 'philosophical about her absence from that gay resort', and she declared that she had 'paid for her new home by what she saved by staying away from the baccarat tables'.[23] And yet, despite these pious claims, it was also reported by Priscilla in *Tatler* that the Dollies continued to make midnight jaunts to Deauville and Le Touquet. They arrived at 2.30 a.m. in time for an hour's flutter at the tables and, perhaps in Deauville, a little socialising with their friend Pearl White, who had settled at the Royal Hotel for the entire season. They may have even enjoyed the company of David, Prince of Wales, who visited Paris and Le Touquet from 8 July.[24] Priscilla also thought that these were costly trips and that they must be jolly lucky in love to have such persistent bad luck with the cards[25] – an obvious reference to the various gentlemen who were in constant attendance at the time. At one all-night session at Deauville, Rosie made substantial losses. During a depressed dinner the next day Gordon Selfridge had two little boxes immaculately gift wrapped and delivered to the sisters' table containing a diamond bracelet for Jenny and a string of matched pearls for Rosie. His note said: 'I hope this will make up for your losses last night darlings.' The Dollies took the whole thing philosophically – it was, after all, only Selfridge's money that had been lost![26]

According to Charles Odet, Rosie was the poorer of the two. That is to say, when losing, she often stopped for a few minutes to reflect and to weigh up if she should continue or not. In contrast, Jenny never hesitated. Even if her pile of chips was evaporating, she would still continue, and surprisingly usually finished well.[27] As a result, Jenny in particular won and lost millions of francs, but, when on a winning streak, she converted much of her winnings into a jewellery collection that was rumoured to be the most extensive in private hands – not including the fabulous gifts she received from all her admirers, including Gordon Selfridge and Jacques Wittouck.

Towards the end of the run of *Paris–New York* rumours began to circulate in Paris about Rosie's secret wedding to Davis Junior, but all efforts to secure an interview by the press and a confirmation of the story met with failure. At the same time it was revealed that Jenny was in difficulty over her decision to marry Jacques Wittouck. She went to the registry office, but the clerk refused to give her a licence on the grounds that she could not prove who she was.[28] This was followed in early October 1927 by a surprising headline in one of the French newspapers that Jenny had in fact married Jacques Wittouck in the town hall of the 16th district of Paris, where she had bought her house.[29] According to the report, it certainly had not been 'love at first sight', since the happy couple had already been engaged for a while under the watchful eye of Gordon Selfridge. A strange comment indeed. Reading between the lines, presumably both men were aware of each other and their affection for the same woman. Needless to say, the report of the marriage was erroneous, but the implication was that it was a close call.

Although it was not intended as such, *Paris–New York*, which drew to a close at the end of November, proved to be the last Parisian show starring the Dolly Sisters. There were plans for another show in 1928 and a variety of other offers and bookings from several sources that stretched into the future, including a rumour that their next immediate project was a revue in Berlin.[30]

But everything was put on hold or cancelled. At first, illness intervened, and then, to the shock of everyone, they announced that they would retire. They explained their retirement in rational terms. It would seem that finally both had had enough and it was time to settle down to a normal life. The bigger picture was of course far more intriguing.

Rosie, who had been feeling unwell during the run of *Paris–New York*, decided to take a holiday slightly earlier than usual on the Riviera. Jenny, also ill and suffering from appendicitis trouble, stayed in Paris. It was intended that as soon as they both felt better they would make an extended trip to Egypt before deciding on the future of their career as the Dolly Sisters. Sadly this was not to be.[31]

Staying at the Carlton Hotel, Cannes, Rosie became critically ill, suffering from appendicitis and stomach and intestinal poisoning, which prevented her from taking food for fifteen days, and she had to be sustained by spinal injections. Surrounded by numerous floral bouquets and a vast Christmas tree, Rosie lay flat on her back packed in ice and attended by four nurses and five doctors, who were initially afraid to operate because of the risk of peritonitis.[32] Immediately she heard the news that Rosie's condition was severe, Jenny rushed to her side, with Davis Junior in attendance. Jenny was told by the doctors that 'the chances of her recovery were reported to be very slight' and she was dying. As it happened, their father was en route for his yearly visit to see his daughters, since he always liked to spend New Year with them.[33]

After a series of operations, the doctors announced that the worst was over and she would recover, although she was faced with the news that she would have to undergo a further operation for appendicitis. 'No one can express the feeling of joy those words gave me, because no one knows how much I love my sister,'[34] Jenny said as she wept profusely.

As Rosie regained her strength, she underwent the appendicitis operation and made a swift recovery. When the Dollies announced that they were retiring from the stage, they also declared that they intended to spend most of their time on the Riviera and planned either to rent or to buy a villa, 'far away from casinos, cafés and bars, and settle down to a retired life. We will just rest for a long time.'[35] If this was indeed their plan, like all good intentions it really did not last long. Although they did stay on the Riviera, leading a quiet life and avoiding casinos were simply impossible.

Rosie's serious condition meant that it suddenly became known she was Mrs Davis Junior. The story of the marriage and the year of secrecy finally came into the open. The news must have been a serious blow to Rosie's 'official' fiancé, François Dupré, although there is no record of what he made of the situation and the year of deception. Davis Senior, instead of being delighted that so well known a person as one of the Dolly Sisters had honoured his family by marrying his only son, was so disgusted that he would not see his new daughter-in-law and became estranged from his son – a strange reaction perhaps given that he had married someone from a similar background. Most annoying of all, the second Lady Davis, who held a high position in American, Canadian and European society, came into contact with her daughter-in-law twice and each time gave her the cold shoulder. Both believed that Rosie was simply a gold digger and had certainly not married for love.

As Rosie recovered she was seen regularly at social events with her husband along with Jenny and her companion Jacques Wittouck and a variety of other guests. They had lost none of their sparkle and allure, as Phillida, the gossip columnist of the *Dancing Times*, observed: 'The doings of the Dolly Sisters have been the subject of the cocktail hour's gossip, and they are supplying all the sensational interest in Cannes. Their clothes, their jewels, their play in the baccarat room are all amazing.'[36]

They attended a lunch party at the Carlton Hotel on 18 January,[37] a gala evening on 26 January[38] and the Fêtes des Mimosas at the Ambassadeurs on 27 January. Here the Dollies and their guests, among 600 others, dined under a tent of mimosa and witnessed a varied programme of attractions that included their co-star from *Paris–New York*, Hal Sherman.[39] Then, on 7 February 1928, the Dollies made their only public appearance on the Riviera at the Ambassadeurs in a charity gala in aid of local charities. The excitement was such that one report announced 'the event promises to be the biggest of the season'. Dressed by their old favourite, Patou, who was in the audience with Jacques Wittouck and Davis Junior, the Dollies wore white diamante hooped dresses festooned with pink roses, headdresses flaunting huge pink feathers and little black gloves. Their entrance was greeted with keen applause, and after dancing they put up for auction a black and diamond vanity case, which was sold first for $2,000, then returned and sold again for $1,200. In total they raised $5,200, which was given to local charities. The following day the Dollies made their appearance in the Battle of the Flowers, dressed alike in white in a carriage, decorated with carnations of various tones and lilac, which was drawn by two black horses. They stole the show and were the immediate target for all the press photographers.[40]

More gala evenings followed, and soon Davis Senior and Lady Davis appeared on the scene, and, at the Gala de la Couture at the Ambassadeurs, where ten leading Parisian couturiers showed off their newest creations, the two parties were forced to be in the same place. Although Davis Senior may well have acknowledged his son out of politeness, it was here that the first public snub against Rosie by Lady Davis occurred, as their private enmity became public knowledge.[41] The atmosphere was electric and yet both parties maintained restraint and no public incident occurred. As the days passed, they organised their social activities to avoid each other in future. Rosie and Davis Junior were certainly not invited to his parents' lavish dinner party at Casanova, which had an extensive guest list and was one of the most splendid parties of the season.[42]

Attending galas and other social events was not the only thing that kept the Dollies occupied, as trips to the casino became their most important activity. One evening, Rosie, irked by the confinement of a severe cold and finding her purse empty and husband away, borrowed a small amount of money from one of her maids and went to the casino. She broke the bank by winning $70,000, the limit at the roulette table. She was told she would have to move to another table. She refused, and eventually the table was reopened for her. She broke the bank again. This time the croupiers insisted the table was closed. Rosie was given two baskets and two police guards to carry the French notes back to the hotel. Three hours later, feeling lonely again, she took $200 and returned to the casino, this time playing at the baccarat table. Her winning streak continued and she won a further $20,000. In total her winnings for the evening were in excess of $90,000.[43] But this was nothing compared with later extravagances. While Jenny lost several million francs one night, Rosie on another winning streak won a colossal $800,000, as King Christian of Denmark and King Carol of Romania watched and applauded.[44]

Their blissful period of early spring frivolity was swiftly terminated when, in mid-March 1928, just after Davis Junior had departed for a business trip to America and Canada, Davis Senior was carried out of the Cannes casino after a heart attack and died at his villa aged 62.[45] Immediately, someone leaked the basic contents of his will, and at first there were stories that Davis Junior had been completely cut off without a cent because of his marriage to Rosie. These stories were then modified, suggesting his share had been reduced and that he had not been totally disinherited. Presumably comments about the content of the will had been made, rather indiscreetly, and indirectly, by Lady Davis. Making a swift return to Paris and in the absence of her husband, Rosie denied all the stories about the will and any disinheritance.

Whatever the situation regarding the will, the enmity between Lady Davis and Rosie and her husband was evident and was regarded by many as a 'smouldering ill feeling', which suggested that there would indeed be a bitter legal contest over the estate. When Rosie met her husband at the boat train, she 'was more voluble and more emphatic regarding the reports of his disinheritance'. Back in Paris, in Lady Davis's apartment at the Hotel Astoria, matters came to a head, and Rosie blamed the leaked reports and any change in the will on Lady Davis, whom she charged with exerting undue influence. This precipitated a stormy scene, and threats of legal action were made. In the middle of the argument Lady Davis stormed out, ordering all her luggage to be shipped to another hotel.[46]

At the end of March Lady Davis accompanied her husband's body on its journey back to Montreal aboard the *Mauretania*. When the boat train left Saint-Lazare station, eleven smart men about town in Parisian society were on hand to bid au revoir, and Baron de Rothschild alone accompanied her to Cherbourg. Lady Davis and her stepson refused to comment to the press, but Rosie said:

> We didn't sail today because we couldn't get accommodation. But we are returning to the United States. Reservations have been made for us now on the *Leviathan* sailing Tuesday. So we will be in Montreal in time for the funeral anyway. As I told you before, I've always understood that Sir Mortimer divided his fortune between Morty and his widow. Any change in the will is news to me. I am sure that nobody will know definitely until the will is probated after the funeral. Quarrel with Lady Eleanor? She is very temperamental and likes to do things her own way, but there has been no quarrel.

In the end, only Davis Junior made the journey and attended the funeral.[47]

Alas for Rosie, her dreams of gold at the end of the rainbow evaporated when Davis Senior's will was read in Montreal after the funeral. Under the direction of the executors, the son and widow were to share on an equal basis the net annual revenue from the estate, which had been estimated at $11,000 a day each. There was a stipulation that the son's interest was to be restricted to him personally and not to be passed on to his wife or issue. Still, as wife of the heir to $75,000,000, Rosie was not going to be too badly off, even though technically she could not benefit from it directly. She did not see it quite like that, and the final straw came when she learned that she would not become a 'Lady', since Sir Mortimer's title was not hereditary.[48] All was not good.

With Rosie's marriage entering turbulent waters and the Dolly Sisters no more, Jenny continued to avoid marriage herself and maintained the best of both worlds with her two admirers. With a little help from both of them, she bought a vast thirty-room chateau in the village of Avon near Fontainebleau, which was still within reasonable distance of the bright lights of Paris. According to Mistinguett, Jenny bought the chateau under the nose of the King of Spain, who had earmarked it for his retirement, although he did find another suitable mansion nearby that became a favourite home of the Queen of Spain.[49] Rosie described it as 'an enormous, beautiful villa with an enormous garden, a big white marble swimming pool, a tennis court and everything else'. Guests entered the villa through a long hall lined with illuminated jewel cases that displayed Jenny's fabulous collection of gems. The decoration was coordinated by the artist Jean-Gabriel Domergue, who adorned the walls of the drawing room with gold and silver designs, depicting eighteenth-century Venetian scenes, at a cost of $100,000.[50]

Here the sisters entertained European royalty, American tycoons and members of the smart international set, including such names as David, Prince of Wales, King Carol of Romania, Vicomte de La Rochefoucauld (a previous beau of Jenny's who had taken her to Corsica) and the wealthy American millionaire Willy Vanderbilt, besides, of course, Gordon Selfridge and Jacques Wittouck. During their parties they served dinner of scrambled eggs, which became famous.[51]

Sophie Tucker was vastly impressed with Jenny's chateau: 'I had an idea that a chateau was a simple little country house.' Instead she was completely surprised as she drove through a huge estate into a magnificent courtyard with a big fountain in the centre. She described the long hall with the jewellery cases and the marble pillars leading into a huge living room with French windows that opened out onto a terrace overlooking the grounds. The interior was sprinkled with antique furniture, priceless crystal and china, but it also had modern touches, with luxurious tiled bathrooms and a kitchen with every modern American household device.[52]

Besides buying property, Jenny decided to spend a few weeks with Gordon Selfridge on his yacht at Deauville for Easter 1928, along with Prince and Princess Serge Wiasensky (his daughter Rosalie). They caused great excitement when they arrived at Le Touquet — a favourite seaside resort of the English, which Basil Woon regarded as exclusive and 'chic — très chic'.[53] One night at 11 p.m., Jenny entered the casino dressed in a white crêpe de Chine gown with a white fur coat and took a seat at the big table. It was widely recognised that Jenny had 'acquired a positively historic collection of jewels', and she showed off some stunning gems with her famous seven-string pearl necklace, two enormous diamond rings and large turquoise bracelets. The *Vogue* reporter was ecstatic about Jenny's appearance. 'Here is a sight which will go down in history. Before her every other woman pales and is silenced in awe or envy . . . for there is certainly no other woman in the world today to be compared with her, the last person of her unique class being the late and lovely Gaby Deslys.'[54] Needless to say, she attracted everybody's attention and in less than two minutes was surrounded by a crowd six deep, which no one else, except Elsa Maxwell, jewelless and in plain black, ever succeeded in attracting. During the evening she paid five visits to the bank and lost well over $20,000.[55]

When Davis rejoined Rosie in Paris after the funeral of his father, they resumed their life together, but things were not the same, and they argued repeatedly. It became perfectly obvious that the relationship was flawed and neither was suited to the other. One of the first signs of dissent was recorded one night at the Liberty Bar in Montmartre. Rosie was dining with the owner of a leading dressmaking and perfume establishment — more than likely Patou. Davis arrived with three ladies allegedly from the Moulin Rouge chorus. He and Rosie were unaware of the other's presence in the restaurant, although everyone else was sitting on the edge of their seats. After fifteen minutes Davis noticed Rosie and went to her table scowling. To the amusement of everyone, he began scolding her and demanded that she should leave the place immediately, with him. Embarrassed and at a loss what to do or say, Rosie followed him outside, where she regained her composure. An argument ensued during which she made some remarks about his 'guests'. Making her excuses to her own dinner guest, Rosie went home alone, and Davis returned to his 'guests', where he remained for the rest of the evening.

Marital arguments continued as the season began in late May with the opening of Billy Reardon's Blue Room (the former Jardin de ma sœur) and The Florida, with a show starring the popular Spanish performer Raquel Meller. But by far the biggest event was the opening of Edmund Sayag's 1928 Ambassadeurs show on 10 May with Jenny and Jacques Wittouck in the inaugural audience.[56] The audience were charged the extraordinary amount of $70 per ticket for dinner and the show (but no champagne). After a few weeks the show was broken into three segments and there were changes of cast, including the addition of the dancers Clifton Webb and Dorothy Dickson, who sang 'Looking for You'. It may well have been Clifton Webb who persuaded Jenny, behind a black mask, to do a turn with him one evening in late June, which proved to be her last public appearance.[57]

After the Paris summer season Jenny arrived in London to spend some time with Gordon Selfridge in preparation for spending August on the Normandy coast. In an interview in the luxurious room of her hotel she claimed that she was only 30 (she was in fact 34) and described how she had won fame and fortune, become rich and then retired. According to the interviewer, 'she spoke in a charming voice which seemed half American, half French, and it seemed that no photograph could do justice to the vitality and the joyful charm of her personality'. Jenny wore two enormous rings, one a diamond the other an emerald, and sipped orangeade as she talked. She explained that she had achieved success because 'my sister and I decided that this was our greatest ambition at the age of 12 and we have worked terribly hard to gain it ever since . . . it is great now to lie back and feel one has been successful.' But it was not all plain sailing.

When you're poor everything is easy – you just go on drawing your salary and dreaming. But when you begin to get a name – to have a reputation – it becomes a struggle to keep up to the same high pitch. You've got to please your public and please the box office and do mostly everything except please yourself. I can tell you a big reputation is a big handicap for any star.

Jenny thought that they had become successful because they were so utterly determined.

Success never sounds so romantic as failure, and ours was achieved in a very practical way – simply by saving our money and getting mother to invest it properly for us. Pennies we found soon became dollars and dollars soon became hundreds when you were clever and did not spend them. We never had yachts and sable coats like other stars – at least not until we could afford them. We always sacrificed the present for the future.

In conclusion Jenny noted that success had brought her independence and freedom. 'It gives you time to see your friends and to help others.' Her determination and drive were clearly illustrated when she explained that she would have been a success at anything because she would have persevered until she got what she wanted.[58]

As August arrived it was time for the Deauville season. Jenny and Gordon Selfridge enjoyed the pleasures of the beach, with Rosie already a perfectly lovely shade of gingerbread.[59] But further public quarrels between Rosie and Davis ensued. By the end of August, Jenny, accompanied by Selfridge, escaped to the Hermitage Hotel in Le Touquet, and every night they were to be found in the casino, where Jenny's gowns and wonderful jewels as usual created much comment.[60]

One of the reasons for Rosie's matrimonial difficulties was that she was yearning to return to the stage and regretted having given up her career. There was considerable curiosity, therefore, when the Dollies announced their intention to open a luxurious cabaret near the Champs-Elysées, where they would be the chief attraction. Some suggested a good name for the venue would be the Dolly Bergères! Unfortunately, Rosie's husband refused point blank to give his consent to the project and did not wish his wife to return to the stage.[61] This became another contributory factor in their estrangement, and by the late autumn, after the public debacles at Deauville, they had separated for good. While Rosie was back in Paris, Davis was staying in New York at the Carlton House Apartments, 47th Street and Madison Avenue. It was rumoured that a divorce was on the cards, and Rosie admitted that 'it could come to that'.[62] However, when Davis arrived back in France in early December aboard the Cunard liner *Aquitania*, he declined to throw any light on dispatches from Paris that a divorce was pending. His name was omitted from the passenger lists, and he did everything possible to keep his identity a secret. When reporters asked for an interview, he sent out word through a mysterious and unidentified woman that he had nothing to say.[63]

FUN, FRIVOLITIES AND 'THE NEW DOLLIES'

Back in Paris without Davis, through her connection with the famous silent-screen actresses the Talmadge sisters, Rosie met the man who was to become her third husband. Constance, Norma and Natalie Talmadge were legends, and their story was a defining part of silent film history. They had become household names but had then been swiftly eclipsed by the advent of sound.[1] Rosie's friendship with the Talmadge sisters, and in particular Norma, dated from Rosie's visit to Hollywood in 1915 when she had been filming *The Lily and the Rose*, and she kept up this friendship back in New York, as they were all part of the same smart Broadway set.

When Constance Talmadge arrived in Paris in September 1928, it had been a year since she had worked on a film. She had recently been divorced from her second husband, Captain Alastair MacIntosh, and was being escorted by Townsend Netcher, whom she married in May 1929.[2] Norma also arrived in Paris and, like her sister and Rosie, was going through tumultuous relationship problems. Norma had married Joe Schenck in October 1916. One of the wealthiest and most influential film executives of his day, Schenck had taken control of Norma's film career and made her a world-famous star, but on the set of *Camille* (1927) Norma met and fell in love with her leading man, the handsome Gilbert Roland, who was ten years her junior. Norma asked Joe for a divorce, but he would not agree. Despite his personal feelings, he was not going to break a successful money-making team and continued to co-star Roland in Norma's next three films.[3]

In early November 1928 Rosie and Norma decided to travel south for several weeks on the Riviera, staying in Cannes and Cap d'Antibes. It must have been either in Paris or on the Riviera that Rosie was introduced to Irving Netcher, Townsend's younger brother, who at the time was footloose and fancy free. Irving was described as a 'bon viveur known internationally for his lavish living'.[4] He was good-looking and intelligent, and it was a bonus that he happened to be one of the wealthy heirs to a Chicago department-store fortune. This time Rosie had really found the gold at the end of the rainbow, and it was love at first sight.

Irving was the third son of Mrs Mollie Netcher, who had been called one of the smartest businesswomen in the world. She had built the famous store in Chicago – called the Boston Store – from a small shop to become one of the biggest department stores in the country and sold it in 1948 for $4 million. Her husband, Charles Netcher Senior, arrived in Chicago in 1873 and became manager of the State Street store owned by Charles and Edward Partridge and bought the store from them in 1878.

The start of the Chicago dynasty came in the Gay 1890s when Charles Netcher Senior smiled at Mollie Alpiner, a talented and ambitious buyer in the underwear department (she had joined the staff at 16 as a sales clerk), and romance blossomed across the counter. They married in 1891 and had four children – Charles Junior, Townsend, Irving and Ethel. Mollie guided her husband in his business career and steered him into several wealth-producing real-estate deals. When he died in 1904, she took charge of all the family business affairs and built a new store on the site of the old one. In 1913 she married Sol Neuberger, a paint salesman and childhood friend, and changed their name to Newberry, saying it was easier to write.

Charles Junior became president of the Boston Store until his death in 1931 at the age of 39. Ethel became Mrs Ethel Netcher Chagnon and lived in Rome. Townsend initially took an active part in the Boston Store, but settled into a life of leisure in his Santa Monica home or in Palm Springs and died in 1955 (a month after his mother's death) at the age of 59. He was married four times and two of his wives, Gertrude Selby and Constance Talmadge, were movie stars. His third wife was Norma Fletcher Hall (heiress to a patent medicine fortune) and his fourth wife and widow was Harriet Smith Netcher, with whom Rosie got on well. Irving was the third son and initially had also worked for the store, but again, like his elder brother, he preferred an easier lifestyle. His first marriage had been to Constance Reed, but this had ended in divorce in 1930 and she died in 1943.[5]

The strong-willed Mrs Mollie Netcher Newberry was a matriarchal ruler who always had the final word. However, she adored her children and made no protest when, following the death of Charles Junior, the eldest, her two surviving sons decided to opt out of the family business and devote themselves instead to a life of leisure and their respective wives. She liked it that way and preferred running the business herself. And, to show her generosity, she gave each of her children an annual Christmas gift of $100,000.[6]

From the Riviera, Rosie, presumably in the company of Norma Talmadge, moved on to enjoy the winter resort of Saint-Moritz in December 1928,[7] and the idea was to join Jenny, Gordon Selfridge and his daughter Rosalie in Cannes.[8] But, when Jenny became very ill, Rosie swiftly returned to Paris. By early January 1929, after an attack of appendicitis, it was decided Jenny had to undergo surgery. Eddie, her brother, and Julius Dolly, her father, had spent the usual family Christmas and so were also in attendance as Jenny's condition deteriorated. She was so ill they had to wait until the end of January 1929 before she was stable enough to endure the operation, and Eddie also underwent surgery for the same condition. Jenny had been suffering from periodic attacks of chronic appendicitis for a number of years but had refused surgery and as a result she had to undergo special treatment for several weeks before the operation, which proved to be of an unusually delicate nature.

Another anxious observer in proceedings, according to one of the Los Angeles newspapers, was Jacques Wittouck, who was noted as being Jenny's primary suitor. There was no mention of Gordon Selfridge this time, although one would assume that he must have cut his vacation short and journeyed back from Cannes to see Jenny.[9]

As Jenny recovered, Rosie once again announced that she was finding it very difficult to keep away from the stage.

> I haven't been near a theatre since I was married, but I feel that travelling round the world and having a good time does not satisfy me. To wake up in the morning and say 'how am I going to kill this beautiful day?' seems to be wicked. I have been working on the stage ever since I was a girl of 12. When I got married I thought I could give it up, but now I find it impossible.

To satisfy her cravings, she was invited back to London by C.B. Cochran to discuss what he could do for her. He took her to see the try-out of his 1929 revue *Wake up and Dream* in Manchester in early March and promised to find her something suitable so she could return to the footlights by September or October of 1929.[10]

As she made the decision to return to the stage, Rosie started divorce proceedings against Davis, with a demand for $2 million as compensation for her brief marriage. Compared with what her friends thought she ought to get, these mere $2 million were regarded as hardly any compensation at all. Interestingly, Rosie, whose sharp bargaining in all sorts of situations had caused everyone in Europe to call the twins the 'Dollar Sisters', was not saying a word. Rosie's friends made the statement and said that Rosie's decision to say nothing was because the Paris courts were being very strict about what they perceived as garrulous Americans seeking divorce with the rule 'if you talk you don't get'.[11] Equally, Rosie was still tight-lipped about her blossoming relationship with Irving Necher.

With the Easter break looming, Rosie took Jenny for a change of scenery after her lengthy period of recuperation from her operation. They went to Dinard on the Brittany coast, which was called 'the Nice of the North' and 'la plage des élégances', as it was blessed with delightful warm spring weather.[12] Gordon Selfridge also took care of her. They were spotted in early May at a performance at the Marigny Theatre in Paris,[13] before departing for a holiday at Pearl White's Hotel du Palais in Biarritz with his daughter, Princess Wiasemsky, and her husband.[14]

From Paris, Rosie denied emphatically that she was seeking a divorce. 'I am not even dreaming of it,' she said.[15] However, Colonel William Hayward, former US Attorney in New York, was retained by Rosie as her legal adviser, and he asked her not to talk to the press because this would jeopardise her case. He had handled the divorce of Marilyn Miller and Jack Pickford but had been forced to abandon his efforts when Miller talked to the press in New York and said she was dashing over to Paris to get a friendly divorce. The French judges looking at her petition, saw the interviews in the Paris press and resented the casual tone of her comments, preventing a quick divorce. Hayward's philosophy was now one of caution and 'no comment' at all to any journalist.[16]

As Rosie flew into London on the Golden Ray (the Paris-to-London shuttle), noticeably without Irving Netcher, she would not be drawn about her divorce, as instructed, but revelled in her return to the London stage after an eight-year absence. Rosie was commère to Noel Coward's compère at Mrs Cochran's charity matinée for the Invalid Children's Aid Association at the London Pavilion with various acts all from C.B. Cochran's enviable stable of stars.

Rosie had brought with her twelve gowns and jewellery worth millions of dollars. With flashing black eyes and ropes of pearls hanging across the front of her silk dress, she looked thoughtfully down at her immense diamond ring but would not say what kind of performance they would give.

'I had to bring over lots of pretty dresses because you see I do not know what colour curtains they will have at the theatre.'

'Just imagine if Miss Dolly appeared in a bright green dress in front of their wonderful purple curtain,' suggested Coward![17]

The performance went without a hitch.

Fully recovered, Jenny flew to London on the Golden Ray to attend Gordon Selfridge's lavish fourth general-election party on 31 May 1929 along with 2,500 other guests, who included the crème de la crème of London society and practically every major stage star: Noel Coward, H.G. Wells, Mrs Norman Holden, Lady Segrave, Lord Churchill of Ascot, Lady Headfort, Lord Fitzwilliam, Margot Aquith, Oliver Hoare, Edward Marshall, the Lord Chancellor, the Crown Prince of Sweden and Princess Ingrid, Princess Arthur of Connaught and Lady Carisbrooke. Selfridge's daughter Princess Wiasemsky was the hostess to an amazing party with dancing and cabaret turns in a miniature theatre. *Tatler* enthused: 'One could send telegrams and cables without paying for them and even telephone New York! It was the nearest approach to a casino party I have seen.'[18] Selfridge's election-night parties were regarded as the most ambitious and entertaining of any given in London, and, although in his seventies, he was still capable of immense social zest and was a perfect host.[19]

After an exciting time motorboat racing near Southampton,[20] Jenny returned to Paris to be confronted by rather caustic comments in the Parisian edition of *Eve*. An editorial had decided that, after years in which it had not been possible to distinguish between the two sisters, it was now becoming a little easier, since it had been observed that one (Rosie) was now lean and the other (Jenny) was becoming larger.[21] For the rest of the year Jenny was preoccupied. In July her absence was noticed at Le Touquet, and there was no mention of her at the various gala evenings in Deauville during August.[22] The reason for her absence from her favourite seasonal haunts would become obvious in late 1930, when she opened her couture establishment. During the second half of 1929 her attention was focused on making this project a reality. In July the purchase of a property that she had earmarked for her business in the fashionable rue de la Paix fell through, but by October new premises had been secured near the Champs-Elysées. At the same time she was employing staff and going on numerous buying trips, which included the purchase of very fine lace in Brussels.[23]

Back on the Riviera, Rosie was soaking up the sun at the Hotel du Cap in the Cap d'Antibes in the summer of 1929 and spent most of her time at Eden Roc, the premier sunbathing resort, in the company of Irving Netcher and a host of other celebrities, including Anita Elson, Tallulah Bankhead, Mrs Reginald Vanderbilt, June (Lady Inverclyde) and Cecil Beaton.[24] She then moved to the Palm Beach Casino in Cannes, where she was spotted with Irving Netcher entertaining a party that included Miss Georgette Cohan (daughter of George Cohan and Ethel Levey), William Fleischmann, the yeast king, and the former movie star Phyllis Haver and her husband the Manhatten millionnaire William Seemen, who were on their honeymoon.[25]

However, her romantic idyll on the Côte d'Azur was broken when she became entangled in a lawsuit as a result of her separation from Davis as two jewellers sued her. In early August 1929 Rosie had to return to Paris to face charges of swindling the jewellers out of pearl necklaces valued at $280,000. The jewellers – Chaumet and Polak's, both located in the aristocratic shopping district of the place Vendôme – asked the court that a trustee be appointed to keep the necklaces, which had been strung together as one, until the case had been decided.

The necklaces had been bought by Davis for Rosie at a time when he was expected to inherit a substantial legacy from his father's estate. With this in mind, both jewellers had relinquished the necklaces to Rosie on the basis that her husband would settle the account. However, since Davis's inheritance was not what had been expected, no payment had been forthcoming. Both jewellers now claimed payment from Rosie, since the necklaces were in her possession. In her defence, Rosie rightly asserted that the necklaces had been gifts from her husband and that he should settle the bill. Davis himself was currently believed to be in Florida, unavailable for comment or to settle the account.[26] Although Rosie tried to avoid reporters, she was confronted outside the court and said simply: 'It is not necessary for me to say anything: it will clarify itself.' Her attorney added: 'A lot of fuss is being made about nothing.'[27]

The tale then took an unexpected twist. When experts from the two jewellery firms examined the necklaces, it was alleged that nearly a third of the pearls were missing. According to press reports, although the Chaumet necklace of 49 pearls was intact, there were 48 pearls missing from the Polak necklace, which had originally contained 115 pearls. It was also alleged that Rosie claimed she might have mislaid the originals, but she promised to try and find the missing pearls.[28] Then in October the proceedings against Rosie by the jewellers for the recovery of the lost pearls were withdrawn. The jewellers notified the examining magistrate that they had found the pearls that they had originally claimed to be missing and stated that the necklaces were intact. Rosie's original statement had stated that the necklaces she handed over were exactly as she had received them and that none of the pearls was lost or removed. As a result Rosie was considering starting a suit against the jewellers and certain newspapers for libel in connection with statements made about the pearls being missing.[29]

After five months of deliberation, a French magistrate directed that complaints against Rosie for obtaining the two pearl necklaces under false pretences be dismissed and that her husband should settle the account or the necklaces be returned to the jewellers.[30] Needless to say, because Rosie was engaged in divorce proceedings, the pearls became an integral part of the settlement.

Presumably Rosie continued her idyll in the South of France with Irving Netcher in early 1930 and then made a three-month trip back to New York in March.[31] In the meantime, Jenny decided to do something rather momentous. To the great surprise of many people, in early 1930, during a trip to Budapest, she decided to adopt two young girls called Manzi and Klari, who were both about 5 years of age. Considering she was unmarried and the subject of gossip concerning her relationships with two public figures, each of whom she had refused to marry, this seems a brave decision to have made. The myth Jenny created was that she found both of them in a Hungarian orphanage, but the truth was that she

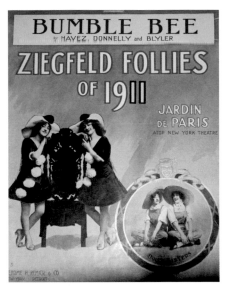

Above left: Sheet music for 'Bumble Bee', *Ziegfeld's Follies of 1911*. *Above right:* Sheet music for 'That Swaying Tango', unidentified show, New York, 1912. *Below left:* Sheet music for the 'Tango Dance', from *The Merry Countess*, with the Dolly Sisters and Martin Brown, 1912. *Below right:* Sheet music for 'There was a Time', from *Maid in America*, Winter Garden Theatre, New York, 1915, featuring Harry Fox and Jenny. *(All author's collection)*

Right: Section from sheet music for 'Waltz Intermezzo', showing the Dolly Sisters in their bridal attire from *His Bridal Night*, Republic Theatre, New York, 1916. *(Author's collection)*

Far right: Sheet music for 'Tell Me Why', from *Oh Look!*, regional USA tour 1918–19. *(Author's collection)*

Above left: Section from sheet music for 'Underneath the Stars', from the *Ziegfeld Midnight Frolic*, New Amsterdam Theatre Roof, 1916. *(Author's collection)*

Right: Advertising slide for the film *The Million Dollar Dollies*, 1918. *(Author's collection)*

Advertising lobby card (1 of 8) for the film *The Million Dollar Dollies*, 1918. *(Author's collection)*

Dolly Sisters and chorus in the tableaux 'La Mine Diamants' (Diamond Mine) in *Paris en fleurs*, Casino de Paris, Paris, 1925. *(Author's collection)*

Design by Zig for promotional leaflet for *Paris en fleurs*, Casino de Paris, Paris, 1925. *(Eric Concklin collection)*

Design by Zig for promotional leaflet for *Paris–New York*, Casino de Paris, Paris, 1927. *(Author's collection)*

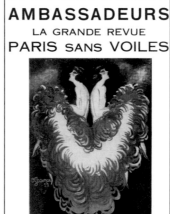

Left: Programme cover designed by Gesmar for *Paris sans voiles*, Ambassadeurs Theatre, Paris, 1923. *(Author's collection)*

Far left: Programme cover design by Gesmar for *Oh! Les Belles Filles*, Palace Theatre, Paris, 1923. *(Author's collection)*

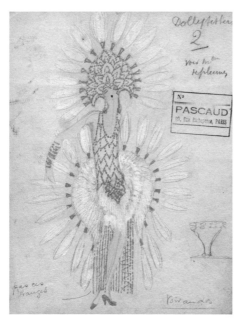

Above left: Costume design (1 of 2) for the Dolly Sisters by Jean Le Seyeux in *A vol d'oiseau*, Edouard VII Theatre, Paris, 1923. *(Author's collection)*

Right: Costume design (2 of 2) for the Dolly Sisters by Jean Le Seyeux in *A vol d'oiseau*, Edouard VII Theatre, Paris, 1923. *(Author's collection)*

Above: Dolly Sisters in their feather creations by Patou in *Oh! Les Belles Filles*. Palace Theatre, Paris, 1923. *(Author's collection)*

Opposite: Dolly Sisters in *Paris sans voiles*, Ambassadeurs Theatre, Paris, 1923. *(Author's collection)*

Left: Jenny in Paris, early 1930s. *(Author's collection from the Towyna Thomas Collection, originally owned by Max Pierce)*

Far left: Jenny in Paris, early 1930s. *(Author's collection from the Towyna Thomas Collection, originally owned by Max Pierce)*

Right: Jenny's two adopted daughters Manzi and Klari, Paris, 1931. *(Author's collection from the Towyna Thomas Collection, originally owned by Max Pierce)*

Far right: Front cover of the press kit for the Twentieth Century Fox film *The Dolly Sisters*, 1945. *(Author's collection)*

adopted the blonde Klari, the child of an actress, first of all. The brunette Manzi was in fact Jenny's little cousin, the daughter of her uncle Marcel Weiss (her mother's brother), who had been a soldier in the First World War and had been badly crippled. On meeting Jenny he said to her, 'you've taken an orphan child. Why don't you take one of my girls and give her advantages I can't?' Big-hearted Jenny, who thought there would always be money and jewels from dancing contracts and admirers, said yes and took Manzi, the youngest, and returned to her chateau in Fontainebleau with her two adopted daughters.[32]

At first Jenny's desire to adopt might seem curious, and yet in 1917, when she was married to Harry Fox and Rosie to Jean Schwartz, both had announced that they intended to raise families. They also thought that the idea of having twins themselves was appealing.[33] At the age of 38, and unmarried, Jenny may have felt the chances of having children herself were slim. She certainly did not appear to want to marry anyone. She had already expressed her view that success had given her freedom and independence.[34] She must have felt that marriage would to some degree diminish her own sense of self-determination and that her ability to control her own destiny would evaporate. Her independent lifestyle clearly meant so much to her that her desire for children could be accommodated only by adoption.

On her return to Fontainebleau, Jenny introduced her daughters to the press, describing them as the 'new Dolly Sisters'.[35] She intended to give the girls all the benefits her wealth and position could provide and explained that they had become 'her chief interest in life'. She added: 'They've got everything I never had and I hope that they'll never have to go on the stage to earn it. But they're learning dancing now – just in case. You know how life is.'[36] At first the two girls were not described as sisters or twins, but three years after their adoption Rosie was referring to them as twins,[37] something that Jenny must have encouraged. Later still, to substantiate their description as twins, it was revealed that they were both born on Christmas Eve 1924.[38]

Jenny went to great lengths to create a myth about her daughters being twins, and, despite denials, she did have theatrical aspirations for both of them. This started from the outset when she described them as the 'new Dolly Sisters' and gave them dancing lessons. Jenny also allowed their English governess to take them to theatrical matinées, and in late February 1932 they were taken to the Empire music hall[39] – a repeat performance of Jenny's early life in Budapest, when she and Rosie were taken to see shows by their nursemaid. Jenny's intent was clear: she wanted her daughters to follow in her footsteps and create a new edition of the Dolly Sisters; this was her way of continuing her career and was a motivation that she maintained for the next decade. Even so, a few years later Jenny said: 'They are not sisters but like to pretend they are twins. They dance sing and play the piano.'[40]

Jenny's new obsession of re-creating the Dolly Sisters certainly did not affect her other compulsion: gambling. Over the summer she spent considerable time at Le Touquet, a resort that she increasingly favoured, just like David, Prince of Wales, whose presence attracted as much interest as Jenny's activities in the casino. Although the season had scarcely started, Jenny and the newly adopted children, accompanied by Gordon Selfridge, spent the end of May and the beginning of June at the Hermitage Hotel and must have seen the Prince, who was visiting during 24–31 May. Like Jenny, the Prince spent virtually every night in the casino, and, although he apparently knew little about the game, he won $10,000. Jenny in the meantime had a distinctly profitable Whitsun holiday weekend (8 June), when in two turns at the baccarat tables her winnings exceeded $250,000. Selfridge was perched on a high stool immediately behind her watching her every movement and feeding her from time to time with neat little wads of money. His presence may have acted as a restraint, because Jenny was described as playing cautiously. Unlike the Prince, she had card sense. 'You see her sitting at the table with a strange inscrutable expression. She will sit for a long while doing nothing and then she will make a plunge, just at the psychological moment and she generally gets away with it.'

Having returned the children to their governess at Fontainebleau, Jenny immediately took a plane back to Le Touquet and, without Selfridge's restraining influence, resumed her winning streak with a further $80,000 and did not leave the casino until dawn, taking her winnings with her.[41] A few weeks later in mid-July, with Selfridge, she was once again playing baccarat and won about $500,000 between 4 p.m. and midnight and then lost practically everything between midnight and 3 a.m. She continued to play, drawing on her reserves, and her luck changed as she broke the bank four times, winning at least $500,000. Her stakes were the highest anyone could remember – at one point $59,000 a stake.[42]

According to Paris press reports, as Jenny gambled at Le Touquet, she became embroiled in a terrific war for the French game casinos. A battle raged between the British millionaire Major J.S. Coats (from the wealthy British cotton family), who had a personal grudge against one of the Battisti Brothers, who owned the casinos at Le Touquet and Juan-les-Pins. Coats was allegedly seeking to undermine their credibility and take control of their operation by breaking the bank. He set out to conduct a personal offensive at Juan-les-Pins while 'others', presumably with his backing, led the engagement at Le Touquet. Tremendous stakes were involved and the Battistis were soon gasping for breath.[43]

Later reports stated that the Dollies 'achieved their top publicity notices as unofficial shills' (someone paid by the casino to play and encourage others to play for publicity purposes) for French casinos, with press releases regularly informing an avid public about their fabulous winnings or losses. They became big draws, with the result that business increased wherever they appeared.[44] It was alleged that the reports of Jenny's winnings at this time were part of an elaborately planned publicity campaign orchestrated by the Battisti Brothers against Coats. Jenny may have been involved in this monumental game, and, although Major Coats appears to have lost his battle to take over the Battisti casinos, she was definitely on a winning streak.

Meanwhile, Rosie was struggling to obtain her divorce and to keep her life out of the public eye, so her romance with Irving Netcher was conducted with discretion, since she could have been cited for adultery. On their return from New York in mid-June, they enjoyed the pleasures of Cap d'Antibes, with parties and social engagements in the casino at Juan-les-Pins, where the company of Norma Talmadge and Gilbert Roland made for a glamorous foursome.[45] At the end of the summer Rosie went to Amsterdam for a short holiday and visited the picturesque villages of Marken and Volendam. She announced that she was about to sign a contract to appear in two talkies for Paramount, which would be filmed in Paris, and was also thrilled to report that the Dolly Sisters were being tempted back to the Paris stage in a play specially written for them by French playwright Saint Granier. In the event neither the films nor the new stage play materialised. Perhaps Rosie was dissuaded from participating in these projects because of her divorce proceedings. Instead she flew to London to catch the latest theatrical offerings before travelling to Biarritz, spending time with Buster Keaton, who was married to Natalie Talmadge. Thereafter Rosie continued her life of self-indulgent leisure with Irving Netcher and Norma Talmadge on the Riviera.[46]

Given the reports of Jenny's wild gains and losses at baccarat, one wonders whether the Wall Street Crash in October 1929 had any direct effect on her. Since the Dollies had much of their money invested in property and jewellery, and always had rich suitors to fall back on, perhaps, at first, the effect was minimal. Yet Paris suffered a huge drop in American visitors and a general slump in business. It was, therefore, strange that in mid-1930, after four years' preparation, Jenny unveiled an extravagant business on the Champs-Elysées. Her preoccupation with this project may explain her low profile during the latter half of 1929 and early 1930.[47]

In November 1930 Jenny finally opened a fashionable lingerie and couture shop at a cost of nearly £200,000, which swiftly became 'one of the very ritziest of salons' in Paris, although some wondered how much lingerie could have been bought for such a sum.[48] Selfridge encouraged the idea, presumably contributed financially and gave advice and guaranteed payment for the goods, while Wittouck too lent a hand.[49]

Jenny explained her decision to open the store by saying that she wished to prove to Gordon Selfridge that she shared his business abilities.[50] This competitive motivation may provide part of the answer. However, both Rosie and Jenny were extremely fond of fashionable attire and lovely things. They had always maintained a lively interest in ensuring that their costumes and gowns were designed effectively. Given this background, it is not really surprising that one of them would find the idea of opening a couture shop appealing. Jenny may have been trying to bring her mother's abortive dream to open a couture establishment in Hollywood in the early 1920s to fruition. She would also have cast an envious eye at her friend, the dancer Florence Walton, who had opened a couture business in May 1928 on the rue St Florentin.[51] Whatever the motivation, given the extravagance of Paris, opening a lingerie and couture establishment as conceived by Jenny may have been a sound idea before the Wall Street Crash in October 1929. But, when the realities of economic recession hit, it turned into an expensive flight of fancy.

Jenny took charge of the decor of her salon with the help once again of Jean-Gabriel Domergue. The wooden walls were painted to look like pink marble with gold edging and were hung with fine paintings. There was a cocktail lounge for clients, and adjoining this was a 'showcase' bedroom ('and she knows her bedrooms,' said *Variety*[52]) with a large mirrored bed. The bed linen comprised a mass of embroidery and lace that 'must have kept a couple of convents working for months'.[53] The chairs, like the bed, were mirrored with deep seats of heavy pink satin, and there was also a dressing table with modernistic mirrors. Thrown carelessly around the bedroom on the chairs, bed and a chaise longue were 'wicked looking' black and white pyjamas, black chiffon nighties and other intimate lingerie. The other rooms contained showcases in which lingerie was plainly displayed and priced. Jenny had ransacked the world for the most expensive merchandise obtainable, from fabulous silks to the rarest ceramics,[54] and the luxury of both salon and wares was 'enough to make you think sinful thoughts', reported *Variety*.[55] It is little surprise that in no time at all Jenny became 'one of the most fashionable modistes in Paris'.[56]

The launch party was well attended, with friends such as Harry Pilcer, Pearl White, Irving Netcher, Gordon Selfridge (Jacques Wittouck was away on business) and Edward Molyneux, and a younger crowd that included the actresses Jannine Crispin and Nina Myral, the actor Jacques Chabannes, along with other celebrities such as Mrs Frank Jay Gould Jennings, wife of the famous American millionaire and Riviera property developer, and the artist George Scott. The mannequin display started an hour and a half after the time announced on the invitation and featured Rosie, Miss Florence (their co-star from their last show at the Casino de Paris) and Gloria, 'a dizzy blonde with plenty of very haughty presence',[57] who was in fact Gordon Selfridge's famous Oxford Street model. But the delay did not appear to matter, since 'by that time everyone felt pretty mellow since all the drinks were on the house'. As the British entertainer Billy Milton observed, 'I never discovered the ingredients of the highly potent cocktails they offered, but they sent the customers on such a "trip" that the results were fantastic sales.'[58]

After the launch, everyone returned to Jenny's chateau at Fontainebleau. Gloria stayed the night in a bed in Jenny's room. She was awakened in the morning by Gordon Selfridge entering with the maid bringing breakfast. 'I was rather embarrassed . . . you know what a stern man he is. Here he was quite different. He was in a dressing gown and slippers. He poured the tea, buttered our toast and sat on Jenny's bed chatting about the shop.'[59]

One friend who did not make the launch was Mae Murray. Murray had expressed an interest in visiting Jenny's chateau to see her daughters. Jenny sent a car to Paris to pick her up, but Mae decided not to go. Needless to say Jenny was not pleased and made her feelings clear by not inviting her to the party.[60] All was not well with Mae, whose unfortunate fourth marriage to the fake prince David Mdivani saw her fleeced of $3 million.

At this point Jenny may well have been feeling the effect of Rosie's yearning for greater independence. Ever since Rosie's marriage to Davis Junior in spring 1927 and the sisters' decision to retire in late 1927, their relationship had entered a new phase. After Rosie had separated from Davis, she had met and fallen in love with Irving Netcher, while Jenny was spending more and more time with Gordon Selfridge. Because of their personal emotional attachments, Jenny and Rosie gradually saw less of each other. Perhaps the diversion of the adopted daughters and the launch of the couture shop may have been necessary to alleviate Jenny's anxiety, as it became obvious that Rosie was edging further away from her.

At the end of 1930, however, both Dollies made a quick trip to London and accompanied Gordon Selfridge to see C.B. Cochran's new production of *Evergreen*,[61] before returning to Fontainebleau for a special Christmas with their father, Sophie Tucker and her husband. Sophie had just played in London, and in early 1931 made plans to make her debut in Paris, asking $7,000 to appear at the Empire Theatre. 'But no artist – American or French – ever got that kind of money in Paris,' the Dollies exclaimed. 'Well kids, your Sophie will get it if she plays there,' she replied. What she did not say was that she had asked such a high price so that the manager would not book her, because for some unknown reason she was terrified of playing Paris. Her plan had backfired, though, and she was booked to appear for two weeks from the end of February. The Dollies, with the help of Maurice Chevalier, busily built up her publicity and called or wrote to every American in Paris. Jenny also made Sophie's entire wardrobe. When Sophie arrived at her suite at Claridge's, it was filled with flowers from the Dollies.

In her dressing room at the Empire was another big box containing soap, towels, perfume, make-up and loo paper. Sophie thought it was one of their crazy jokes. 'There's nothing to laugh at,' Rosie said; 'you'll soon find out that this is the most useful present anybody can give you in a French theatre. Have you taken a look at the toilet yet?' On opening night Sophie observed that the clothes Jenny Dolly had made 'were the most beautiful and as chic as anything a Paris audience ever saw'. At the end of her performance ushers presented her with fifteen floral bouquets. She later found out that all of them had been sent by the Dollies, since 'they were determined to put me over with the Paris audience if they possibly could'.[62]

Immediately after Sophie's Paris debut, Jenny travelled to the Riviera, where she was part of Gordon Selfridge's party, along with his daughter

Rosalie and son-in-law Serge (Prince and Princess Wiasemsky), staying at the Miramar instead of the usual Carlton Hotel in Cannes. At one of the gala dinners at the Ambassadeurs restaurant during April 1931 there was great excitement at the arrival of the great comic film star Charlie Chaplin.[63]

For Rosie, 1931 followed the same pattern as the previous year, and with Irving Netcher as her constant companion she continued enjoying the pleasures of the Cap d'Antibes, regular visits to Maxim's at Juan-les-Pins[64] and trips to Monte Carlo.[65] They were also guests at the social event of the summer season: the Cannes wedding of opera singer Grace Moore to the Spanish film actor/director Valentine Parera, where the other guests included the MGM director Eddie Goulding, Sophie Tucker, Maurice Chevalier, Gloria Swanson and Charlie Chaplin.[66]

Later in the summer, after enjoying the pleasures of Deauville with old friends Pearl White and Florence Walton,[67] Jenny spent some time with Rosie at Eden Roc, Cap d'Antibes.[68] In the company of Gloria Swanson, Maurice Chevalier and Cecil Beaton, they both made a great impression at the gala for the opening of the summer season at the Monte Carlo casino, which comprised a two-hour dinner with a continuous cabaret. Rosie, brown and sophisticated in white lace, was weighed down by fabulous jewels, while Jenny, much less sunburnt, wore a girlish frock of pink taffeta and a string of green beads.[69]

On her return to Paris, Jenny met the MGM film star and singer Jeannette MacDonald, who was about to appear onstage in Paris and Berlin, and began designing and executing her costumes.[70] Then, Rosie joined her for their birthday celebrations on 25 October,[71] and shortly afterwards Jenny went to London. Jenny would have met Charlie Chaplin again at Gordon Selfridge's fifth election party on 27 October 1931 for 3,400 guests. There was a huge list of the rich, titled and famous, including Winston Churchill, Noel Coward and the Aga Khan. Selfridge with his son, daughters and their husbands, was accompanied by Jenny in a chinchilla cape he had given her worth nearly $20,000 and covered in jewelled bracelets on both arms.[72] At this fifth party within a decade, everyone danced to the bands of Jack Hylton, Marius B. Winter and Jack Allan in two ballrooms, with entertainment by the comedians Nervo and Knox and the juggling Rigoletto Brothers, as the election ushered in a Conservative government with a huge majority.[73]

Finally, in November 1931, Rosie won her divorce after accusing her husband of unfaithfulness with an allegedly beautiful girl in a Miami hotel through the help of her chief witness Jack Renault, the Canadian heavyweight boxer. Immediately Rosie and Irving announced their plans at an engagement party in Ciro's restaurant in Paris. The prospective groom was reported to have received a cable protest from his mother, Mrs Netcher Newbury. Facing the possibility that his $100,000-a-year allowance would be cut to a mere $30,000, young Netcher told party guests he would marry Rosie first and worry about money afterwards. The marriage was expected to take place on 18 February 1932, the day Rosie's divorce from Davis Junior would become final.[74]

During the winter of 1931 and early 1932 Rosie, Irving and Jenny spent a pleasant holiday in Saint-Moritz with a host of other celebrities, including Charlie Chaplin and Gloria Swanson,[75] but soon moved south to enjoy the Riviera season. They were at Rosie's villa at Saint-Jean on the exclusive Cap Ferrat when her divorce became final in February 1932. A large settlement was made out of court, estimated at the original quoted sum of $2 million in lieu of alimony, plus the payment for the two pearl necklaces. Davis was reported to have persuaded the trustees of his father's estate to pay him the next four years' income in advance in order to meet the settlement, which must have caused him a few lean years thereafter.[76] He returned to Montreal, Canada, and in October 1932 Texas Guinan, the nightclub hostess and friend of the Dollies, announced that she was to marry him. 'He is the only man in the world who can make me laugh,' she said. Alas, no wedding took place, and Davis died in 1940, in a car crash on the Montreal–Quebec highway.[77]

Immediately after the divorce settlement, despite a terrible cold that she had caught skiing at Saint-Moritz, Rosie began finalising her wedding plans.[78] She had been with Irving Netcher for three years, so was eager to legitimise their relationship and get married as soon as possible. However, she discovered that it was not as easy as she thought, since there were legal obstacles to remarrying so soon after an American divorce. When she went to the French authorities, she was told that, under French law, she must reside for 300 consecutive days in the country before the marriage could be legalised; the same applied to Belgium. She then went to Switzerland, where three months' residency was necessary, and in England her American divorce was not even recognised as valid. So in desperation she realised that they would have to return to New York for the ceremony. Jenny commented:

> Well she changes her mind so often that I really do not know even now if it is fixed. We have been chasing everywhere fixing things up for her and as soon as anything was fixed sure enough a call would come through to say it was all off and we would get busy somewhere else. She is so afraid now that if she marries anywhere else she'll suddenly awake one morning and find she is a bigamist. But anyway they are going to get married.[79]

Jenny bought the tickets for the happy pair to sail back to America in early March with their father, who had been staying with them for his annual Christmas and New Year visit.[80]

Rosie was followed everywhere by her two dogs Bonzo and Poupée, much to the polite dismay of elevator attendants, barmen and Irving Netcher's English valet, who no doubt was frequently left holding the leads. Bonzo was a recalcitrant but affectionate black and white French bulldog and Poupée was one of the smallest of champion Belgian griffons. Thinking of her impending transatlantic crossing, Rosie assured reporters: 'They will be very happy on the *Olympic*, especially at this time of the year.' Both Rosie and Jenny adored dogs.[81] Like so many wealthy women of the time, they were obsessive about their pets, which became what can only be described as 'fashion accessories'.[82] Their first dog, a Pekinese named Tsin, had appeared in their arms when they arrived in New York in October 1922, but another identical Peke was swiftly acquired, and the pair were frequently observed with their mistresses until late 1929. Jenny insisted that her Peke was descended from one of Rudolph Valentino's.

Before sailing from Cherbourg, Rosie announced to the press that they would not purchase joint property in France because of the high taxes and because their future life would include too much travelling, so she must have already sold her properties in Paris. 'If this marriage doesn't take, I am entering a nunnery,' Rosie added, as she sailed away aboard the *Olympic* with 12 trunks containing 40 hats, 50 pairs of shoes, 15 evening gowns and 20 dresses in green, black and white and beige made specially for her honeymoon.[83] On arrival in New York, Rosie and Irving were guests of Mr and Mrs Nate B. Spingold, a motion picture executive and his wife, who had formerly been the famous New York modiste Mme Francis, in their apartment at the Waldorf Astoria.[84]

At a civil wedding ceremony on 17 March 1932, conducted by Mayor James J. Walker of New York, Rosie, wearing an almond green gown, green shoes and a hat to match, tied the knot with Irving. Irving's brother Townsend, his wife Constance Talmadge and the Manhattan millionnaire William Seemen and his wife, former movie star Phyllis Haver, were witnesses. Norma Talmadge was also one of fifty intimate friends in the wedding party.[85] Rosie said that she was prepared to be a playmate bride not a drudge to her new husband: 'Men want companions when they marry . . . they want their wives to play, to be merry and happy, not to take life too seriously . . . You see I've had experience . . . I think I know what men want. I've tried marriage before, so I should be better qualified to make this marriage successful.'[86]

The happy couple spent their honeymoon at Palm Beach, the exclusive resort that had originally been purely a wintering place for society, but, like the French Riviera, was fast becoming more of an all-year-round location. The peak of the Florida boom and of Palm Beach was in 1924–6. After that there were two hurricanes and a collapse in real estate, but things had picked up again by the 1930s. The newlyweds would have enjoyed an endless round of cocktail parties, benefits, concerts and lounging on the beach, before moving on to Havana, Cuba. They arrived back in Paris on 6 May aboard the *Olympic* and decided that this was where they would like to make their main home, contradicting earlier announcements.[87] Rosie was reported as being the focal point of everyone's attention when she arrived at a party with her new husband, looking 'exactly like what most of us believe the beauty salons of Paris can turn out. Inky black hair, sun-tanned complexion, scarlet lips, flawless eyebrows. And of course, a slinky black gown and long earrings.'[88]

From Paris the Netchers travelled to Berlin,[89] before settling in for a lengthy stay on the Riviera, basing themselves in Monte Carlo and using their super-cruising speed boat, a present from Irving Netcher's mother and the envy of all their friends, to convey them every morning to Cap d'Antibes.[90] In Cannes one day, while a tennis tournament was in progress, an ape escaped from a gypsy camp and shuffled onto the courts, where it proceeded to terrorise international society with a set of sharp flashing teeth and arms of prodigious strength, as he bit or scratched a number of famous people, including Rosie, the much-married Peggy Hopkins Joyce, Lady Cunningham-Reid, wife of a Conservative MP, and the Russian Princess Sherbatoff. In the confusion various men, including Maurice Chevalier, Lord Charles Cavendish, husband to the dancer Adele Astaire, and the novelist Maurice de Kobra, led an assault with the aid of the Cannes fire brigade and managed to capture the marauding ape.[91]

Rosie's marriage to Irving Netcher proved to be enduring, and they were very happy together, although, as the years passed by, Chicago and New York, not Paris, became their home. The Netchers also travelled throughout the world to such places as Egypt, India and China besides the usual attractions of the South of France. But, as the Second World War loomed in Europe and the appeal of the Riviera faded, American society found other pleasure pastures in home-grown resorts, and the Netchers, following the trend, began to spend more time in such places as Palm Beach, Hollywood and Palm Springs. More importantly, this marriage meant that the two sisters for the first time in their lives lived totally separately. Rosie may have been deliriously happy, but things were not so good for Jenny.

15

TRAGEDY AND THE TRINKET SALE

While Rosie married Irving Netcher and settled into a new life, moving between Paris, Chicago and the usual society resorts, Jenny was left in Paris with her two young daughters. Her relationships with Jacques Wittouck and Gordon Selfridge were more episodic than in previous years. She settled into a quieter life, punctuated with financial and emotional difficulties, as a new, somewhat elusive, if not sinister, man emerged as her escort.

In early January 1933 a rumour swept Paris that Jenny had committed suicide. According to various press reports Jenny had been suffering from depression for several months and had been staying periodically in a private clinic near her home in Fontainebleau for treatment and care. This alarming story followed a declaration at the local police station by Dr Lesieur, her doctor at Fontainebleau, that she had disappeared, and everyone jumped to the wrong conclusion. Naturally the police followed up the report by telephone and discovered that it was erroneous: Jenny had simply gone away for a few days.[1] An enterprising reporter managed to contact her by phone and was reassured that she was perfectly alive and seemingly in good spirits. She told him she had just eaten a marvellous breakfast and was waiting to hear the date of her funeral.[2]

Jenny's condition can be explained by events that took place in 1932, when she was forced to close her couture establishment after little more than a year, despite being hailed as 'one of the most fashionable modistes in Paris'.[3] She explained to the press that the venture had initially been successful but had then suffered from the general slump. She could not devote all her time to the shop, since her two children had the right to share her time; instead of the business, she was going to help establish and maintain an orphanage in Paris. Clearly the economic depression following the Wall Street Crash in October 1929, which affected everyone in Paris, had also made its mark on Jenny.

As Rosie enjoyed her honeymoon in America, Jenny was in Nice with Gordon Selfridge. One day they were having lunch with Grand Duke Boris of Russia, Paul Dubonnet (the third son of the famous aperitif king) and his wife, the former Jean Nash (known as the best-dressed woman in the world, who was fond of marrying and divorcing[4]), several high French government officials and other dignitaries at the Beaulieu restaurant. Jenny suddenly discovered that one pearl about the size of a sparrow's egg was missing from her necklace. Although Jenny often said that she really did not care much for her jewellery, this pearl was an exception. Before long, in a rather hilarious and incongruous scene worthy of a Hollywood slapstick comedy, all her lunch companions were scrambling around on their hands and knees together with the waiters, peeping under tables and feeling in the cuffs of gentlemen's trousers trying to find the precious item. The excitement continued until Jenny's chauffeur finally discovered the missing pearl on the floor of her car.[5]

Jenny was still solvent enough to enjoy her favourite pastime, gambling. She was spotted at the baccarat table in the Palais de la Mediterranée on the Promenade des Anglais, Nice, a vast casino opened by the American millionaire Frank Jay Gould in 1930. She was reminded by a reporter of a pledge she had allegedly made to quit gambling, and replied that her comment had been slightly exaggerated and wailed: 'Oh why didn't I keep my promise . . . I have lost $8,000.'

'Was it your money?' the reporter enquired respectfully.

'Why bless my soul, of course it was my money!' she replied indignantly. 'Whose money do you suppose it was? I have always worked for my living and I am still doing so. But don't you worry. I will work some more and get it back.'[6]

Jenny was decidedly 'in the luck' and swiftly recouped her losses by winning $200,000.[7]

Even so, Jenny was not pleased at continued reports that she had won small fortunes at baccarat. She dismissed them as nonsense, saying she was worried instead about one of her daughters, who in February 1932 had accidentally caught some of her fingers in the door of Jenny's car in Paris and had had to undergo an operation. Despite her concern, she was in fact on the Riviera, not in Paris looking after the injured child.[8] Before this accident, Jenny had decided to abandon Paris and move back to the USA with her two daughters, but this medical emergency and the lengthy process of sorting out her financial affairs put her plans on hold.[9]

The closure of her couture shop and her concern for her daughters masked a serious financial situation that became evident later. The worldwide depression following the Wall Street Crash had in fact played havoc with her investments.[10] Jenny herself explained:

I loaned money with only promises as security. When I wasn't repaid, I myself borrowed, giving actual guarantees. I did that to give time to those people whose word I trusted. I am now compelled to make good my own commitments. Nevertheless I would rather be in my place than in that of those to whom I loaned, for at least I can still keep my head up. It would break my heart to tell them.[11]

It is quite possible that her past financial security had been compromised by the loss of help from her generous benefactors. As a direct result, she was in the process of selling part of her remarkable collection of jewellery, which she had kept for a rainy day, and was trying to sell her luxurious property at Fontainebleau in order to pay off various debts.[12]

These financial setbacks must have contributed to her illness and depression. The fact that she had not made a commitment to either of her two benefactors, Jacques Wittouck and Gordon Selfridge, and that Rosie was now happily married to Irving Netcher, may have also caused her anxiety. After years of erring on the side of caution and always considering her sister when it came to matrimony, she was now adrift. At the same time, Rosie was at ease being apart from her sister. Rosie's happiness may have been partly responsible for Jenny's misery.

Yet there was light at the end of the tunnel: with Rosie's agreement, Jenny had decided that they would return to the stage and screen.[13] Clearly Jenny's reasons were primarily financial, but Rosie had always missed the life of a performer; back in 1930 she had declared that she would make movies and that the Dolly Sisters would make a stage comeback. To this end, in the spring of 1933, Rosie was in Hollywood discussing a film deal. Given Rosie's contacts, this could have been either with the top brass at Paramount, with Joseph Schenck (estranged husband to her friend Norma Talmadge) at United Artists/20th Century Productions or with another friend, such as Jack Warner at Warner Brothers. Rosie was also negotiating for the Dolly Sisters to mark their comeback on the New York stage in a show specially devised for the première of the film, and another New York stage offer was under consideration.[14] All rather exciting stuff for two 41-year-old ex-dancers who had given up the exhausting life of performers to indulge themselves with an easy life of leisure.

As Rosie negotiated deals in America, Jenny, as part of her recovery, appears to have taken a holiday away from Paris, most probably a sojourn in Biarritz. She was accompanied by Max Constant, a rather enigmatic, naturalised American who had been born in France on 20 October 1899 and at 34 was seven years Jenny's junior.[15] According to later stories, during Jenny's relationship with Gordon Selfridge she met and fell in love with

Max Constant. She was torn between the two and spent one last weekend with Max before planning to agree to be Selfridge's bride.[16] The truth is actually far more intriguing.

Constant had served in the French artillery during the First World War and became an aviator in England.[17] Apart from his career as a pilot, he was also described as a film star, although he appears to have starred in only two movies – *Trilby*, an adaptation of George Du Maurier's novel released in 1923 by First National, and *Why Get Married?* (1924), a French-Canadian production. He was also an uncredited still photographer working on Charlie Chaplin's *A Woman of the Sea*, released by United Artists in 1926.[18]

Cholly Knickerbocker, the society columnist, claimed that the relationship between Jenny and Constant 'was a torrid love affair, full of heavy promises, loud quarrels and abrupt breaks that never lasted'.[19] Disturbingly, according to one Parisian newspaper, Constant was 'un vague gangster', and his association with Jenny was viewed with suspicion by many.[20]

It is not known where or how Jenny met Constant, but she would have been introduced to him in the early 1930s in Paris. At the ritzy opening of the new show at the Casino de Paris in late 1931, for example, the Dolly Sisters with Gordon Selfridge, Irving Netcher and other high-profile guests were in the inaugural 'celebrity' audience along with Max Constant.[21] The implication was that he was most definitely a member of the Dollies' party. He then turned up at a cocktail party that was thrown in Paris in February 1932. Rubye de Remyer, an old friend of the Dolly Sisters and now Mrs Ben Throop, arrived with her husband in Paris and settled at their new apartment on the rue Jean-Goujon. They immediately gave a lavish party in honour of Mrs Albert Kaufman, wife to the Paramount executive, and the New York couturier Hattie Carnegie. There was an impressive guest list that included Florence Walton, Jenny Dolly, François Dupré (Rosie's ex-fiancé) and Max Constant. Jenny was at the head of the guest list and Max Constant at the bottom.[22]

As Jenny and Max returned to Paris by car on the misty dawn of 2 March 1933, Jenny's chauffeur Noel apparently dozed at the wheel and the car left the road at 75 miles an hour just outside Cavignac, 30 miles from Bordeaux. The car bounced from one tree to another along the roadside before overturning and hitting another tree, throwing Jenny 30 feet. Her injuries were extensive. The entire right side of her face was terribly torn and mutilated, and she had an eye injury. One of her lungs was punctured. Several ribs were shattered. She had concussion, and her skull was fractured. But most seriously she had severe internal injuries, which included a displaced stomach. She was in a coma for five days and delirious for one month.[23] Max Constant was in a coma for forty-eight hours but was less critically injured. Noel, the chauffeur, also survived the crash, but there were no reports of his condition.

The reports of Jenny's injuries and what happened next are confusing. The newspaper *Écoutes*, the first to report the accident, asked why news was being kept secret and was astonished by the apparent mystery being attached to what was happening.[24] Later, *Paris Midi* also observed that Jenny's 'entourage' were desperately trying to preserve some form of secrecy about the accident and complained about the difficulty of finding out precise information.[25] In desperation, the reporter turned to Jenny's secretary, who was still in Paris, and claimed that there had been daily telephone calls to say that Jenny was getting much better and played down her injuries. However, the *Chicago Tribune* gleaned that Jenny was at a hospital in the rue Théodore Ducos, Bordeaux, and was described as being 'in a desperate condition'.[26] Meanwhile, in Paris, Jenny's English governess, who was looking after her two daughters, stated that she knew nothing of the accident. 'I am quite certain that I would have been informed if any accident had taken place,' and added that Jenny's 'whereabouts at the present time are unknown to me but I believe she is still motoring in France'.[27]

Despite the fact that the French press reported the accident immediately, there were no further reports until June. It was the same overseas. *Variety* simply reported that Jenny had been injured in a car accident in Bordeaux, that she was recuperating in Spain and that she had sent word that no bones were broken.[28] Jenny's injuries and condition were mysteriously played down. Rosie heard the news through a copy of *Paris Midi* and telephoned Paris and

Bordeaux, but was told that Jenny was only slightly injured and that there was no need to worry – it had been only a slight mishap.[29] Given their closeness and their earlier claims that they had an intuitive bond and knew when the other was in difficulty, perhaps Rosie may have felt something was amiss.

Why all the secrecy? After several initial reports, why did press coverage evaporate until June? And why was Rosie not informed about the serious nature of Jenny's injuries? Rosie did not really give an explanation and simply said that it was only later, when she tried to correspond with Jenny, that she suspected the truth. Jenny had been in the hands of local doctors, her broken limbs had knitted badly and her internal injuries had developed adhesions.[30] The implication was that there had simply been a case of medical negligence and lack of communication.

Cholly Knickerbocker offered a more dramatic explanation, suggesting that there had in fact been a sinister plot that would make a movie thriller to end all thrillers. He alleged that after the accident Constant – 'a rotter and a criminal' – and a group of friends had kept Jenny captive in Bordeaux and tried to keep her condition secret from everyone for the sole purpose of gaining possession of her legendary collection of jewellery, estimated to be worth over $1 million. He further suggested that she had been administered habit-forming drugs to keep her sedated and unaware of her condition and was unable to communicate directly with anyone. He also added that Constant had a 'stormy' disposition and that some of Jenny's friends had whispered accusations that he had tried to kill her and that the accident had not been an accident at all.[31] Some of Knickerbocker's facts are wrong, and he does make some strange statements: throughout his report he refers to Constant as being Italian, he describes how Jenny had been kept in a filthy garret of an Italian hovel and claims that her jewellery was later found beneath a pile of rubbish nearby.

However, could there be some element of truth in Knickerbocker's story? It certainly would provide an explanation for the strange events following the accident. And the motive is a strong one. *Écoutes* had already rather pointedly suggested that Jenny's companion appeared to be moving within her circle at a rather good time – just as she was about to liquidate most of her assets – so there had already been some suspicion about his motives.[32] Perhaps it might also be relevant to this apparent plot that, just before the fatal excursion, Jenny had decided she would abandon Paris in favour of a return to America, where Rosie was arranging their 'comeback' by appearing in a film and a stage show. With this momentous change in her life, she clearly had no intention of marrying Selfridge, who had firm roots in London, and viewed her relationship with Constant as just a passionate affair that would evaporate when her 'comeback' plans with Rosie materialised. The time had come for the so-called gangster and his friends to act before it was too late.

Despite being told that all was well, Rosie and Irving Netcher decided to return to Paris to discuss all the arrangements for the return of the Dolly Sisters to the footlights with Jenny and to investigate what was going on. As they made preparations to return to Europe, Rosie received another telegram, which told her that Jenny was in fact gravely ill. They immediately left for Europe. If Knickerbocker's story is to be believed, Jenny's captors must have given up or were exposed, but whatever happened was not made public and Constant and his friends disappeared.[33]

Rosie arrived in Paris on the boat train in late May 1933 and swiftly went to Bordeaux to collect Jenny and supervise her transfer to the American Hospital in Paris. When Rosie discovered the truth and the extent of Jenny's injuries, she said: 'It is not at all a question of her reappearance on the stage. It is simply a problem of saving her life. At present she is disfigured in a ghastly way and it may be permanent. Our dancing team has probably broken up for all time.'[34] Referring to the fact that Jenny had postponed her return to America the previous year because of her daughter's injury, Rosie concluded that 'the tragedy of it is that it was her love for her little adopted daughter which brought this on her'[35] – not the most helpful of comments, placing responsibility and guilt on the child.

Jenny did indeed come back from the doorway of death: 'I stared at that grim fellow, death, until I stared him down and he went away. But he left souvenirs. He arranged things so I would never dance again. And, while I lay between life and death undergoing an operation from which, so the surgeon said, I had but one chance in a hundred to emerge alive, my fortune toppled.' This was, of course, not quite true, since her fortune had already been dissipated, and she was in debt before the accident, but nevertheless a convenient metaphor.[36]

She was hospitalised throughout the summer and on 17 June underwent her first major operation to adjust the displacement of her stomach to its normal position,[37] before embarking on seventeen painful and expensive plastic surgery operations to her face in an attempt to restore her beauty. Doctors, family and friends tried to maintain Jenny's will to recover by making her believe that she would be able to dance again and return to the stage. To this end C.B. Cochran visited her from London and promised her a London engagement, but it was a merciful deception to bring her hope.[38] A friend said: 'We don't dare tell her she cannot go back on the stage for several years more at least, if ever. We cannot reveal that to her, because the hope of resuming her career is giving her the energy to carry on.'[39] Jenny never really recovered mentally or physically, and the accident and subsequent medical attention left deep emotional scars.[40] Her beauty was almost restored, but her spirit was broken. She had become a different woman.

Edward Dolly had also made the trip back to Europe to see Jenny. Eddie had made Hollywood his home and had been signed to Fox Studios as a choreographer by studio head Winfield Sheehan during the latter's visit to Paris in November 1929.[41] He worked on various projects, including *Are You There?* (1930) with his old friend, the costume designer Dolly Tree, who had also signed a contract with Fox, and moved to Hollywood. After seeing Jenny in Paris, Eddie spent the summer with Rosie and Irving Netcher on the Riviera, and they were seen together aboard the Netcher speedboat outside Cannes harbour.[42] This might sound rather heartless, but it had been decided to take Jenny's adopted daughters, Manzi and Klari, away from the trauma of their mother's hospitalisation for a holiday. Nevertheless Jenny was left all alone.

At the end of July 1933 Rosie and Irving gave a dinner party at the Juan-les-Pins casino, followed by a party at the Hollywood nightclub. Things got a bit out of hand when Mrs Roy Royston, the former Mrs George J. Gould Junior, informed Lord and Lady Milford Haven, cousins of King George V, that champagne applied to the feet cooled them and made them dance. This was disputed by Fred Proctor, who had recently won the Irish sweepstakes prize, and Doris Dickson. Laura Royston promptly slipped off a sandal and plunged her foot into the champagne bucket and poured a bottle of fizz all over her feet. The effect proved so cooling and dance-provoking that the idea swiftly caught on, provoking great merriment, and the party did not disband until the early hours. The next day Netcher discovered that 'the Champagne for feet' was an item billed at about $100. He was not amused and protested. The owners insisted that those who used the champagne were his guests and therefore he was liable.[43]

As the autumn drew closer, Eddie returned to Hollywood, and Rosie and Irving went to New York for a few weeks before also going to Hollywood to visit the actress Bebe Daniels and Irving's brother Townsend and his wife, the former actress Contance Talmadge.[44]

After almost a year of preparation, Jenny's jewellery was finally set to be auctioned at the Hotel Drout on 16 November 1933. Jenny's fabulous collection had been a talking point for years, and the sparkling diamonds, rubies, emeralds and sleek pearls were estimated to be worth in excess of a million dollars, although it is unlikely that she auctioned every item. 'There is a separate story to so many of these jewels, but it would break my heart to tell them,' she said.[45]

The sale included a brooch of platinum set with diamonds, sapphires and rubies; a square-cut emerald (40 carats) mounted as a ring; a cut brilliant (51 carats) mounted as a ring; a black pearl weighing 134 grains that had been owned by Gabys Deslys; a pendant made of a carved emerald with a tiny brilliant-set watch at the base; a brooch of platinum and diamonds; a pair of earrings set with diamonds, rubies and emeralds; a necklace set with diamonds and four large brilliants, one as a pear-shaped pendant; a necklace of 75 pearls weighing 1,749 grains with small pearl 'entre-deux' and a clasp set with pear-shaped diamond and numerous small stones; a necklace of three rows of 298 pearls and a 51.75-carat diamond ring, estimated at $176,000, a gift from Gordon Selfridge that later caused Jenny enormous problems and a lengthy lawsuit from the French government.[46] The sale made only $300,000, and the highest price paid for a single article was $110,000 for the 51.75-carat diamond ring.

Jenny had not been present at the sale and was tearful as she was told the news, saying: 'A number of people had got beautiful things for nearly nothing', and in this way she believed, rather generously, that she had done a lot of good.[47] She added, 'In a month's time I shall be myself once more . . . after I had resigned myself to die. Then I was horrified at the thought that I might be disfigured for life and now I am happy that it is not to be. What more can one ask of life?'[48] Later, when Jenny recalled these events, she said: 'I was not interested any more in jewels. It meant nothing. I wanted my face back. I sold the jewels to pay for the plastic surgery which restored my face – or gave me what you call a mask. It will suffice. It is all right. I can see, I breathe, I live, I have my daughters, I did not die. So I am happy.'[49]

Rosie told the reporter Sheila Graham that Jenny sold her jewels to care for her children, since they were now her major worry. The sale was a sacrifice she made willingly in order to retain guardianship of the two girls. According to Rosie, Jenny was still dangerously ill in the American Hospital in Paris, lying on her back, broken in health and pocket. 'Yes it is true Jenny may never be able to dance again . . . but at the moment she is too ill to think or care about returning to the stage. The only thing urging her to get better at all is the remembrance of the two motherless orphans she adopted.' Sheila Graham asked if it was true that she was destitute and without money, and Rosie answered:

She is very hard up but not quite destitute. You see even when the money was pouring in Jenny had a hunch times wouldn't always be so good so she invested about $1 million in jewellery. The bad times came for Jenny all right and then to crown everything America went off the gold standard. That meant every five dollars we had was only worth three and what with investments going bust things began to look very unpleasant. Jenny was worried she wouldn't be able to keep the twins and although I offered to help her financially, she was too proud to accept my money. So she sold her jewels and is trying to sell her chateau at Fontainebleau.[50]

Of course, there is artistic licence at play here. Jenny had already been forced to sell her jewellery before the accident. Her injuries and the scale of hospital and surgery bills had clearly increased her debt and had therefore bought into focus how she would care for her two adopted daughters.

By the end of the year Jenny was in London recovering from an operation in a West End nursing home. She was treated by a famous English plastic surgeon, and a skin graft was performed. The surgeon insisted that in a month or so only the faintest line would show on the face – a line that would completely vanish with make-up. Jenny was extremely grateful to the British medical profession, and she made a statement saying that she wanted to make some return by working for medical charities, but there is no evidence that she actually did anything. Jenny also announced that she would make her home in London and was looking for a house for herself and her two children. Her aim was to see that her daughters received a first-class education in England before being trained for the stage. She was contemplating going into theatrical management in the West End,[51] although she also announced: 'As soon as I am quite well I shall appear in a play, probably in London.'[52]

Presumably Jenny's desire to move to London indicates her intention once again to come under the protection of Gordon Selfridge, who may well have helped her through this difficult period, despite the affair with Max Constant.

Shortly after her visit to London, when she was back in Paris, she became ill again, and it became necessary for her to undergo surgery on her diaphragm.

Gordon Selfridge was with her at this time and for some reason insisted that Dr Soupault, who was her surgeon and had conducted her previous operations, with a team of three assistants, perform this operation at her chateau in Fontainebleau. When it was over, Selfridge was nervously waiting for news downstairs, smoking a cigar. But all went well.[53] However, Selfridge's benevolence by this time may well have been on the wane. In 1929 the Selfridge family was forced to leave Lansdowne House and moved into a less ostentatious residence in Carlton House Terrace, although even here he still entertained lavishly beyond his resources. His financial situation was not as robust as it had been, and his affairs were in a critical state, as he was in debt to the company – Selfridge's Store – to the sum of over $500,000.[54] He was forced to curb his expenditure, which must have included his generosity to Jenny.

Jenny's life was quite simply in turmoil, and the case of the 52-carat diamond ring, which had been sold at the auction, became an unbearable burden. One winter morning in early 1928 Jenny was strolling down the esplanade at Cannes on the arm of Gordon Selfridge followed by an admiring crowd thrilled at getting a free look at a celebrity. It was whispered that he would buy her anything she fancied – and it was about to happen. Jenny's bright eye had caught something even brighter, a diamond, flashing at her like a small sunset, from the window of Maison Chaumet, the famous jewellers of Paris. To the delight of the audience, Jenny instantly took Selfridge shopping, and the two were in the store for some time. M. Vigier, the manager, took the glittering trophy from the window, and, when the two shoppers emerged from the store, 'the spectators almost cheered in their enthusiasm. M. Vigier had not returned the treasure to the window and the contrasting expressions of Jenny and her admirer suggested why. They had seen history being made in the diamond business.'[55]

Selfridge had bought the diamond for $160,000.[56] Perhaps if she had known how much trouble it was going to cause, Jenny might have strolled right past and resisted the temptation. For the next few weeks the gorgeous gem glittered on Jenny's finger, but she soon realised that she needed to pay a luxury tax of

12 per cent, amounting to $20,000, but not if the item was bought for export. With M. Vigier, Jenny thought that she could save paying this tax by exporting the gem to England, and so it was sent across the Channel to the London branch of Chaumet, together with one-half of a torn playing card, the ace of diamonds. Like many other spendthrifts, Jenny had her own thrifty moment that proved more expensive than her extravagance. A few days later, M. Felix Rosenberg, Jenny's secretary, was dispatched to London, presented the other half of the card, collected the gem and headed back to Paris, where it was continually shown off in public by Jenny.

A few years later, in early 1931, someone anonymously claimed that Jenny had played an ingenious trick on French customs to avoid paying the luxury tax. At a court case on 6 May 1931, Jenny indignantly denied the story and claimed that she was a model taxpayer and the victim of a scurrilous anonymous letter. She narrowly missed being made to pay fines and duty that had accrued to the staggering value of $120,000. Instead, on the basis that another swindle had been perpetuated with another diamond, M. Rosenberg was charged with the offence, and the case went forward to an examining magistrate.[57]

After the publicity that the auction of her jewellery had created, the French government continued its case against Jenny, and in April 1934 demanded the unpaid tax, which had escalated in value. Jenny again testified that her secretary, who had since died, was responsible for the transaction, taking the ring to England and bringing it back to France, and claimed she had no knowledge of the fact that the tax had not been paid.[58] Her story was not believed, and on 9 June she was sentenced for breaches of customs regulations to three days' imprisonment, suspended indefinitely because she was a first-time offender, but she was fined $750,000.[59]

In spite of pleas and criticism from both sides of the Atlantic, the French government insisted that Jenny must pay every franc of the staggering fine. 'She evaded a debt to the French government,' a spokesperson said. 'It is execrable, like those disgusting Germans who are evading their indemnity to France.'

Some suggested that, since France repudiated its own debts to the United States, it might be a bit lenient with Jenny, who, with her sister Rosie, spent millions of dollars in France, to say nothing of attracting many of the world's richest men, who left millions more. The French thought this was an 'abominable thought' and argued: 'Our war debts are another matter and France needs the money herself.' The argument followed that Jenny needed the money even more than the French government, since she had not only lost her great wealth but her health and beauty too.[60]

Jenny appealed against the ruling and fled to London, saying she had not got such a vast sum of money and that she now had to live on a mere $1,330 a week, which was simply not enough. At the same time she was equally distraught to discover that she had lost her acquired American citizenship because she had forgotten to return to the United States within the required year. Since she had been born in Hungary, she managed to obtain a Hungarian passport, without which it would have been impossible to obtain sanctuary in London.[61]

While Jenny suffered the indignity and humiliation of this lengthy court case, Rosie and her husband were enjoying themselves in Palm Beach, Florida's famous playground for celebrities, with Norma Talmadge and her new fiancé George Jessel.[62] Afterwards they went on a lengthy pleasure trip, eventually joining Jenny in Paris for a while, before visiting Havana and then travelling on to Los Angeles aboard the Grace liner *Santa Elena*.[63] They arrived in Hollywood in May 1934 en route for Hawaii, perhaps in an attempt to revitalise their film project.

As Rosie and Irving stepped out into the glamorous world of Hollywood, they would have found an incredibly vibrant nightlife. The exclusive Colony and Clover clubs were packed nightly until dawn, but the premier event of 1934 was the opening of Billy Wilkerson's Trocadero café. Wilkerson, the owner of the *Hollywood Reporter* was also the owner of the popular Vendome, on Sunset, famous for its luncheon trade. He needed a place for the night crowd on the stretch of Sunset between Hollywood and Beverley Hills. He found

La Bohème, bought it and employed Harold Grieve, the decorator of the stars, to renovate the interior as a smart French café. Myron Selznick, the famous agent, hosted an opening-night party, which was a private affair before the club's official opening. Joe Schenck and Rosie Dolly did the rhumba, and other guests included the Bing Crosbys, the Fred Astaires, writer Dorothy Parker, and film stars William Powell, Jean Harlow, Myrna Loy (with her husband Arthur Hornblower), Ida Lupino, Jeannette MacDonald and Gilbert Roland (with whom Rosie and Irving had spent some summers on the Riviera when he was involved with Norma Talmadge).[64]

After a few weeks they were due to visit Hawaii before returning to Paris, but, because they spent so long having fun in tinsel town, they were forced to cancel their trip and return to Chicago.[65] Four years later in 1938 they were back and did make the trip to Honolulu after a few weeks as guest of the movie mogul Jack Warner. They had known Warner for some time and had been guests at his wedding in January 1936 in New York. An invitation to the Warner house on Angelo Drive was the Hollywood equivalent of visiting the White House or Buckingham Palace.[66]

In early March 1935, Rosie and Irving sailed on the French liner *Île de France* from New York to Europe, being waved *bon voyage* by their friend the film actress Dorothy Mackail. Jenny arrived at Croydon airport with her daughters from Paris and was met by Rosie. Manzi and Klari were placed in the care of St Margaret's School, London, while Jenny and Rosie talked over plans with C.B. Cochran to appear in a semi-musical play called *Sisters* that was scheduled for late 1935 but never materialised.[67] Despite the excitement of a possible return to the London stage, Rosie persuaded Jenny to return to America, and without any explanation to the press they both took the boat train to the *Majestic*, moored at Southampton, and, at the beginning of April 1935, for the first time in ten years, Jenny arrived in New York. 'When my darling sister and her husband came 3,000 miles to take me home, I decided I would put myself in their hands. Believe me I'm jolly glad to be back,' she told the press.[68]

Jenny's position must have become very difficult. Her precarious financial affairs, the law suit from the French government and presumably Gordon Selfridge's inability to continue his protective shield[69] all contributed to her agreement with Rosie that she would have a better life back in America. Arriving back in New York, they were met by Dorothy Mackail and their father, Julius Dolly, who burst into tears when he hugged Jenny. As she settled into the Netchers' suite at the Ritz Towers, New York, Jenny said with a smile that she had written her life story entitled *Time Off* while recovering in bed and that it would make 'some sensational revelations'.[70]

After a few weeks in New York, Jenny followed Rosie and Irving back to Chicago and began to make plans to visit Hollywood, but suddenly her agenda changed. She had met Bernard Vinissky, aged 42, a prominent Chicago attorney, a graduate of the University of Illinois, a bachelor and a friend of Irving Netcher, at a dinner party on 3 June that George Thorne had given for Prince Purachatra, an uncle of the ex-king of Siam.[71] Thorne, the wealthy Chicago traveller and millionaire whose estate Vinissky handled, said: 'I guess it was love at first sight. Jenny and Bernard are being married. Sure it's definite. I've already bought them a present.' Jenny said: 'It isn't definitely decided yet. It would be very embarrassing if it were announced.' Vinissky simply commented that he and Jenny 'were very good friends'. The news made headlines, and even Louella Parsons, the famed journalist for the Hearst newspaper group, observed: 'We know now why Jenny Dolly did not come to Hollywood as per schedule. Jenny had other plans . . .'.[72]

On 29 June 1935 Jenny married Vinissky at 6 p.m. in Rosie's apartment at the Drake Hotel. It certainly must have been love at first sight, because Jenny had all her trunks packed to go to Hollywood. 'But after meeting the lawyer she decided to stay right in Chicago and forgot her Hollywood engagements.'[73] Feeling her life was now settled, Jenny sent to London for her daughters, and they arrived in New York aboard the *Berengaria*, to be met by their mother and their new foster father. Manzi's foot was bandaged, since she had caught it in the electric horse of the ship's gymnasium and had had to have six stitches. 'I hope you're not going to imitate me,' said Jenny.[74]

Six months after her marriage, Jenny was still entangled with the French government, the case jumping from French to American courts. As a consequence of the latest battle, Jenny had to prove her American citizenship, which Federal authorities claimed had lapsed through her long residence in Europe. Luckily she was able to obtain several signed affidavits from Harry Fox, her first husband, that aided her case.[75] The outcome of this battle is vague, but it would appear that at some point Jenny did pay part or all of the fine.

A happy domestic life seemed possible, and at first the marriage did go well. There were holidays at Coral Gabes, Florida,[76] social outings into the nightlife of Chicago, visits from friends such as C.B. Cochran,[77] Fanny Brice, Sophie Tucker and others, and in August 1936 Vinissky filed a petition to adopt Jenny's two daughters in the County Court.[78] Yet, despite a good quality of life, Jenny was not happy. She was prone to periods of depression and self-pity, when she cursed the doctors for not allowing her to die on the operating table after her accident.[79] As Sophie Tucker observed: 'All her friends hoped she was going to have happiness after so much trouble and suffering, but I guess happiness was not for Jenny.'[80] Five years after her marriage to Bernard Vinissky, sometime in 1940, they separated, and she made preparations to visit Hollywood as her destiny reached its dramatic conclusion.

A Lonely Glamour Girl Checks Out

Jenny's first appearance in Hollywood in early January 1941 was a major news story. She was described as a glamorous ghost, albeit a charming, vivacious and indomitable one, from a world that was no more. Jenny had decided to fly to Hollywood on a whim, partly to visit her brother Eddie, who now worked for America's largest purveyor of general merchandise via mail order – the Sears Roebuck Company in Los Angeles. She also wanted to introduce her two 16-year-old daughters to the city that she regarded as the international capital of entertainment. Much was made of her 'close friends', such as the Duke of Windsor, Alfonso, King of Spain and the Aga Khan, her spectacular gambling feats and the sale of her jewellery to pay the expenses of her trip 'back from death'.

Despite the dramatic embellishments, Jenny's story was a poignant one that brought into focus the fact that the world in which she and Rosie had found fame, fortune and romance had disappeared. The old world of Europe and the carefree days of the 1920s and early 1930s full of revelry and fun were no more. 'Yes,' Jenny said, with no trace of nostalgia:

that world has vanished – zut – like that. Where once the croupiers cried, the air raid sirens wail. It is the airmen who make killings with bombs, instead of the gamblers with their systems. In Europe the men and women are equal now. The grimy concierge and the great man of title. The hell of war is an interlude between two worlds. It is a furnace in which a new world is being forged. Out of the flames peace will come at last and then just as now that old world will become a memory. There will be democracy. There will be a building from new foundations. The waste and reckless gaiety, the prodigal spending and the gambling that followed the last war will find no place in the world that is to come. So even from the evil of war, good will come.

Talking about Hollywood as she perceived it now, Jenny said, rather naively: 'This is better. The men and women of motion pictures live soberly and sanely, not recklessly and sometimes foolishly, as we did in the old world.'

Once again, Jenny made reference to her colourful life story and mentioned that she had been writing an autobiography. Several magazines, including *Cosmopolitan* had apparently already bid for the rights. It was agreed that it would make sensational reading, since the Dollies had known everybody in Europe worth knowing, they had been fêted by all the leading celebrities and in their heyday they had been the talk of two continents.[1]

Touching on more intimate matters, Jenny was completely frank about her plastic surgery and insisted on placing the interviewer's fingers on her face near the left eye to feel the cavity beneath the skin. 'You see,' smiled Jenny, 'you would not know it unless you felt it, so?' The interviewer regarded the mask as 'a true masterpiece of the surgeon's art, for Jenny Dolly remains a beautiful woman'.[2]

Although she was estranged from her husband Bernard Vinissky, it was arranged that he would join them at her residence in the Shelton Apartments, 1735 North Wilcox Avenue, Hollywood (a few blocks off Hollywood Boulevard). Bernard had been ill and in the summer of 1940 had gone into a sanatorium to seek a cure for arthritis and at the time he was still unwell, but he thought that he would eventually improve and would make the journey west.

Jenny's dream had been that her daughters would become another edition of the Dolly Sisters. She believed that visiting Hollywood would do some good for her girls and she hoped that she would be able to utilise her contacts to get them into the movies. But, according to one reporter: 'Like most things unlucky Jenny had elected to do, the idea didn't pan out.' Manzi did not come up to New York and Hollywood standards of beauty and had no urge whatever to be an actress. Klari, on the other hand, appeared to have some theatrical skill, and Jenny had secured a place for her in the chorus of a new Earl Carroll show.[3]

A very old friend from Jenny's New York days, Earl Carroll had become one of Ziegfeld's major competitors in New York, but he had relocated to Hollywood and opened his world-famous theatre-restaurant in December 1938. His spectacular venue situated on Sunset near Vine had a capacity for over 1,000 guests and became the most celebrated place in Hollywood, featuring a glamorous chorus of over sixty showgirls.[4]

Jenny had telephoned many Hollywood celebrities and friends about Klari's scheduled appearance and was very happy about it. Also, Rosie, with her husband Irving Netcher, had arrived via Mexico for an extended stay, taking the Hal Roach home at 610 North Beverly Drive. Despite this family reunion and the good news of Klari's theatrical debut, something was amiss.

On Sunday 1 June 1941, while Manzi and Klari enjoyed themselves on the beach, Jenny telephoned her aunt, Mrs Frieda Bakos (sister to her mother Margarethe), about 1 p.m., telling her that she did not feel well and that she was in great pain as a result of having had a tooth extracted. Mrs Bakos promised to come and see her immediately. In the meantime Jenny fashioned a noose from the sash of her dressing gown and hanged herself from an iron curtain rod in her living room. Her aunt Mrs Bakos and her daughter Stephany arrived at 1.45 p.m. In the apartment was Jenny's bulldog 'Sonny', whose barking aroused Mrs Bakos's curiosity when there was no response to the doorbell. Mrs Dorothy Bray, manager of the apartment, let Mrs Bakos in, but it was too late. Jenny was dead. The coroner's office was undecided whether to hold an inquest. The owner of the apartments said that she had heard no commotion, and Detective Lieutenant Byron Diller said that, although there had been no note to give a motive, it was 'undoubtedly suicide', which allayed any fears of foul play.[5]

What was it that drove Jenny to take her own life? There was no simple explanation but rather a series of events that gradually overwhelmed her. First, there was the worry over the financial difficulties she had endured since the beginning of the 1930s that culminated in the sale of her jewellery collection and her chateau at Fontainebleau. The court case against her for evading customs duty by the French government was also stressful, as was the huge fine. All these financial constraints made her fearful that she might lose her two daughters, which added to her anxiety. But by far the biggest influence was the serious injuries she received in the car accident in 1933. Physically and emotionally she never recovered and described herself as a broken shell.[6] She often wished she had been left to die rather than having to endure dozens of painful operations. Her aunt said that Jenny had told her that the doctor who saved her life after the accident did not do her any favours and that 'she used to cry and tell me she wanted to die'. But her aunt never thought she would take her own life. Her uneasy state of mind was aggravated by the fact that she had neither as much money nor as much grace nor as much beauty as she had once known. These were the crucial factors that plagued her mind and drove her to have serious bouts of self-doubt and melancholia.

She was also troubled by her relationship with Rosie. For twenty-six years Jenny had been with Rosie in the whirl of life. Everyone thought of the Dolly Sisters as one. As Rosie married Davis Junior and then Irving Netcher, they became two separate individuals, and for the first time they truly began to lead different lives. Jenny believed that, because of all her bad luck, she was now on a side street, while Rosie, always the luckier of the two, continued in a gala parade.

Since the late 1920s there had been growing tension between the two sisters. Jenny had always taken the lead but had always considered her sister and their career before making decisions, while Rosie, perhaps in deference to Jenny's dominance, just did things without consulting her. Jenny had come to believe that all the world, including her own sister, had turned its back on her. When Rosie and Irving Netcher settled into the Hal Roach home in Beverly Hills, it became 'a mecca for the merrymakers of film land', but Jenny was not invited often, and, when she was, her aunt related that she 'felt like a disembodied spirit sitting in the background while her twin danced and laughed with important folk from all over the world. Those same people had been Jenny's intimates too.' Jenny believed that Rosie was negligent of her emotional needs, and, although Rosie had helped her financially, that was all Rosie had given. What Jenny wanted was the attention, love and a sense of involvement with her sister that they used to enjoy.

As Jenny arrived in Hollywood, she firmly believed that the friends she had known in Europe and entertained at her chateau in Fontainebleau, friends who had drunk her champagne, accepted her gifts and laughed at her jokes during her heyday, would flock to her assistance and make it easy for her and the girls. She learned all too quickly the Hollywood theme that a man is never kicked when he is up and never noticed when he is down. Now they passed her by with no recognition. Her aunt observed: 'I know actors and actresses who lived for weeks at a time with Jenny in Paris, but they wouldn't give her a telephone call when she came out here.' Jenny had had a very rude awakening.

From the perspective of the twins' many friends, Jenny was simply not the same person she had been, and, because of her period as an invalid, she had started to think more like a recluse. The plastic surgery had restored some of her beauty, but she was unable to walk with her former grace. It was hard for her not to feel sorry for herself and hard for her not to try and enlist the sympathy of others. She was not a welcome guest even at the home of her sister, primarily because she complained about everything. She thought that the apartment she had taken was too small, that she was 'cooped up' and that she could hear all the arguments that went on up and down the street. She did not even like California: 'This damned weather out here doesn't agree with me. I've been sick ever since I came,' she told her aunt. She had acquired the habit of repeating things over and over again almost as if she were talking to herself, which proved more than irritating.

In her short stay in Hollywood Jenny had become the loneliest person in the world in her double apartment where no one visited her, not even Rosie. Privately she confided to her aunt that she was upset at not being included in Rosie's gay social whirl, and could not understand why. Describing her last few days, her aunt said that she had been lonely over the Memorial Holiday weekend, because, when Rosie and her husband went to Santa Barbara, Jenny was not invited. 'She said to me, "Why didn't they ask me? I know those people as well as Rosie does." I told her not to bother with them – that some day Rosie might find herself in the same boat and think back on it. But Jenny said Rosie always had better luck. She never would be in the same boat.'

On the Saturday of the holiday, because Jenny thought Rosie and her husband were out of town, she planned a swimming party at their home, inviting friends of her two daughters so she could watch them swim. When she called the house on Saturday morning and told the maid about her plans, she was informed that Rosie had come home early. Jenny asked the maid to have Rosie call her as soon as she got up. Jenny waited all day but Rosie never called. 'Jenny was terribly hurt and cried bitterly. "My own sister. My twin. Did you ever think she would do that to me?"' she asked her aunt over and over again. Her aunt did her best to console her, but it was no use.

Later that evening Manzi telephoned her aunt Mrs Bakos and told her that Jenny was very sick and asked if she would send a doctor. The aunt sent her own family physician over to examine Jenny. He phoned her afterwards and told her that there was nothing at all wrong with her. 'It's all in the mind,' he said. The doctor gave Jenny something to make her sleep and warned Klari that her mother was facing a nervous breakdown. Even with the medication Jenny could not sleep because of the pain as a result of having had a tooth extracted. Round and round in her kaleidoscope of thoughts went the memory of Rosie's thoughtlessness: she did not call, her own sister.

On the fateful Sunday morning Manzi called the aunt again. The aunt agreed that she would go over in the afternoon and pick Jenny up, so she could spend the rest of the day with them, while the girls could spend the day at the beach. When they received the last call from Jenny at 1 p.m., they rushed over. But Jenny was dead. They managed to contact Manzi, who was at the beach, but Klari had gone to rehearsals. When they reached her by telephone, Klari was stricken dumb for a few minutes and then said, 'What will I do now?' Someone suggested that she go to Rosie's, but she answered that she might as well carry on with the rehearsals. 'That's what mother would want me to do. She told me the work I was doing was more important to me than anything else in the world.'

When they told Rosie, she was prostrate with grief. The night after Jenny died, Rosie was taken to Aunt Frieda's house. Apparently this was the first time that Rosie had ventured to her aunt's house since she had been in Hollywood, and she cried in Frieda's lap as she had done when she was a little girl. But it was too late. Jenny was gone. Irving Netcher took charge of funeral plans and Jenny was buried on 4 June 1941 at the Wee Kirk o'the Heather, Forest Lawn Memorial Park. The service was a simple but profound Episcopal ritual. There were about seventy-five mourners, who included Rosie, Irving Netcher, his brother Townsend Netcher, Eddie Dolly, Aunt Frieda and scores of theatrical and film celebrities, including Fanny Brice, Sophie Tucker, the Duncan sisters and many others. Jenny's husband Bernard Vinissky was too ill to attend,[7] and her father, Julius Dolly, was too frail to make the journey from New York, where he still lived. Rosie was on the verge of collapse and, following the service, was virtually carried to a waiting car.[8]

Almost a month later, at the beginning of July 1941, Klari Dolly finally appeared in the chorus of Earl Carroll's spectacular new show *Something to Shout About*. Klari was proud of what she had achieved and said: 'I felt that was what mother wanted me to do. She had always planned for me to go into show

253

business.' Asked about losing all her luxury, Klari replied: 'I'm going to try and get as much of it back as I can, as well as working all my life to carry on the Dolly name.' She claimed her ambition was not to follow in her mother's footsteps but to create her own style, including singing semi-torch songs with an eye on the screen.[9] Although Manzi took a business job and had no interest in the stage, Jenny would have been proud of her daughter's efforts, even if they were short-lived, for Klari was not destined for stardom like her mother.

The Rhythm, the Rhyme
and the Dance

After Jenny's death it is not clear what happened to Jenny's two daughters, Manzi and Klari. It is likely that their adopted father, Bernard Vinissky, looked after them in Chicago until they were able to lead their own lives. Presumably Rosie would also have helped in their upbringing. Although Rosie and Irving appear to have made Chicago their main home, they also spent a lot of time on the West Coast. Like Irving's brother Townsend, they bought a house in Beverly Hills and spent the war years giving large parties and enjoying life. Following the whims of the Hollywood set, they also spent a lot of time in Palm Springs, probably staying at the El Mirador Hotel, a favourite of Townsend's, before buying a home at 1200 Vista Vespero.[1]

On first sight, Palm Springs appears disappointing. It was an isolated location in a windswept oasis located 100 miles from Los Angeles on the edge of a desert backed up against the 11,000-foot Mount San Jacinto, which Cleveland Amory thought resembled 'an abandoned Cecil B. DeMille set'. And yet, as the doors closed on the old-world resorts, Palm Springs became the new mecca for the rich and famous and all the major Hollywood stars. During the silent film era the Desert Inn, the only hotel at the time, was frequented by film stars such as Charlie Chaplin, Rudolph Valentino and Alla Nazimova, who made movies in the desert. But the town's popularity as a resort really began with the construction of the El Mirador Hotel in 1928. Through the 1930s Palm Springs became more and more fashionable and was regarded as the Palm Beach of the West, and soon private villas were being built by the glitterati of Hollywood. Tradition dictated that on 15 October the actor Charles Farrell, fully clothed in his white tie, top hat and tails, dived into the pool at the Racquet Club, launching the official Palm Springs social season, which ran through to April.[2] Rosie and Irving made this an annual event and became firm fixtures.

It was inevitable, with Rosie mixing with all the right people in Hollywood, that sooner or later the idea of making a movie about the Dolly Sisters would become a hot property. By the beginning of 1943 Rosie had sold the rights to the story of the Dollies for $52,500 to Twentieth Century Fox, no doubt through her connections with her old friend Joe Schenck, who had been chairman of the company and was at that time a producer. The screenplay by John Larkin and Marian Spitzer was partly based on a fourteen-page biography written by Rosie, and partly on scrapbooks, correspondence and newspaper clippings that Rosie supplied.[3] As part of the deal, the studio was forbidden to include any information about Jenny's adopted daughters or her suicide. Before signing the contract, Rosie also obtained releases from family and friends, allowing for the use of name, likeness, actions and activities, in fact or in fiction.[4]

George Jessel, another old friend of Rosie's who had been married to Norma Talmadge, made his debut as producer and may have had a hand in getting Rosie to sign with Fox. The starring roles were allotted to the super-glam blonde babes Betty Grable and June Haver, with the addition of the handsome John Payne in the male lead. The result was a highly fictionalised biopic, where historical chronology and biographical accuracy evaporated.[5] What emerged was a nostalgic musical that bore a slight resemblance to the true story of the Dolly Sisters but pandered to the post-war taste for fluffy romantic stories.

The film successfully resurrected the golden era of the theatre and the international set from the 1910s to the 1920s, but for some it was a disappointment. Robert Wennersten, who interviewed Rosie in later years, was scathing. 'The film turned out to be a boring, hack musical. Its feeble attempt to provide a 1920s background failed. The girls' career and private lives, once the source of so many vicarious thrills, came off seeming dull and uninteresting.'[6] Wennersten had a point, but the film has to be seen as a product of its period, and, despite the disregard for accuracy, it became a huge box-office hit. There was praise for the costumes by Orry Kelly, the imaginative dances staged by Seymour Felix, Irving Cumming's expert direction, Jessel's 'well seasoned and veteran showmanship' and some fantastic production numbers, including 'Dark Town Strutters Ball', which might seem racist by today's standards, and the lipstick sequence.[7] There was also a fabulous selection of songs, of which 'I'm Always Chasing Rainbows' became a hit, repeating Harry Fox's original success with the same song in *Oh Look!* with the Dollies from 1918.[8]

The world première was screened rather aptly in Chicago on 5 October 1945. Despite all the precautions, there were clearly quite a few people who felt misled or misrepresented. In March 1946 Harry Fox filed suit against the studio, Jessel and Rosie, claiming that his reputation had been adversely affected by the representation of his character as 'lowly songwriter'. There were also suits by Klari, one of Jenny's daughters, and Beatrice Fox White, Harry Fox's third wife.[9] But they all swiftly evaporated.

By far the most damaging case was the highly publicised suit by Jean Schwartz, which came to court in March 1947. Schwartz demanded $100,000 in damages, even though he had been paid $2,000 by the studio for his consent to be named and characterised. The point of the suit was that he had not been portrayed and had been effectively written out of history. For

Schwartz it raised the issue of whether the movies had the right to take liberties when portraying actual characters and events. Schwartz made numerous allegations: that his career had been damaged because he had not been included in the movie; that the studio was in breach of contract because it had not employed him as a technical director; that Rosie had misled him into believing that his songs would be included; that he had lost a substantial sum (estimated at $40,000–$50,000) in revenue because his songs had not been included, and that the film had grossly distorted history by representing Harry Fox as a songwriter when it had been Schwartz who had written the songs.[10]

At the Federal Court, Schwartz cited his visit to Rosie's suite in the New York Ritz Carlton, where he had discussed the film with his former wife, who told him about negotiations with the studio. He insisted that Rosie had said 'you are the only husband I really want in the picture', when in the end Schwartz had been left out and Netcher had been included. She had told him she was receiving $50,000 for the rights to the Dolly Sisters' story and that she was doing it 'mostly' for Jenny's adopted children. She had also said, 'they'll use a lot of your songs and you'll make a lot of money'. To back his claim that he or his work was to be included in the film, Schwartz introduced as evidence a telegram sent by Jessel saying, 'I wish you would send me a list of the hits you wrote with Billy Jerome. I have an idea you might make some money out of them.' Schwartz also testified that he visited Jessel during the production of the film to play him some new melodies that Jessel was thinking of using.[11]

Schwartz claimed that he became ill when he learned he had been left out of the picture: 'I got sick. I had to go home. I got a doctor. I lost all ambition. I had a terrible mental reaction. I couldn't write any more songs.' He added that the shock had even affected his fingertips, so that he could not tap out tunes that in forty-nine years had earned him $1,000,000! Harold F. Collins, presumably restraining himself from laughter, cross-examined him and wanted to know the details of his illness. But all Schwartz would add was that he suffered a pain in his fingertips and nervousness.[12]

In defence, Rosie testified in court and provided a wealth of peripheral background information that essentially 'dipped into her champagne and caviar past' and also said that she had been happy about the film, 'because it was sort of a memorial' to Jenny.[13] The thrust of the defence was made by executives at Twentieth Century Fox. Darryl Zanuck said the only purpose of the Dolly Sisters' film was to give the public 'the glamorous magic' of the dancers' lives, not to present a biography.[14] George Jessel claimed that Hollywood can do anything when characterising a person for the movies: 'I am not under oath when I produce a picture . . . I can make a character anything I like – an acrobat or a violinist.' Robert Daru (counsel for Schwartz) wanted to know why Harry Fox, a comedian, was portrayed as a songwriter in the picture, while in fact Schwartz had been Rosie's first husband and the only songwriter in the life of either sister. In answer Jessel contended that he was privileged to represent a comedian as a songwriter, or anything else for that matter.[15]

After five weeks Federal Judge Campbell E. Beaumont directed the jury to return a verdict for the defendants, Twentieth Century Fox, George Jessel as producer and Rosie. The defence attorney Harold F. Collins moved for dismissal of the suit on the grounds that a case had not been sufficiently presented for consideration by the jury. Judge Beaumont upheld the contention and said: 'I have viewed the picture . . . and the plaintiff was not named or characterised.'[16] Schwartz lost his case.

After the excitement of the court case, the Netchers boarded the Sante Fe Super Chief for their journey back east, but rather dramatically the train was involved in a serious accident at Raton, New Mexico. Rosie and Irving were both injured, although not badly, and luckily for Rosie her $300,000 worth of jewellery and all her personal effects were retrieved from their wrecked compartment.[17]

For the next few years they continued their life of travelling and began visiting Europe again. On one of these trips they decided to spend a summer holiday with Mr and Mrs Bob Considine in Capri, Italy. Bob Considine

(1907–75) was the popular American journalist, author and talk-show host, famous for his syndicated column 'On the Line'. A few days after their arrival, on 26 June 1953, Irving, aged 52, died suddenly of a heart attack. Millie (Mrs Bob Considine), who was one of Rosie's long-time friends, commented: 'Their 21 year marriage was a very happy one . . . Rosy was prostrate with grief.'[18] Rosie gave Millie a necklace worth $150,000 for being so nice to her during her ordeal.[19] Rosie was flown back to the USA with Irving's body, and the funeral took place in Chicago.[20] Rosie was named sole heir in Irving's will, which left her gross assets of $657,188 (net $596,640).[21]

After Irving's death, Rosie's life followed a familar pattern. She would spend the winter months at her house in Palm Springs and visiting the casinos in Las Vegas, and then summer in her apartment at 470 Park Avenue, New York, and the Hamptons on Long Island. In between she would take holidays abroad, perhaps visiting some of her old haunts in Europe.[22]

It was shortly after Irving's death that she became friendly with the dapper singer George Allardice, whose career had begun in New York supper clubs and Broadway musicals with his debut at the Blue Angel on 54th Street. Allardice became friendly with Jolie Gabor, the mother of the Gabor sisters in Long Island, and sang at her wedding, swiftly becoming the darling of New York's society set. At the same time he became great friends with Rosie, who had become another Long Island society darling. In late 1954, when he was 25, Rosie took him to Palm Springs and gave a party in his honour at the exclusive Biltmore Hotel, where he also performed to great success. He became her constant companion, spending the summer in Long Island and the winter in Palm Springs. As George put it, Rosie 'kept' him. They travelled the world together, and Rosie always picked up the bill. Later, in 1959, Allardice moved to Palm Springs permanently and became the premier charity entertainer, dubbed 'Mr PS' by the local press.

Described by a friend as 'smooth as a good martini', Allardice was able to orchestrate a fabulous atmosphere resembling an intimate house party, and his friendship was readily given. 'He was always one of those guys you are glad to see with a happy face and a good disposition,' said Frank Bogert, former mayor of Palm Springs. Bruce Fessier, the entertainment editor of the local paper, observed that Allardice learned the secrets of people living in high society by living a life that also had to be kept secret from people outside the community. Allardice was openly gay at a time when gay nightclubs were very discreet. To George's crowd, being gay was nothing remarkable. Many of them came to Palm Springs just for its sexual freedom, and Allardice once said that Palm Springs was 'Sin City' in the strait-laced Eisenhower era, where Howard Hughes, Liberace and others owned multiple local homes to hide multiple lovers.[23]

Although Rosie had a new companion, her life in the 1950s was punctuated with further deaths. In 1955, just two years after Irving's death, the great Netcher matriarch Mollie died, followed a month later by her sole surviving son, Townsend.[24] In January 1956 Rosie's brother Edward died in Los Angeles after a long illness,[25] and in July 1959 her first husband, Harry Fox, died aged 76 at the Motion Picture Country Home Hospital after a three-year illness.[26]

Despite all this sadness, Rosie appeared on Ed Murrow's *Person to Person* CBS-TV show, screened on 24 October 1958. Murrow opened this edition with a peep into her Park Avenue apartment, before she talked about her past and all her showbiz encounters with the rich and famous. John A. Aaron, co-producer, recalled that she had been a person with 'a great verve for life' and as a guest 'extremely good, easy to work with' and 'not one who threw her wealth or jewels around'. Aaron had known her from his visits to the Hamptons, Long Island, where Rosie had held court at the Bath and Tennis Club in Westhampton, where she 'lived casually', but whatever she did she did big, said Aaron. 'If this meant swimming six times around the pool while younger people were puffing after a single go-round, six times it was.' He also remembered that at one New York party she had one caveat for the assembled carousers: 'If you drink scotch, make it Black and White. It will never hang you over.'[27]

Jo Ranson, reviewing the programme, said that Rosie lived 'like a silken dowager dame in tufted surroundings with abundant memories of riotously rich stage door admirers and also knee-deep in precious gems . . .'. Rosie was ensconced in a peau de soie gown, cap sleeved and off the shoulder with the sculptured bodice criss-crossing into an Empire. The opulent bell-shaped skirt ended in intriguing knots at each side of the hemline. She was weighted down with a heavy glittering three-strand necklace and long-drop two-strand earrings. She also wore a wide matching bracelet. On her bosom she displayed a stunning brooch in the form of a flower basket, a gift from her late husband. With her adornments and the severity of her centre-parted coiffure tightly drawn into a full, low chignon, she was indeed a dramatic sight.[28]

Perhaps it was the grim realities of life that drove her to attempt suicide on 20 April 1962 in a rather dramatic way one hour before a dinner party. Rosie had just returned from her winter vacation in Palm Springs when she was found at 5.35 p.m. on the floor of her bathroom in a coma, dressed in a nightgown, with sleeping pills strewn all over the floor. Her maid said that Rosie had been despondent and had talked of suicide. That evening she was expecting five guests for dinner and an hour before they were due to arrive she had told the maid: 'I won't be around for the party.' The maid and her first dinner guest found her in the bathroom, and she was rushed to the Roosevelt Hospital for treatment for an overdose. Her condition was at first reported as fair but then deteriorated and fear was expressed for her life, but she eventually pulled through. Two of her dinner guests – her niece Manzi (Mrs Lee Kantro)[29] and a close friend Richard Hall – went to the hospital, but offered no explanation of the incident.[30]

Elements of her despondency can be gleaned from her last interview, given to Robert Wennersten in a suite of the Beverly-Wilshire Hotel in the late 1960s. Wennersten said that 'there was no bitterness in her dark, sometimes rasping voice. But there was a certain sadness, a note of passive acceptance'. As she told him:

They never forget you in England. You can retire for twenty-five, thirty years. You go back, and they meet you with open arms, as if you'd just left yesterday. Here they forget very easily. I found out that America has changed. I must say it's not bad, but it's not the same world we used to live in. Today it's different, entirely different. Whether I come here, or whether I'm in New York, old friends you call up when you arrive – they've forgotten you. They don't call back. They don't do that in England. They don't do that in France. Here is very selfish people. They forget very easily.

Perhaps she was beginning to feel the pain that Jenny had gone through when she arrived in Hollywood in 1941 shortly before she took her own life. But, on a more positive note, Rosie added: 'It's been a beautiful life. Life has been grand to me and I thank God every day, every night, that He's given me a beautiful, wonderful life. I miss my family. They're all gone now.'[31]

Six years after her suicide attempt she became an invalid after a hip injury that never healed properly, and at the end of January 1970 she became so ill with flu that she was taken to Leroy Hospital at 40 East 61st Street, where she died of a heart attack on 1 February 1970, aged 77. Rosie's funeral service was held at the Frank E. Cambell funeral church between Madison Avenue and 81st Street and her ashes were taken to California for interment in the entrance hall of the Great Mausoleum of Forest Lawn. Here she was interred with Jenny and her brother Edward, all encased in the pedestal of a lifesize statue of a young woman with her hands on her hips, one foot before the other, her head tossed back and her hair and long skirt swirling behind her. The statue was appropriately named: 'The Rhythm, The Rhyme and the Dance'.[32]

18

EPILOGUE

When the Dolly Sisters retired in late 1927, numerous imitators followed in their wake. In Berlin, Marlene Dietrich and Margo Lion performed a sexually ambiguous spoof that made fun of the Dollies as wholesome girls in the 1928 revue *It's in the Air*.[1] But none was more outrageous than the Norwegian Rocky Twins, two boys who dressed up in drag as the Dollies and parodied their routines. Throughout their career the Dollies and then the Rockies attracted a large gay audience.[2] It is not difficult to understand why. In the purest terms they epitomised camp, and, even during the 1930s and beyond, their legend as gay icons lived on.

After their deaths, the Dolly Sisters were not forgotten, and in 1973 MGM TV with the Production Company entered into an agreement with CBS to produce an original musical based on their life. The script by William Bast (who wrote the Lizzie Borden TV movie) was going to focus on their rivalry, their show-business careers and their feat of breaking the bank at Monte Carlo.[3] Alas, the project never came about.

Then in June 1980 the Women's Interart Center in New York produced *Yesterday is Over*, a play inspired by the Dolly Sisters that used their lives as a highly theatrical metaphor. The play was set at a fictional 1955 reunion of two former stars, who were called 'perfect mirror images' and 'whose gold sister fever during the Scott Fitzgerald days infected an already dizzy, reeling generation. The sisters' plumed fans, fabulous diamond headdresses and reckless nights at Monte Carlo's casinos underscore a bitter show business tango that fatally seduced the beautiful bodies who danced it.'[4]

More recently the magic of the Dollies has remained undimmed. Bill Bryson fell under their spell, writing in *Notes from a Small Island* that Gordon Selfridge fell into rakish ways with a Dolly Sister on each arm – a nicely phrased story that perpetuates their mythlike status.

But most resonant for me is my own story about Angela Carter. Working at Pan Books in the late 1980s, I promoted Angela's novel *Nights at the Circus*, arranging talks and signing sessions for her in UK bookstores. One of these publicity jaunts was at the Andromeda bookshop in Birmingham. I met Angela at her house and journeyed to Birmingham, loitered as she did her stuff at the bookshop and then whiled away a few hours with her at a rather marvellous lunch waiting for our return train to London. It was a wonderful experience and Angela was charming and interesting but far more intrigued by my research about the Dolly Sisters. We talked for hours and I told her their story. Then *Wise Children*, her novel about the twins Nora and Dora Chance, mistaken identities and the tangled fortunes of two theatrical families, was published in 1991. The Dollies had clearly been an inspiration. Interestingly, the cover and the poster for the launch of the book featured a painting of the Dolly Sisters based on a photograph of them wearing the brightly coloured costumes in which they danced the mazurka in the 1923 show *Paris sans voiles* at the Ambassadeurs, Paris. Although Angela Carter may already have had the idea about writing a novel about twins before I met her, I was delighted that she, like me, had succumbed to the magic of the Dolly Sisters.

CHRONOLOGY

1892   Born in Budapest, Hungary, 25 October

1902   April: see Isadora Duncan dance in Budapest

1903   8 May: Julius Dolly arrives in New York

1905   30 May: Margarethe Dolly and the Dolly Sisters arrive in New York

1906   First dancing performance in Boston

1906   Engagements with Gertrude Hoffman

1906   Autumn: engagement in Havana, Cuba

1907   June: *The Maid and the Millionaire* at the Madison Square Roof Garden, New York

1908   Spring: touring with *The Strolling Players*

1908   April: touring vaudeville act

1909   Summer: vaudeville act at Henderson's and the New Brighton Music Hall, Long Island

1909   Autumn: engaged by Lee Shubert for *The Midnight Sons* and toured through early 1910

1910   August: Margarethe returns from trip to Budapest with brother Edward

1910   August–October: *The Echo*, the Globe, New York, presented by Charles Dillingham; toured into 1911

1911   May: Jenny's romance with the driver Harry Knight

1911   June–September: *The Ziegfeld Follies of 1911*, Jardin de Paris/New York Theatre Roof Garden, toured through early 1912

1912   April–September: *Winsome Widow*, New York Theatre, New York

1912   Summer: buy house in Bensonhurst

1912   August–November: *The Merry Countess* (reworking of *Die Fledermaus*) for the Shuberts at the Casino Theatre, New York; toured into early 1913

1913	February: Jenny and Harry Fox in *The Honeymoon Express*, Winter Garden Theatre, New York
1913	March: Rosie in *The Beggar Student*, Casino Theatre, New York
1913	10 April: Rosie marries Jean Schwartz
1913	12 May for two weeks: Rosie and Martin Brown in Hammerstein's, New York
1913	June: Jenny and Harry Fox start twenty-four-week vaudeville tour
1913	June–September: Rosie and Martin Brown in *Ziegfeld Follies of 1913*, New Amsterdam Theatre, New York
1913	November: Rosie in *Miss Caprice*, the Studebaker Theatre, Chicago
1914	January: Rosie in *The Whirl of the World*, Winter Garden, New York
1914	March: Jenny and Harry Fox in new vaudeville tour including the Palace, New York
1914	May: New York Theatre Roof Garden/Jardin de Danse, New York, with Carlos Sebastian
1914	28 August: Jenny marries Harry Fox
1914	9 September: Jenny and Harry Fox at the Palace Theatre, New York
1914	20 October: Rosie and Martin Brown in *Danceland* at the Palace Theatre, New York
1914	December: Jenny and Harry Fox at the Palace Theatre, New York
1914	December: Rosie and Martin Brown in *Hello Broadway* at the Astor Theatre, New York
1915	February: Jenny and Harry Fox in *Maid in America* at the Winter Garden Theatre, New York
1915	February: Universal release *Dance Creations*, a short film of Rosie and Martin Brown dancing
1915	May: Jenny and Harry Fox leave cast of *Maid in America*
1915	July–August: Jenny filming *The Call of the Dance*
1915	July–September: Rosie in Hollywood filming *The Lily and the Rose*
1915	September: Kalem release *The Call of the Dance*
1915	Late: Jenny and Harry Fox in new vaudeville tour
1915	December: release of *The Lily and the Rose* (D.W. Griffiths's first film for Triangle), starring Rosie and Lillian Gish

1916   January: Ziegfeld's *Midnight Frolic*, New Amsterdam Theatre Roof Garden, New York

1916   February: Keith Circuit, Palace Theatre, New York

1916   February: consider film offers from Pathe and Fox

1916   March–April: shows in and around New York: Alhambra, Orpheum Brooklyn, Colonial and Prospect

1916   August: Rosie and Jenny in *His Bridal Night* at the Republic Theatre, New York

1917   13 April: death of Diamond Jim Brady

1917   June: Jenny files for divorce from Harry Fox

1917   July: Jenny and Harry Fox are reconciled

1917   July–November: vaudeville contract with Keith Circuit, including the Palace, New York

1917   November: dancing at the Knickerbocker Grill and Murray's Roman Gardens, New York

1917   November: signed for Hitchcock–Goetz revue *Words and Music* to follow *Hitchy Koo* at Raymond Hitchcock's 44th Street Theatre or Fulton Theatre; subsequently withdrew

1918   January: performance for Red Cross at Palm Beach, Florida

1918   February: filming *The Million Dollar Dollies*

1918   April: release of *The Million Dollar Dollies* produced by Emerald Pictures

1918   May: cabaret in *The Midnight Revue* at the Shuberts' Century Roof Garden

1918   May: signed as co-stars with Webber and Fields in *Back Again* at the Chestnut Street Opera House, Philadelphia; show cancelled

1918   14 July: join revised version of *Oh Look!* at Belasco Theatre, New York (originally opened 7 March at Vanderbilt Theatre, New York); until 1920: regional tour

1920   April: Dollies close their 31-week tour of *Oh Look!*

1920   April: leave for London onboard the *Baltic*

1920   16 June: *Jigsaw*, first appearance on the London stage at the London Hippodrome, produced by Albert de Courville (the show ran until 11 December)

1920	End August: leave cast of *Jigsaw* to spend time in Deauville and Paris
1920	10 October: death of Olive Thomas in Paris
1920	20 October: Jenny arrives in New York on the *Adriatic*; starts divorce proceedings from Harry Fox; announces she will marry an English duke
1920	November: Jenny returns to London
1921	17 January–26 November: *League of Notions* at the New Oxford Theatre, London, presented by Charles B. Cochran
1921	March: meet Lord Beaverbrook; attend Philip Sassoon's party and meet David, Prince of Wales
1921	17 October–13 May 1922: *Fun of the Fayre* at the Pavilion Theatre, London; Pony Trot number with Clifton Webb
1921	12 November: Victory Ball at the Albert Hall; the appearance of the four sets of Dollies
1921	November: Rosie's liaison with Lord Ashley, the 9th Earl of Shaftesbury
1921	November: Jenny's liaison with the prominent American millionaire Alexander Smith Cochrane
1921	21 December–21 January: *Babes in the Wood* at the New Oxford Theatre, London, presented by Charles B. Cochran
1922	Late January: leave for New York; 3 February: arrive on the *Aquitania* from Cherbourg
1922	February: New York $25,000 contract to appear for Keith vaudeville at the Palace, Riverside, Colonial and Alhambra theatres, New York
1922	19 April: arrive in London on the *Aquitania*
1922	May–July: Rosie's liaison with Percy Brooke and trip to Spain and Morocco
1922	Summer: Jenny performs at Elsa Maxwell's Acacias nightclub, Paris, with Clifton Webb
1922	July: booked for Cochran's variety show at the Palace but cancelled
1922	August: *Phi-Phi* at the London Pavilion; the Dolly Sisters arrange the dances with Eddie Dolly
1922	August: Deauville casino and liaison with King Alfonso of Spain
1922	27 September: leave Cherbourg for New York on the *Majestic* for eight-week vaudeville engagement

1922	November: cabaret at Lew Leslie's Monte Carlo restaurant, New York
1922	December–January 1923: vaudeville tour with Harry Richman
1923	January: farewell party for Pearl White at Texas Guinan's Beaux Arts nightclub
1923	30 January: leave for Europe on the *Berengaria*
1923	March: cabaret at the Ambassadeurs, Cannes
1923	March: cabaret at Edouard Baudoin's casino, Juan-les-Pins
1923	May: *Dover Street to Dixie* at the London Pavilion; Jenny arranges dances with Eddie Dolly.
1923	June: *Paris sans voiles*, Ambassadeurs, Paris
1923	June: death of their mother, Margarethe
1923	Summer: Jenny's love affair with Vicomte de La Rochefoucauld
1923	September: Rosie in Biarritz
1923	September: Jenny in Corsica and the Riviera with Vicomte de La Rouchefoucauld
1923	November–spring 1924: *Oh! Les Belles Filles* at the Palace Theatre, Paris
1923	December: Jenny's liaison with Henri Letellier
1924	7 April: wedding of Rubye de Remer to Ben Throop in Paris
1924	May–June: cabaret show at Le Seymour, Paris
1924	June–July: at leisure in Deauville
1924	26 July: return to New York aboard the *Aquitania*
1924	August–September: visit of David, Prince of Wales, to New York
1924	16 September: *Greenwich Village Follies* (sixth edition) at Shubert Theatre, New York
1924	18 September: appearance in cabaret for David, Prince of Wales, at the Lido-Venice Club, New York
1924	October: rumours of Rosie's engagement to Edgar Allan Woolf
1924	Autumn–early 1925: regional American tour of *Sitting Pretty*
1925	9 May: Rosie arrives back in Europe on board the *Olympic*; Jenny follows later
1925	May: Rosie announces engagement to François J. Dupré

1925   June: Jenny meets Jacques Wittouck in Paris

1925   6 July–end August: cabaret show at the Kit Kat Club, London; Jenny meets Gordon Selfridge

1925   September: rehearsals for *La Revue Mistinguett*, Mistinguett's first show at the Moulin Rouge; public disagreement

1925   November: *Paris en fleurs* at the Casino de Paris, Paris

1925   November–December: nocturnal partying with Rudolph Valentino in Paris

1926   Spring: with Gordon Selfridge at Le Touquet

1926   July: *Dolly's Revels* cabaret show at the Kursaal, Ostend

1926   August: at leisure in Deauville and Le Touquet

1926   Late summer: Jenny buys a house at 8 rue Pomereu, Paris

1926   November: *A vol d'oiseau* at the Edouard VII Theatre, Paris

1927   January–February: at leisure, first in Saint-Moritz and then Cannes

1927   31 March: Rosie marries Sir Mortimer Davis Junior in America

1927   April: Jenny in Le Touquet with Gordon Selfridge

1927   22 April: Rosie arrives back from New York on board the *Olympic*

1927   End May: *Paris–New York* opens at the Casino de Paris, Paris

1927   October: rumours that Jenny has married Jacques Wittouck

1927   November: Leon Volterra stages *Le Diable à Paris* at the Theatre Marigny; dances arranged by the Dolly Sisters

1927   December: Rosie in Cannes, Jenny in Paris

1927   December: Rosie seriously ill in Cannes and undergoes several operations; Jenny joins her in Cannes with Jacques Wittouck

1927   December: announce that they intend to retire

1928   Spring: at leisure in Cannes

1928   March: death of Sir Mortimer Davis Senior

1928   Spring: Jenny buys chateau in Fontainebleau

1928   April–May: Jenny with Gordon Selfridge in Deauville and Le Touquet

1928   July: Jenny in London with Gordon Selfridge

1928   August: Jenny with Gordon Selfridge and Rosie with Mortimer Davis in Deauville and Le Touquet

1928   November–December: Rosie with Norma Talmadge on the Riviera; Rosie meets Irving Netcher

1928   December–January 1929: Rosie in Saint-Moritz

1929   January: Jenny seriously ill in Paris

1929   March: Rosie in London

1929   April: Rosie and Jenny in Dinard

1929   May: Jenny with Gordon Selfridge in Biarritz

1929   May: Rosie appears in charity matinée in London with Noel Coward

1929   31 May: Jenny at Gordon Selfridge's election party in London

1929   Summer: Rosie staying at the Cap d'Antibes and Cannes

1929   Summer–autumn: Jenny in Paris planning the opening of her couture establishment and buying trips to Brussels

1929   August: Rosie sued by two Paris jewellers

1929   Autumn–spring 1930: Rosie in Cap d'Antibes

1930   March–June: Rosie in New York

1930   Spring: Jenny in Budapest and adopts Manzi and Klari

1930   May–June: Jenny takes trips to Le Touquet with Gordon Selfridge

1930   August: Rosie in Amsterdam and Paris

1930   September: Rosie in Biarritz

1930   November: Jenny opens lingerie and couture shop on the Champs-Elysées

1930   December: visit to London to see C.B. Cochran's production *Evergreen*

1930   December: Christmas at Fontainebleau with Sophie Tucker

1931   Spring: Rosie and Jenny on the Riviera

1931   June: Jenny in Deauville

1931   Summer: Rosie and Jenny on the Riviera

1931   27 October: Jenny attends Gordon Selfridge's election party

1931   18 November: Rosie wins divorce from Mortimer Davis

1931   December–January 1932: Rosie and Jenny in Saint-Moritz

1931   February: Rosie on the Riviera

1931   Late: Jenny meets Max Constant in Paris

1932   17 March: wedding of Rosie Dolly and Irving Netcher in New York; honeymoon in Palm Beach, then Havana, Cuba

1932   April: Jenny in Nice with Gordon Selfridge

1932   6 May: Rosie and Irving arrive back in Paris; travel to Berlin and spend the summer on the Riviera

1933   January: rumour that Jenny has taken her life in Paris

1933   Spring: Rosie (with Irving) in Hollywood discussing film deal and stage comeback

1933   March: Jenny in car accident near Bordeaux with Max Constant

1933   Late May: Rosie and Irving arrive back in Paris and bring Jenny to Paris from Bordeaux

1933   Summer: Jenny in hospital undergoing surgery; Rosie and Irving on the Riviera

1933   Late: Rosie and Irving visit New York and Hollywood

1933   16 November: Jenny sells her jewellery

1934   9 June: Jenny fined heavily for not paying duty on a diamond ring

1934   Spring: Rosie and Irving in Palm Beach

1934   Summer: Rosie and Irving visit Paris, Havana and Hollywood

1935   March–April: Rosie and Irving visit Europe, collect Jenny and return to USA

1935   29 June: Jenny marries Bernard Vinissky in Chicago

1941   January: Jenny arrives in Hollywood

1941   1 June: Jenny commits suicide in Los Angeles

1945   5 October: *The Dolly Sisters*, musical biopic, released by Twentieth Century Fox; world première in Chicago

1947   March: lawsuit over the film *The Dolly Sisters* by Jean Schwartz

1953   26 June: Irving Netcher dies in Capri, Italy

1956   January: Edward Dolly dies in Los Angeles

1959   July: Harry Fox dies

1962   20 April: Rosie found unconscious after suicide attempt

1970   1 February: Rosie dies in New York

Acknowledgements

My thanks are extended to all those poor souls who have had to endure my obsession over the years, including family, work colleagues and friends.

Particular thanks must go to the following people:

Colin Prince (for doing all things domestic and financial while I slaved at my i-book and for always listening to my daily revelations with nonchalance)

Shirley and Donald Chapman (cleaning fairies and parents extraordinaire)

Christopher Feeney (for his immense enthusiasm, for steering me in the right direction and for attempting to diminish my 'encyclopaedic tendencies')

Hilary Walford (for her diligence in editing the text and for being able to cope with my many moments of incomprehension)

Robert Smith (for taking me on as a client and clearly loving the Dollies as much as I do)

Alex McCormack (for reading the manuscript with her usual attention to detail and insight and giving me incredibly helpful comments on thousands of post-it notes)

Andy Orr (for absolutely everything – advice, contacts, leads and for sharing all his material on the Dolly Sisters)

David Roberts (for reading the manuscript and telling me it was like a fluffy soufflé – which I took as a compliment))

David Smith (for always locating all the British theatre material I needed)

Mike Everson (for unreservedly copying anything in his extensive Parisian Music Hall collection that was of relevance and for offering so many helpful leads and advice)

Randy Bigham (for sharing the content of his unpublished biography on Lucile)

Krystyna Green (for reading the various drafts and always telling me the truth)

Jenny Hammerton (for sharing all her knowledge about the *Eve* Film Review/British Pathé Newsreels from the 1920s and for being so encouraging and helpful in every respect, including reading all drafts and offering so much encouragement)

Denise Strains (who helped me with most of the French translations and made our trip of discovery to the Côte d'Azur and Le Touquet such a pleasure)

Mark Swartz at the Shubert Archive (for his unfailing help, advice and support over the years)

Kristine Krueger at the Margaret Herrick Library, Academy Foundation, Beverly Hills (who has always come up trumps with my requests with unfailing thoroughness)

Raye Virginia Allen (for her inspiration, encouragement and advice)

Ami Kranc (for my dose of fun and frolics, and a bed after too many hours at the Lincoln Centre Theatre Library in New York)

Scott Martin in Chicago (for doing so much local research)

Katherine Arai, whom I 'met' through Ebay (for providing help in obtaining Dolly memorabilia and valuable information about the Dollies from her collection about Ruth St Dennis and Denishawn)

Elsie Gordon in Port Saint Lucie, Florida, whom I 'met' through Ebay (for sending me so many useful clippings and information)

Max T. Pierce (who wrote a wonderful article about the Dollies in *Classic Images*, sold me a wonderful photo album of the Dollies and became a friend)

Café de Fleurs on the Fulham Palace Road (where I spent many lunchtimes writing and having lovely nosh)

Sue Fletcher and Michael Cudlipp at the History of Advertising Trust (Selfridge Collection)

Richard Mangan at the Mander and Mitchinson Collection

Susannah Benedetti at the Wisconsin Center for Film and Theater Research

Christophe Gauthier, Bibliothèque de l'Arsenal, Paris (for his amazing generosity of time and invaluable assistance)

Dace Taube, University of Southern California, Specialized Libraries and Archival Collections

Mireille Cealac (for selling me so many wonderful things on Ebay from Paris)

Ray Perman, Sevenarts Ltd/Grosvenor Gallery (regarding Erté)

Marie-Louise Foucart, Bibliothèque Royal de Belgique (regarding Jacques Wittouck)

Annette Fern, at the Harvard Theater Collection, Houghton Library, Harvard University

Sarah McSkimming, Syndication, Express Newspapers, London
Elaine Hart, formerly at the Illustrated London News Picture Library
Joe Yranski at the Donnell Media Centre, New York
Shelley Thacker at Palm Springs Public Library
Sally McManus at the Palm Springs Historical Society
Eric Concklin, New York (for sharing his incredible collection of Dolly Sisters photos)
Eve Golden (for sharing her collection of papers, for introductions and for her usual wonderful wit and advice).

A huge thank you to Ebay and Abe.com (without which it would have taken an eternity to research this book and collect photographic material)

Finally, enormous appreciation should go to the deceased Basil Woon for writing such wonderful books, which captured the spirit of an era.

I would also like to extend my gratitude to the following archives and libraries:

UK
British Film Institute Library
British Library
British Newspaper Library, Colindale
Getty Images
History of Advertising Trust
Illustrated London News Picture
  Library
Kingston University Library, Knights
  Park
Mander and Mitchenson Theatre
  Collection
Theatre Museum, Covent Garden
Westminster Central Reference
  Library

France
Bibliothèque d'Arsenal
USA
Academy of Motion Picture Arts &
  Sciences
Centre for American History at the
  University of Texas at Austin
Harry Ransom Humanities Library,
  University of Texas at Austin
Harvard Theater Collection
Lincoln Center Performing Arts Library
Shubert Archive
USC Hearst Newspaper Collection
Wisconsin Center for Theater and Film
  Research

Every effort has been made to trace copyright holders. Any omissions should be notified to the publishers for correction in any subsequent edition.

NOTES

Abbreviations and Sources

AMPAS	Academy of Motion Picture Arts & Sciences, Los Angeles,
DSS/NY	Dolly Sisters Scrapbooks, Robinson Locke Collection, NYPL
DSS/P	Dolly Sisters Scrapbook, Bibliothèque de l'Arsenal, Paris
EI	Ellis Island website at www.ellisisland.org
GHS	Gertrude Hoffman Scrapbook, Robinson Locke Collection, NYPL
HFS	Harry Fox Scrapbook, Robinson Locke Collection, NYPL
HUL	Harvard University Library, Cambridge, Mass.
JDC	Jenny Dolly, clippings file, NYPL
M&M	Mander and Mitchenson Theatre Collection, Greenwich, London
NYJAA	New York Journal American Archive, The Collection in the Center for American History, The University of Texas at Austin
NYPL	New York Public Library for the Performing Arts, Lincoln Center Plaza, New York
RDC	Rosie Dolly, clippings file, NYPL
SA	Shubert Archive, New York
SC	Selfridge Collection, History of Advertising Trust, Norwich
USC	University of Southern California, Hearst Newspaper Collection, Los Angeles
WCFTR	Wisconsin Center for Film and Theater Research, Madison

Other newspapers and magazines listed were viewed at the British Library, the British Newspaper Library, the British Film Institute Library or are press clippings in the author's collection.

Clippings from the University of Southern California, Hearst Newspaper Collection, Los Angeles, are frequently stamped *LA Times* and so all clippings have been listed as the *LA Times*, but some might be from another Hearst newspaper such as the *LA Examiner*.

Introduction

1. Michael Mok, *New York Post*, 30 September 1939 (WCFTR).
2. Unidentified clipping dated *c*. 1945 via Eve Golden (NYPL).
3. Richard Lamparski, *Whatever Became of . . .* (New York, 1985).
4. Michael Mok, *New York Post*, 30 September 1939 (WCFTR).
5. Charles B. Cochran, *Showman Looks On* (London, 1945).
6. *New York Review*, 3 September 1916 (SA).
7. Robert Wennersten, 'The Last of the Dollys', *Performing Arts* (May 1972).
8. Meredith Etherington-Smith, *Patou* (London, 1983).

Chapter 1

1. Unidentified, undated clippings (SA).
2. *Ibid.*
3. *Dance Lovers' Magazine* (September 1924).
4. *The World*, 22 March 1914.
5. Unidentified, undated clippings (SA).
6. *Ibid.*; *The World*, 22 March 1914; *Picturegoer* (April 1921).
7. Unidentified, undated clippings (SA).
8. Peter Kurth, *Isadora: A Sensational Life* (Boston, 2001).
9. Unidentified, undated clippings (SA).
10. 'A Wise Little Dolly of Broadway', *Cosmopolitan* (April 1915); *Dance Lovers' Magazine* (September 1924).
11. *Stage Pictorial* (January 1914) (DSS/NY).
12. Unidentified, undated clippings (SA).
13. *The World*, 22 March 1914.
14. Unidentified, undated clippings (SA).
15. His address was given as 73 Lexington Street, which must be Lexington Avenue near Gramercy Park (EI).
16. Unidentified, undated clipping (DSS/NY).
17. EI.
18. *The World*, 22 March 1914.
19. Robert Wennersten, 'The Last of the Dollies', *Performing Arts* (May 1972); unidentified, undated clippings (SA); advert in *New York Dramatic Mirror*, 20 May 1916; Fred Astaire, *Steps in Time* (New York, 1959). Other 'star' pupils at this school included Gertrude Hoffman, Fred and Adele Astaire, Dazie, Harry Pilcer, Nora Bayes, Ethel Levy and Joseph Santley.
20. Unidentified, undated clippings (SA).
21. *Ibid.*
22. *Ibid.*
23. *New York Review*, 30 September 1916; unidentified, undated clipping (DSS/NY).

24. Unidentified, undated clippings (DSS/NY).
25. Unidentified clipping, dated 16 June 1906 (GHS).
26. Unidentified, undated clipping (WCFTR); unidentified, undated clipping (SA); *Theatre Magazine* (November 1913).
27. Unidentified, undated clipping (DSS/NY).
28. Doremy Vernon, *Tiller's Girls* (London, 1988).
29. Gerald Bordman, *American Musical Theatre* (New York, 1978).
30. *Variety*, 20 July 1907.
31. *Ibid.*, 28 March 1908.
32. Unidentified, undated clippings (SA).
33. Unidentified Cleveland newspaper, 9 February 1908 (DSS/NY).
34. *Theatre Magazine* (July 1915); unidentified, undated clippings (SA).
35. Lee Davis, *Scandals and Follies* (New York, 2000).
36. *New York Review*, 30 September 1916.
37. According to later reports, their Broadway debut was at Keith's Union Square Theatre in 1909.
38. *Variety*, 12 June 1909.
39. *Ibid.*, 12 June and 10 July 1909; unidentified, undated clippings (DSS/NY).

Chapter 2

1. Unidentified, undated clippings (SA); *Variety*, 29 May 1909; Gerald Bordman, *American Musical Theatre* (New York, 1978).
2. Unidentified, undated clippings (SA).
3. *Ibid.*
4. Brooks McNamara, *The Shuberts of Broadway* (New York, 1990).
5. Programmes (SA).
6. Unidentified, undated clippings (SA).
7. Henry Tyrrell, 'The Delectable Dollys', *Cosmopolitan* (September 1912).
8. EI.
9. Obituary, *New York Times*, 29 January 1956.
10. *Dance Magazine* (February 1927).
11. *Morning Telegraph*, 14 and 21 May 1911 (DSS/NY).
12. Lee Davis, *Scandals and Follies* (New York, 2000).
13. *London Magazine* (July 1924).
14. Robert Wennersten, 'The Last of the Dollies', *Performing Arts* (May 1972).
15. *Variety*, 1 July 1911.
16. Herbert G. Goldman, *Fanny Brice: The Original Funny Girl* (New York, 1992).
17. The first had been *Over the River*.
18. Tyrrell, 'The Delectable Dollys'.
19. *Variety*, 20 April 1912.
20. Davis, *Scandals and Follies*.

21. Tyrrell, 'The Delectable Dollys'.
22. Unidentified, undated clipping (DSS/NY).
23. 'Rosie Dolly Story of Love, Glamour, Career Read in Trial', unidentified clipping dated 28 March 1947 (AMPAS).
24. An address was given during their transatlantic voyages as 2215 Bay View Park or Place, Brooklyn (EI).
25. Tyrrell, 'The Delectable Dollys'.

Chapter 3

1. *New York Review*, 30 September 1916.
2. *Ibid.*; *Washington Times*, 13 May 1916.
3. See H. Paul Jeffers, *Diamond Jim Brady: The Prince of the Gilded Age* (New York, 2001), and Parker Morell, *Diamond Jim: The Life and Times of James Buchanan Brady* (New York, 1934).
4. Robert Wennersten, 'The Last of the Dollys', *Performing Arts* (May 1972).
5. Morell, *Diamond Jim.*
6. Cleveland Amory, *The Last Resorts* (New York, 1948).
7. Jeffers, *Diamond Jim Brady.*
8. Unidentified clipping dated 1917 (DSS/NY); Anthony Slide, *The Encyclopedia of Vaudeville* (Washington, 1994).
9. Brooks McNamara, *The Shuberts of Broadway* (New York, 1990).

10. Morell, *Diamond Jim.*
11. Jeffers, *Diamond Jim Brady.*
12. *Town Topics*, 23 July 1914 (DSS/NY); Jeffers, *Diamond Jim Brady*; information about racing venues from the Internet.
13. Unidentified clipping dated 29 September 1914 (DSS/NY).
14. Unidentified, undated clipping (DSS/NY).
15. *New York Review*, 30 September 1916.
16. *Variety*, 23 August 1912.
17. *Evening Sun*, 21 August 1912.
18. *Variety*, 23 August 1912.
19. Unidentified, undated clipping (AMPAS).
20. Detail about the trip and performance at Newport from Jose Collins, *The Maid of the Mountains* (London, 1932).
21. Unidentified, undated clipping (DSS/NY).

Chapter 4

1. Unidentified, undated clippings (SA).
2. *Ibid.*
3. *The World*, 22 March 1914.
4. *Variety*, 23 August 1912; Jean Schwartz had written songs for Harry Fox in *The Passing Show* of 1912.
5. *Variety*, 27 July 1913.
6. It was the sixth production at the Winter Garden Theatre since its

opening in March 1911. The first
five shows were *La Belle Paree*
(1911), *The Revue of Revues* (1911),
Vera Violetta (1911), *The Passing
Show* (1912) and *Broadway to Paris*
(1912).

7. Detail about Pilcer and Deslys
from James Gardiner, *Gabys Deslys*
(London 1986).

8. *Variety*, 14 February 1913;
Gardiner, *Gabys Deslys*; Gerald
Bordman, *American Musical Theatre*
(New York, 1978).

9. Gardiner, *Gabys Deslys*.

10. Sophie Tucker, *Some of these Days*
(London, 1948).

11. *Variety*, 14 February and 7 March
1913.

12. *Ibid.*, 28 March 1913.

13. 'Rosie Dolly Story of Love,
Glamour, Career Read in Trial',
unidentified clipping, 28 March
1947 (AMPAS).

14. Unidentified clipping dated 1915
(NYJAA)

15. *Theatre Magazine* (October 1916).

16. *The World*, 10 April 1914.

17. Unidentified clipping dated 1915
(NYJAA)

18. Unidentified, undated clipping
(DSS/NY).

19. *Cosmopolitan* (September 1914).

20. Unidentified, undated clippings
(SA).

21. Unidentified, undated clipping
(DSS/NY).

22. Unidentified clipping dated
10 June 1913 (DSS/NY).

23. *Variety*, 20 June 1913.

24. *Ibid.*, 27 July 1913.

25. Lee Davis, *Scandals and Follies* (New
York, 2000); Richard Ziegfield and
Paulette Ziegfeld, *The Ziegfeld
Touch* (New York, 1993). After
1919 Pennington appeared in five
editions of George White's *Scandals*
and several movies.

26. Gerald Bordman, *American Musical
Theatre* (New York, 1978).

27. Unidentified, undated clipping
(DSS/NY).

28. *Variety*, 20 June 1913.

29. Unidentified, undated clipping
(SA).

30. Unidentified clipping dated
September 1913 (DSS/NY).

31. *Cosmopolitan* (September 1914).

32. *Ibid.*

33. Undated clipping from *Variety*
(DSS/NY).

34. Unidentified, undated clipping
(DSS/NY). Although a press story
states he appeared in *Hello Tango*,
there is no mention of him in any
of the programmes.

35. Bordman, *American Musical
Theatre*; Davis, *Scandals and Follies*.

36. Unidentified, undated clipping
(SA).

37. *Variety*, 16 January 1914.

38. Marian Spitzer, *The Palace* (New
York, 1969).

39. *Variety*, 29 May 1914.
40. Unidentified, undated clipping (DSS/NY).
41. *Ibid.*
42. *Ibid.*
43. *Variety*, 15 May 1914; *Dramatic Mirror*, 3 June 1914.
44. Doremy Vernon, *Tiller's Girls* (London, 1988).
45. *Variety*, 17 April 1914.
46. It was adapted by Mistinguett and Harry Pilcer in *Paris Qui Jazz* (1920) and Jenny Golder and Harry Pilcer in 1927, where it was renamed the 'cob trot' with just one 'filly' and the trainer. Information about the 'cob trot' from Jenny Golder by Alan Black.
47. Unidentified clipping dated 9 May 1914 (HFS).
48. *Variety*, 15 May 1914; Gardiner, *Gabys Deslys.*
49. *Ibid.*
50. Unidentified clipping dated 8 August 1914 (HFS).
51. Unidentified clipping dated 27 August 1914 (DSS/NY).
52. 'Rosie Dolly Story of Love, Glamour, Career Read in Trial'.
53. *New York Review*, 30 September 1916.
54. Unidentified, undated clipping (SA).
55. *Ibid.*
56. *Theatre Magazine* (October 1916).
57. *Variety*, 4 September 1914.
58. *Ibid.*, 11 September 1914.
59. *New York Telegraph*, 20 October 1914.
60. Information derived from *New York Telegraph*, 20 October 1914; unidentified, undated clippings (DSS/NY); *Variety*, 24 October 1914.
61. *Variety*, 31 October 1914.
62. *Variety*, 24 October 1914.
63. Both sisters toured through the autumn, and on 16 November the two vaudeville acts appeared on the same bill at the Colonial Theatre, New York.
64. *Variety*, 1 January 1915.
65. Bordman, *American Musical Theatre.*
66. Unidentified, undated clipping (DSS/NY).
67. Unidentified, undated clipping (WCFTR); unidentified, undated clipping (DSS/NY). Costumes designed by Lamberti of Paris but executed in New York.
68. Davis, *Scandals and Follies.*
69. *Variety*, 27 February 1915.
70. *Ibid.*, 6 March 1915.
71. Unidentified, undated clipping (DSS/NY); *Variety*, 10 January 1913.
72. Unidentified clipping dated 14 May 1915 (DSS/NY).
73. *Variety*, 24 September 1915.
74. *New York Review*, 21 August 1915 (DSS/NY).

75. *Variety*, 23 July 1915.
76. Description from Gloria Swanson, *Swanson on Swanson* (New York, 1980).
77. H. Paul Jeffers, *Diamond Jim Brady: The Prince of the Gilded Age* (New York, 2001).
78. Jim Heimann, *Out with the Stars* (New York, 1985).
79. Charles Chaplin, *My Autobiography* (London, 1966).
80. *New York Telegraph*, 16 July 1915 (DSS/NY).
81. *Moving Picture World*, 31 July 1915.
82. *Variety*, 23 July and 30 July 1915.
83. Kevin Brownlow, *Hollywood: The Pioneers* (London, 1979).
84. Alfred A. Cohn, 'What They Really Get Now', *Photoplay* (March 1916).
85. All information and sources about Ruth St Denis, Denishawn and Rosie Dolly's association with them has been provided by Kit Hoenig, who studied with Ruth St Denis and taught dance for her in the 1960s. Denishawn evolved into both a dance company and a chain of nationwide schools. The artistic partnership of St Denis and Shawn endured until 1968, when St Denis died at the age of 91. Shawn died in 1972.
86. *Dance Lovers' Magazine* (October 1924).
87. Ted Shawn, *One Thousand and One Night Stands* (New York, 1960); Walter Terry, *Ted Shawn: Father of American Dance* (New York, 1976).
88. *Dramatic Mirror*, 11 October 1915 (RDC).
89. Unidentified, undated clipping (DSS/NY).
90. Unidentified, undated clipping (DSS/NY).
91. *Motography*, 25 September 1915 (DSS/NY).
92. *Ibid.*, 11 September 1915 (DSS/NY).
93. Heimann, *Out with the Stars*.
94. Unidentified, undated clipping (DSS/NY).

Chapter 5

1. *New York Clipper*, 18 December 1915 (DSS/NY).
2. It is possible that Lucile was responsible for the screen attire of each Dolly in *The Lily and the Rose* and *Call of the Dance* filmed in 1915.
3. I am very grateful to Randy Bigham for helping me write this brief summary of Lucile. His biography *Lucile: Her Life by Design* is pending publication. Lucile's American branches closed in 1922, the London house in 1924, and the Paris salon in 1932. Lucile's memoir, *Discretions and Indiscretions*, was published the same year. Lucile died of breast cancer at a nursing

home in London on 20 April 1935, at the age of 71.

4. Unidentified, undated clipping (DSS/NY).

5. Richard Ziegfeld and Paulette Ziegfeld, *The Ziegfeld Touch* (New York, 1993).

6. *Variety*, 28 January 1916.

7. *Ibid*.

8. Unidentified, undated clipping (DSS/NY).

9. *Variety*, 28 January 1916.

10. Lewis A. Erenberg, *Steppin' Out: New York Nightlife and the Transformation of American Culture 1890–1930* (Chicago, 1981); unidentified, undated clipping (DS/RLC/NPL).

11. *New York Telegraph*, 14 March 1916 (DSS/NY).

12. *Dramatic Mirror*, 11 March 1916 (DSS/NY).

13. *Variety*, 10 March 1916.

14. *New York Star*, 23 February 1916 (DSS/NY).

15. Unidentified, undated clippings (DSS/NY).

16. *Washington Times*, 13 May 1916 (SA).

17. *Ibid*.

18. *Ibid.*, 11 May 1916 (SA).

19. *New York Review*, 30 September 1916 (SA).

20. *Ibid*.

21. Unidentified, undated clipping (DSS/NY).

22. *Vanity Fair* (December 1916).

23. *Ibid*.

24. Charles Higham, *The Duchess of Windsor: The Secret Life* (New York, 1988), pointed out by Randy Bigham, Lucile's biographer.

25. *Theatre Magazine* (October 1916).

26. *New York Review*, 30 September 1916 (SA).

27. *Ibid*.

28. *Ibid*.

29. *Ibid*.

30. Unidentified, undated clipping (DSS/NY).

31. Interview with Mary Pickford, *Baltimore American*, 9 November 1916 (DSS/NY); repeated in interview with Ashton Stevens, unidentified, undated clipping Chicago newspaper *c*. mid-1918 (HFS).

32. H. Paul Jeffers, *Diamond Jim Brady: The Prince of the Gilded Age* (New York, 2001); Parker Morell, *Diamond Jim: The Life and Times of James Buchanan Brady* (New York, 1934).

33. Robert Wennersten, 'The Last of the Dollies', *Performing Arts* (May 1972).

34. Unidentified clipping dated 1917 (DSS/NY).

35. Unidentified, undated clippings (DSS/NY).

36. *Variety*, 22 June 1917.

37. *San Francisco Sunday Chronicle*, July 1917 (HFS).

38. *Variety*, 15 June 1917.

39. *Ibid.*, 17 August 1917; unidentified, undated clipping (HFS).

40. *Variety*, 20 July 1917.

41. Marian Spitzer, *The Palace* (New York, 1969).

42. *Washington Star*, 11 September 1917 (DSS/NY).

43. *Theatre Magazine* (September 1917).

44. *Journal American*, 1 October 1941 (NYJAA).

45. *Variety*, 10 August 1917.

46. *New York American*, 14 August 1917 (DSS/NY).

47. *Variety*, 31 August 1917.

48. The September 1917 issue of *Vanity Fair* advertised a new production with the Dolly Sisters called *Welcome Stranger* – this could well have been the new Woods show.

49. *Variety*, 31 September 1917.

50. Unidentified clipping dated 16 October 1917 (DSS/NY).

51. *Motion Picture World*, 27 April 1918 (AMPAS).

52. *Variety*, 12 October 1917; unidentified, undated clipping (DSS/NY).

53. *New York American*, 16 November 1917 (DSS/NY).

54. *Ibid.*

55. *Variety*, 28 September 1917.

56. *New York American*, 21 November 1917 (DSS/NY). Lewis A. Erenberg, *Steppin' Out* (Chicago, 1981).

57. *Theatre Magazine* (April 1918).

58. *Ibid.*

59. Stuart B. McIver, *Yesterday's Palm Beach* (Miami, 1976); Theaodore Pratt, *That Was Palm Beach* (St Petersburg, Fla., 1968); Carolyn Hall, *The Twenties in Vogue* (London, 1983).

60. *Photoplay* (November 1918); *Motion Picture World*, 27 April 1918 (AMPAS).

61. *Moving Picture World*, 27 April 1918.

62. Unidentified, undated clipping (WCFTR).

63. *Photoplay* (July 1918).

64. Also cast were Bradley Barker, Huntley Gordon, Paul Doucet and Dolores Cassinelli.

65. *Chicago Herald*, 20 May 1918.

66. Unidentified, undated clippings (DSS/NY).

67. *New York World*, 3 June 1918.

68. *Bioscope*, 27 May 1920.

69. *Variety*, 7 June 1918.

70. Kendall later moved to London and produced cabaret shows including the *Midnight Follies* in 1926.

71. Unidentified, undated clipping (DSS/NY) and programme (NYPL).

72. Unidentified, undated clipping (SA).

73. Strangely the June 1918 issue of *Vogue* stated that Weber and Fields were appearing together in *Back Again with the Dolly Sisters* in their

own inimitable 'Guess Again'
number.

74. *Variety*, 5 July 1918.

75. *Ibid.*, 29 March 1918.

76. *Variety*, 16 August 1918.

77. *Ibid.*

78. Unidentified, undated clipping
    (SA).

79. *Kansas City Times*, 11 November
    1918 (DSS/NY).

80. Interview with Ashton Stevens in
    unidentified clipping dated mid-
    1918 from a Chicago newspaper
    (HFS).

81. *Variety*, 4 July 1919.

82. *Theatre Magazine* (October 1919).

83. *New York Star*, 7 April 1920
    (DSS/NY).

84. 'Rosie Dolly Story of Love,
    Glamour, Career Read in Trial',
    unidentified clipping, 28 March
    1947 (AMPAS).

85. Unidentified clipping dated
    February 1922 (DSS/NY).

86. 'Rosie Dolly Story of Love,
    Glamour, Career Read in Trial'.

87. *Evening World*, 13 February 1922
    (JDC).

Chapter 6

1. One friend would have been Jose
   Collins, with whom they appeared
   on Broadway. She was at the time
   appearing in *The Southern Maid* at
   Daly's Theatre.

2. They thought it was the house of

the Conservative British statesman
Lord Curzon at 1 Carlton Terrace.

3. *The World*, 7 December 1924;
   Titbits, 24 January 1925.

4. *The World*, 30 November 1924;
   Titbits, 24 January 1925.

5. *The Stage*, 24 June 1920.

6. *Eve*, 13 July 1920.

7. Jenny Dolly, 'Secrets of a Star',
   Sunday Dispatch, 19 August 1928
   (M&M); de Courville, *I Tell You*
   (London, 1927).

8. *Eve*, 12 August 1920.

9. *Bystander*, 2 July 1920.

10. Jenny Dolly, 'Secrets of a Star'.

11. *Eve*, 8 July 1920.

12. *Tatler*, 7 July 1920.

13. *Bystander*, 28 July 1920.

14. *The Stage*, 24 June 1920.

15. *Eve*, 15 July 1920.

16. *The Stage*, 24 July 1920.

17. *Eve*, 15 July 1920.

18. *The World*, 7 December 1924;
    Titbits, 24 January 1925.

19. Robert Wennersten, 'The Last of
    the Dollys', *Performing Arts* (May
    1972).

20. Unidentified clipping dated
    13 August 1920 (DSS/NY).

21. *Variety*, 1 October 1920.

22. *The World*, 26 September 1920.

23. Margaret L. Talmadge, *The
    Talmadge Sisters* (London, 1924).

24. All information from the
    invaluable website Taylorology
    (www.angelfire.com/

az/Taylorology) issue 33 (September 1995).

25. Jose Collins, *The Maid of the Mountains* (London 1932).

26. Unidentified clipping dated 20 October 1920 (DSS/NY).

27. *Picturegoer* (April 1921).

Chapter 7

1. James Harding, *Cochran: A Biography* (London, 1988).

2. Charles B. Cochran, *The Secrets of a Showman* (London, 1929); Harding, *Cochran*.

3. Robert Wennersten, 'The Last of the Dollys', *Performing Arts* (May 1972).

4. Charles B. Cochran, *Showman Looks On* (London, 1945).

5. *The Sketch*, 3 June 1925; Cochran, *The Secrets of a Showman*.

6. Ibid.

7. *Bystander*, 2 February 1921.

8. Programme (author's collection).

9. Unidentified, undated clipping (DSS/NY).

10. *Bystander*, 2 February 1921.

11. *The Stage*, 20 January 1921.

12. Ibid.

13. *The Sketch*, 3 June 1925; Cochran, *The Secrets of a Showman*.

14. Charles Graves, *The Cochran Story* (London, 1951).

15. *The Sketch*, 3 June 1925; Cochran, *The Secrets of a Showman*.

16. EI.

17. John Murray Anderson, *Out without My Rubbers* (New York, 1954).

18. Descriptions from Frances Donaldson, *Edward VIII* (London, 1974); Philip Ziegler, *King Edward VIII* (London, 1990); John Parker, *King of Fools* (New York, 1988); Rupert Godfrey, *Letters from a Prince* (London, 1998). The quote from Lord Mountbatten comes from Frances Donaldson; the quote from Lady Loughborough from Rupert Godfrey.

19. *The World*, 30 November 1924; *Titbits*, 24 January 1925; *Evening World*, 2 March 1928. The date of this party has caused some concern. The Dolly Sisters believed that Philip Sassoon's invitation and subsequent party happened shortly after their debut in *Jigsaw* in June 1920. Unfortunately the Prince of Wales was not in the country at the time and returned to London only in early October 1920, after they had withdrawn from the show. That autumn the Dollies were in Paris, and Jenny made a trip to New York. Therefore the logical date for these events is after the launch of *League of Notions. Daily Mail*, 5 March 1921, listed Sir Philip Sassoon entertaining a large number of guests for dinner and a dance on 4 March 1921, and this is most likely this event.

Equally, their meetings with Lord Beaverbrook and Sir Thomas Lipton are more likely to have occurred at this time; indeed, the photograph of Lipton in the feature in *The World* magazine is signed and dated 1921.

20. *The World*, 30 November 1924; *Titbits*, 24 January 1925.
21. A.J.P. Taylor, *Beaverbrook* (London, 1972).
22. *The World*, 7 December 1924.
23. *Ibid.*
24. James Mackay, *The Man who Invented Himself: A Life of Sir Thomas Lipton* (Edinburgh, 1998).
25. *Titbits*, 3 January 1925.
26. *Evening World*, 2 March 1928 (DSS/NY).
27. *Dancing Times* (August 1920).
28. 'Nightlights' feature in *Bystander* (July and August 1921).
29. Taylor, *Beaverbrook*.
30. *Eve*, 20 April 1921.
31. Photograph, dated 4 May 1921 (SC).
32. *Bystander*, 6 July 1921.
33. Jacques Pessis and Jacques Crepineau, *The Moulin Rouge* (London, 1989).
34. Mistinguett, *Mistinguett: Queen of the Paris Night* (London, 1954).
35. Peter Noble, *Ivor Novello* (London, 1951).
36. Charles Castle, *The Folies Bergère* (London, 1982).
37. *League of Notions* ended 26 November 1921.
38. *The World*, 7 December 1924; *Titbits*, 24 January 1925.
39. *Eve*, 16 February 1927.
40. After his divorce from Jenny, Harry Fox married Evelyn Brent in 1931. Following a successful Broadway stage career, Fox switched to the screen and was placed under contract by Cosmopolitan Pictures (perhaps because of his friendship with William Randolph Hearst) and also worked for Warner Brothers and Twentieth Century Fox. In later years he was a photo laboratory technician for Douglas Aircraft until his retirement in 1956. He died in 1959 aged 76 at the Motion Picture Country Home Hospital after a three-year illness. After Jean Schwartz divorced Rosie, he married Sally Long in the early 1930s and died in 1956 in Los Angeles.
41. Smith Cochran gained a divorce from Walska in June 1922 in a Paris court. He died of tuberculosis in 1929. Obituary in *New York Times*, 21 June 1929.
42. *Variety*, 3 February 1922.
43. Unidentified clipping dated 25 November 1921 (DSS/NY).
44. *Buffalo Illustrated Express*, 11 December 1921, and other clippings (HFS).

45. Mini-biography in *Chicago Tribune*, Paris edition, 10 August 1927.
46. Interview with Kit Peters, who was in the chorus of *Humpty Dumpty*, produced by Julian Wylie in Manchester, 1926–7.
47. Eddie choreographed *Mayfair to Montmartre* (1922), *Phi-Phi* (1922), *Dover Street to Dixie* (1923) and *Little Nelly Kelly* (1923) for Cochran. He then became one of London's leading producers of cabaret with his *Dolly's Revels* shows at the Piccadilly Hotel from the spring of 1924, all dressed with impeccable taste and creativity by Dolly Tree. As London took to the idea of cabaret, he launched other shows at the Grafton Galleries, Café de Paris and the Blue Peter Club. Eddie then joined Cochran's rival, Julian Wylie, through his relationship with Dolly Tree, who was Wylie's exclusive dress designer. Gus Scholke had staged most of Julian Wylie's earlier shows, but, with his death in June 1924, Eddie took his place and worked on all Wylie's pantomimes, musicals and revues well into the early 1930s. At the same time Eddie helped choreograph many of his sisters' shows in Paris.
48. *The Stage*, 20 December 1921.
49. *Bystander*, 11 January 1922.
50. *Ibid.*
51. Charles Graves, *The Cochran Story* (London, 1951).

Chapter 8

1. Unidentified, undated clipping (SA).
2. *Variety*, 10 March 1922.
3. *Ibid.*, 24 February 1922.
4. *Ibid.*
5. *Variety*, 3 March 1922.
6. *Ibid.*
7. *Ibid.*, 10 March 1922.
8. *Ibid.*, 17 March 1922.
9. Unidentified clipping dated 11 March 1922 (RDC).
10. Roger Kaln, *A Flame of Pure Fire* (New York, 1999).
11. Unidentified, undated clipping (DSS/NY).
12. Interestingly nothing can be found about this titled gentleman, and even Debrett's could not trace any details. Perhaps Percy Brook was not his real name and Rosie invented him for the press. He could be Lord Ashley, with whom she was romantically linked in November 1921.
13. *The World*, 21 December 1924; *Titbits*, 31 January 1925.
14. Maurice Mouvet was divorced from Florence Walton in 1920 and Walton shortly afterwards married Leon Leitrim, her new dancing partner.

15. Basil Woon, *The Paris that's not in the Guide Books* (New York, 1926).
16. Kaln, *A Flame of Pure Fire*.
17. General information about Paris derived in part from Tony Allan, *The Glamour Years: Paris 1919–1940* (London, 1977); William Wiser, *The Crazy Years: Paris in the Twenties* (London, 1983).
18. Bricktop, *Bricktop* (New York, 1983).
19. Peter Leslie, *A Hard Act to Follow* (London, 1978).
20. Woon, *The Paris that's not in the Guide Books*.
21. Meredith Etherington-Smith, *Patou* (London, 1983).
22. *Ibid.*
23. Woon, *The Paris that's not in the Guide Books*.
24. *Eve*, 21 June 1922.
25. Elsa Maxwell, *RSVP: Elsa Maxwell's own Story* (Boston, 1954).
26. *Tatler*, 7 July 1922.
27. *Eve*, 14 June 1922.
28. *Variety*, 7 July 1922.
29. Information in part from Lew Leslie clippings file (NYPL).
30. Woon, *The Paris that's not in the Guide Books*.
31. Information about Molyneux's dinner party from Cleveland Amory, *Who Killed Society?* (New York, 1960).
32. *Variety*, 16 June 1922.
33. *Eve*, 21 June 1922; *Tatler*, 21 June 1922.

34. *The Stage*, 15 June 1922.
35. *The World*, 21 December 1924; *Titbits*, 31 January 1925.
36. Information about Deauville, the 'season' and Eugene Cornuche from Woon, *The Paris that's not in the Guide Books*; Basil Woon, *From Deauville to Monte Carlo* (New York, 1928).
37. Woon, *From Deauville to Monte Carlo*.
38. *Eve*, 16 August 1922; *The Sketch*, 16 August 1922.
39. Woon, *The Paris that's not in the Guide Books*; Lorimer Hammond, 'Debutante Deauville', *Chicago Tribune*, Paris edition, 3 August 1924.
40. A.J.P. Taylor, *Beaverbrook* (London, 1972).
41. *The World*, 21 December 1924; *Titbits*, 31 January 1925.
42. *The Sketch*, 23 August and 6 September 1922.
43. *Variety*, 29 September 1922; photograph dated 4 October 1922 (USC); EI.
44. Unidentified, undated clippings (SA).
45. Unidentified, undated clippings (SA).
46. Held by the Grosvenor Gallery, who act as Erte's agents.
47. *Variety*, 20 October 1922.
48. *Ibid.*, 25 December 1922.
49. *Theatre Magazine* (March 1923).

50. Harry Richman, *A Hell of a Life* (New York, 1966).
51. Ashton Stevens, in *Chicago Herald American*, 15 October 1948, brought to my attention by Elsie Gordon in Port Saint Lucie, Florida.
52. EI.

Chapter 9

1. Mary Blume, *Côte d'Azur: Inventing the French Riviera* (London, 1992); Jim Ring, *Riviera, the Rise and Rise of the Côte d'Azur* (London, 2004).
2. Stella Margetson, *The Long Party* (Farnborough, 1974).
3. Xan Fielding, *The Money Spinner: Monte Carlo and its Fabled Casino* (Boston, 1977).
4. Basil Woon, *The Paris that's not in the Guide Books* (New York, 1926); Basil Woon, *From Deauville to Monte Carlo* (New York, 1928).
5. Woon, *From Deauville to Monte Carlo*.
6. *The Sketch*, 7 February 1923; *Tatler*, 21 February 1923.
7. *The Sketch*, 21 February 1923.
8. *Ibid.*, 28 February 1923.
9. *Tatler*, 21 March 1923.
10. Woon, *From Deauville to Monte Carlo*.
11. *Ibid.*
12. Dressed by Pascaud and Gaston Zanel after designs by Montedoro, Zinoview, Villepelle and Jean Aumont.
13. It is unclear when they performed this number in New York, but the famous photograph of them gazing at each other through a mirror, which was a feature of this particular tableau, was seen in *His Bridal Night* (1916) and reproduced in *Vanity Fair* (December 1916).
14. Unidentified, undated clippings (DSS/P).
15. *The Stage*, 7 June 1923.
16. *Sunday News*, 15 June 1941 (JDC).
17. Jenny Dolly, 'Secrets of a Star', *Sunday Dispatch*, 19 August 1928 (M&M).
18. *The Stage*, 7 June 1923.
19. EI.
20. *The World*, 28 December 1924.
21. *Ibid.*
22. *Ibid.*
23. *Ibid.*
24. Unidentified, undated clipping (M&M).
25. Robert Robert, *Paris Restaurant* (New York, n.d. (*c.* 1926)).
26. *Bystander*, 12 September 1923.
27. *Chicago Tribune*, Paris edition, 21 September 1923.
28. *Dancing Times* (August 1926).
29. *The World*, 4 January 1925; *Titbits*, 7 February 1925; Marjorie Farnsworth, *Ziegfeld Follies: A History in Text and Pictures* (London and New York, 1956).
30. Woon, *From Deauville to Monte Carlo*.

31. *Chicago Tribune*, Paris edition, 4 October 1923.
32. They married in August, but the marriage did not last the year.
33. *Chicago Tribune*, Paris edition, 2 November 1923.
34. *Picturegoer* (October 1923). No trace of these films can be found in French or British Film Archives.
35. With thirty-three spectacular scenes and costumes by Gaston Zanel from designs by Aumont, Zamora, Dolly Tree, Montedoro and Lafugie and gowns by Patou.
36. *The Stage*, 22 November 1923.
37. *Eve*, 5 December 1923.
38. *Ibid.*
39. *Chicago Tribune*, Paris edition, 8 December 1923.
40. Information about Letellier from Woon, *The Paris that's not in the Guide Books.*
41. Constance Rosenblum, *Gold Digger: The Outrageous Life and Times of Peggy Hopkins Joyce* (New York, 2000).
42. *Chicago Tribune*, Paris edition, 19 January 1924.
43. *Eve*, 26 March 1924.
44. *Ibid.*, 9 April 1924.
45. Woon, *The Paris that's not in the Guide Books.*
46. *The Sketch*, 30 January 1924.
47. *Chicago Tribune*, Paris edition, 5 February 1924.
48. *Ibid.*, 31 May 1924.
49. *Ibid.*, 3 April 1924.
50. *Tatler*, 15 April 1924.
51. *Chicago Tribune*, Paris edition, 28 May 1924; advertising card (DSS/P).

Chapter 10

1. *Chicago Tribune*, Paris edition, 6 July 1924.
2. *Ibid.*, 3 August 1924.
3. *Sunday Express*, 20 July 1924; *The Sketch*, 30 July 1924.
4. Marjorie Farnsworth, *The Ziegfeld Follies: A History in Text and Pictures* (London and New York, 1956).
5. Robert Wennersten, 'The Last of the Dollys', *Performing Arts* (May 1972).
6. Unidentified clipping dated 27 July 1924 (DSS/P).
7. James Gardiner, *Gaby Deslys* (London, 1986).
8. Information on Fruity Metcalfe from Anne de Courcey, *The Viceroy's Daughters* (London, 2000); Frances Donaldson, *Edward VIII* (London, 1974); Philip Ziegler, *King Edward VIII* (London, 1990).
9. *Chicago Tribune*, Paris edition, 7 January 1924; *International Herald Tribune*, 9–13 January 1924.
10. *Chicago Tribune*, Paris edition, 4 April 1924; *International Herald Tribune*, 3 April 1924.
11. *Écoutes*, May 1924 (DSS/P).
12. *International Herald Tribune*, 15–16 April 1924.

13. *Chicago Tribune*, Paris edition, 19 April 1924; *International Herald Tribune*, 21 April 1924.

14. *Chicago Tribune*, Paris edition, 4 July 1924.

15. *International Herald Tribune*, 5 July 1924.

16. *American Vogue*, 15 May 1925.

17. *Écoutes*, 27 July 1924 (DSS/P).

18. *The Sketch*, 5 September 1923; *The Sketch*, 9 January 1924.

19. *Variety*, 8 April 1924.

20. *Tatler*, 25 June 1924; *Variety*, 28 May 1924.

21. *The Sketch*, 30 July 1924.

22. Meredith Etherington-Smith, *Patou* (London, 1983).

23. *Dance Lovers' Magazine* (September 1924).

24. *Variety*, 2 July 1924.

25. *Dance Lovers' Magazine* (October 1924).

26. 'Dolly Sisters Tell about the Prince of Wales', *New York Tribune* (August 1924) (NYJAA).

27. Donaldson, *Edward VIII*.

28. Ziegler, *King Edward VIII*.

29. Cleveland Amory, *Who Killed Society?* (New York, 1960).

30. Information about the movements of the Prince of Wales's social events from *The World* (September–October 1924); Donaldson, *Edward VIII*.

31. Lewis A. Erenberg, *Steppin' Out: New York Nightlife and the Transformation of American Culture 1890–1930* (Chicago, 1981).

32. Louise Berliner, *Texas Guinan: Queen of the Nightclubs* (Austin, Tex.,1993).

33. Ziegler, *King Edward VIII*.

34. Alan Tommy Lascelles to Godfrey Thomas, 5 March 1945, Godfrey Thomas papers, quoted in Ziegler, *King Edward VIII*.

35. Lee Davis, *Scandals and Follies* (New York, 2000).

36. *Variety*, 22 October 1924.

37. *The World*, 17 September 1924.

38. Robert Baral, *Revue* (New York, 1962).

39. Davis, *Scandals and Follies*.

40. *Variety*, 22 October 1924; John Murray Anderson, *Out without My Rubbers* (New York, 1954).

41. At $2,500 a week, a total of $50,000.

42. *Variety*, 22 October 1924.

43. Charles Samuels and Louise Samuels, *Once upon a Stage: The Merry World of Vaudeville* (New York, 1974).

44. According to *The World* he left New York on 31 October 1924 aboard the *Olympia*, arriving Southampton 2 November 1924.

45. *Variety*, 29 October 1924.

46. *The World*, 29 October 1924; *Variety*, 5 November 1924.

47. *Variety*, 14 January 1925.

48. *Ibid.*, 7 January 1925.

Chapter 11

1. *Chicago Tribune*, Paris edition, 20 May 1925.
2. *Ibid.*, 27 May 1925.
3. *Ibid.*, 11 June 1925.
4. See the story on p. 123.
5. *Écoutes*, 8 October 1927 (DSS/P).
6. Jules Dupre Senior was born 1811 and died 1889.
7. Edward Berenson, *The Trail of Madame Caillaux* (Berkeley and Los Angeles, 1992).
8. *Jazz*, 15 June 1927.
9. *Variety*, 2 May 1925.
10. *Tatler*, 8 July 1925.
11. Basil Woon, *The Paris that's not in the Guide Books* (New York, 1926).
12. *Evening World*, 2 March 1928 (SA).
13. Unidentified clippings dated 26 November 1933 and 3 June 1941 (USC).
14. It is not known exactly when Jenny met Wittouck but it is likely she met him during this season.
15. Information by email from Bibliothèque Royale de Belgique.
16. Woon, *The Paris that's not in the Guide Books.*
17. *Vogue* (USA), 15 May 1925; Woon, *The Paris that's not in the Guide Books.*
18. Woon, *The Paris That's Not in the Guide Books.*
19. *Referee*, 5 July 1925.
20. Sophie Tucker, *Some of these Days* (London, 1948).
21. *Tatler*, 29 July 1925.
22. Manuel Weltman and Raymond Lee, *Pearl White: The Peerless Fearless Girl* (New York, 1969)
23. Eve Golden, 'Little White Lies, the Elusive Life of Pearl White', *Classic Images* (July 1997).
24. Information about Gordon Selfridge and his relationship with Jenny Dolly derived from Gordon Honeycombe, *Selfridges* (London, 1984); A.H. Williams, *No Name on the Door* (London, 1956); Reginald Pound, *Selfridge: A Biography* (London, 1960).
25. Gordon Honeycombe in his book *Selfridges* says they met at the Kit Kat Club in 1923, but the Kit Kat opened in 1925 with the Dolly Sisters. The Dolly Sisters also spent 1923 in Paris not London.
26. Janet Aitken Kidd, *The Beaverbrook Girl* (London, 1987).
27. *Jazz*, 15 June 1927.
28. Victor Seroff, *The Real Isadora* (New York, 1971).
29. James Gardiner, *Gaby Deslys* (London, 1986).
30. Williams, *No Name on the Door.*
31. *Ibid.*
32. Pound, *Selfridge.*
33. Williams, *No Name on the Door*; Bill Bryson, *Notes from a Small Island* (London, 1995).
34. J.A. Maxtone Graham, *Eccentric Gamblers* (London, 1975).

35. *Evening World*, 2 March 1928 (SA).
36. Maxtone Graham, *Eccentric Gamblers*.
37. Jenny Dolly, 'Secrets of a Star', *Sunday Dispatch*, 19 August 1928 (M&M).

Chapter 12

1. Charles B. Cochran, *Showman Looks On* (London, 1945).
2. A.H. Williams, *No Name on the Door* (London, 1956).
3. Unidentified clipping, possibly from *Daily Express* (August 1926) (M&M).
4. Some information about this incident from Jacques Pessis and Jacques Crepineau, *The Moulin Rouge* (London, 1989).
5. *Chicago Tribune*, Paris edition, 14 November 1925.
6. *Ibid.*, 8 November 1925.
7. *Ibid.*, 14 November 1925.
8. *Ibid.*
9. *Ibid.*, 8 November 1925.
10. *Ibid.*, 14 November 1925.
11. *Ibid.*, 11 November 1925.
12. Mistinguett, *Mistinguett: Queen of the Paris Night* (London, 1954).
13. *Illustrated Sporting & Dramatic News*, 21 November and 26 December 1925.
14. Bryan Hammond and Patrick O'Connor, *Josephine Baker* (London, 1988); Bricktop, *Bricktop* (New York, 1983).
15. *Illustrated Sporting & Dramatic News*, 28 November 1925.
16. *Chicago Tribune*, Paris edition, 14 November 1925; programme (author's collection).
17. *Dancing Times* (January 1926).
18. *Illustrated Sporting & Dramatic News*, 19 December 1925.
19. *Dancing Times* (January 1926).
20. *Illustrated Sporting & Dramatic News*, 19 December 1925.
21. Sophie Tucker, *Some of these Days* (London, 1948).
22. John Murray Anderson, *Out without My Rubbers* (New York, 1954).
23. Emily W. Leider, *Dark Lover: The Life and Death of Rudolph Valentino* (London, 2003); S. George Ullman, *Valentino as I Knew Him* (New York, 1926).
24. *Tatler*, 13 January 1926.
25. *New York Herald*, 1 January 1926.
26. *Tatler*, 14 April 1926.
27. Photograph dated 14 April 1926 (SC).
28. *Tatler*, 2 June 1926.
29. *Ibid.*, 10 February 1926.
30. *Dancing Times* (July 1926).
31. *Ibid.*
32. *The Stage*, 3 June 1926
33. *Ibid.*
34. *Eve*, 16 June 1926
35. *Era*, 21 July 1926.
36. *The Sketch*, 25 August 1926.
37. *Chicago Tribune*, Paris edition, 15 August 1926.

38. Unidentified, undated clipping (SC).
39. Schedule of the Prince of Wales from the *Times* index.
40. *New York Herald*, Paris edition, 28 October 1926; *Chicago Tribune*, Paris edition, 29 October 1926.
41. Bricktop, *Bricktop*.
42. *Era*, 20 November 1926.
43. *Illustrated Sporting & Dramatic News*, 27 November 1926.
44. Unidentified, undated clipping (M&M).
45. *Dancing Times* (January 1927).
46. *Illustrated Sporting & Dramatic News*, 27 November 1926.
47. *Ibid.*
48. Advert, 16 November 1926 (DSS/P).
49. *Écoutes*, 5 December 1926 (DSS/P).
50. Unidentified clippings dated 6 and 12 December 1926 (DSS/P).
51. *Paris Soir*, 17 December 1926 (DSS/P).
52. *Ibid.*
53. *Chicago Tribune*, Paris edition, daily theatrical listings.
54. *Variety*, 2 June 1931.
55. *Dancing Times* (September 1928).
56. Unidentified clipping dated 16 December 1926 (DSS/P).
57. *Tatler*, 12 January 1927.
58. *Variety*, 2 June 1931; unidentified, undated press clipping (SA); clippings (DSS/P).
59. Copy of certificate (SC).
60. Reginald Pound, *Selfridge: A Biography* (London, 1960).
61. Clippings (DSS/P).
62. Unidentified, undated clipping (M&M).
63. *The Sketch*, 7 September 1927.
64. *Evening World*, 2 March 1928 (SA).
65. The author made a visit in September 2002 and was graciously given a tour by one of the occupants – it is now divided into several apartments. The roof garden was incredible!
66. Williams, *No Name on the Door*; unidentified clipping dated December 1926 (DSS/P).
67. *The Sketch*, 5 January 1927.
68. Carolyn Hall, *The Twenties in Vogue* (London, 1983); *American Vogue*, 1 January 1932.
69. *The Sketch*, 2 March 1927.
70. *The Sketch*, 9 and 23 February 1927; *Tatler*, 19 and 26 January 1927.
71. Letellier and Yola married 8 January 1927 – report in *Chicago Tribune*, Paris edition, 10 January 1927; additional information in Basil Woon, *From Deauville to Monte Carlo* (New York, 1928).
72. Gloria Vanderbilt and Thelma, Lady Furness, *Double Exposure: A Twin Autobiography* (London, 1959).
73. Elsa Maxwell stated that the location was Monte Carlo. But in spring 1927 all the people that Maxwell

described were in Cannes not Monte Carlo, including the Dollies, and they were all gambling at the casino. The account of Thelma, Lady Furness, also supports my sequence of events, since her observations took place in Cannes at this time.

74. *Eve*, 9 March 1927.

75. *Menton and Monte Carlo News*, 12 March 1927.

76. *Chicago Tribune*, Paris edition, 5 March 1927.

77. *The Sketch*, 2 March 1927.

78. The list included the King and Queen of Sweden, the King and Queen of Denmark, the King and Queen of Portugal, Prince and Princess Nicholas of Greece, Prince and Princess Bourbon-Parme, Prince and Princess Paul of Serbia, Grand Duke Michael of Russia, Princesses Elizabeth and Marina of Greece, Prince Louis d'Orléans-Bragance, Princess Josepha de Bourbon-Caserte, Prince and Princess Rénier de Bourbon-Siciles, Prince and Princess Christian of Hesse, Lord Derby, La Marquise du Bourg de Bozas, La Comtesse de la Salle, Lady Orr-Lewis, Lady Wolverton and many others.

79. *Eve*, 23 March 1927; *Tatler*, 23 March 1927.

80. Constance Rosenblum, *Gold Digger: The Outrageous Life of Peggy Hopkins Joyce* (New York, 2000).

81. *Variety*, 23 March 1927.

82. *Eve*, April 1927.

Chapter 13

1. *Variety*, 23 March 1927.

2. *Tatler*, 14 May 1928.

3. *American Weekly* (March 1929).

4. *Ibid.* (March 1929).

5. *New York Journal*, 28 April 1928 (NYJAA).

6. Information about Sir Mortimer Davis Senior and Lady Davis from American Weekly (1928; March 1929) (SA).

7. *American Weekly* (March 1929) (SA).

8. *New York Herald*, 22 April 1927.

9. *Variety*, 10 July 1928; *Chicago Tribune*, Paris edition, 29 January 1929.

10. *Eve*, 27 April 1927; *Eve*, 4 May 1927; *Tatler* 27 April 1927.

11. *Daily Mail*, 14 and 19 April 1927; *New York Herald*, Paris edition, 18 April 1927.

12. *Variety*, 30 March 1927.

13. *Jazz*, 15 June 1927.

14. *The Sketch*, 13 July 1927.

15. *Illustrated Sporting & Dramatic News*, 18 June 1927.

16. *The Stage*, 14 July 1927.

17. *Ibid.*

18. *Dancing Times* (August 1927).

19. *Tatler*, 8 June 1927.

20. Billy Milton, *Milton's Paradise Mislaid* (London, 1976).

21. *Jazz*, 15 June 1927.
22. *Eve*, 29 June 1927.
23. *The Sketch*, 7 September 1927.
24. *Times* index.
25. *Tatler*, 17 August 1927; *Chicago Tribune*, Paris edition, 31 June 1927.
26. J.A. Maxtone Graham, *Eccentric Gamblers* (London, 1975).
27. *Jazz*, 15 June 1927.
28. Unidentified, undated clipping from summer 1927 (NYJAA and Theatre Museum Archive).
29. *Écoutes*, 8 October 1927 (DSS/P).
30. *Tatler*, 17 August 1927.
31. Unidentified clippings dated 27 and 28 December 1927 (DSS/P).
32. Unidentified clipping dated 27 December 1927 (M&M); *Chicago Tribune*, Paris edition, 2 December 1927.
33. Unidentified clipping dated 31 December 1927 (DSS/P).
34. Jenny Dolly, 'Secrets of a Star', *Sunday Dispatch*, 19 August 1928 (M&M); *Evening World*, 2 March 1928.
35. Unidentified clipping dated 28 December 1927 (HTC); *Chicago Tribune*, Paris edition, 24 December 1927.
36. *Dancing Times* (March 1928).
37. *Chicago Tribune*, Paris edition, 23 January 1928.
38. *Ibid.*, 27 January 1928.
39. *Ibid.*, 2 February 1928.
40. *Ibid.*, 11 February 1928.
41. *Ibid.*, 22 February 1928.
42. *Ibid.*, 23 February 1928.
43. Unidentified, undated clipping (RDC).
44. *Los Angeles Times*, 3 March 1928 (USC); *Evening World*, 2 March 1928 (SA).
45. *Chicago Tribune*, Paris edition, 22 March 1928.
46. *Ibid.*, 29 March 1928; unidentified clippings dated 29 March 1928, 1 April 1928 and 11 April 1928 (USC).
47. *New York American*, 2 April 1928 (NYJAA).
48. *American Weekly* (1929) (SA); *Evening Standard*, 2 October 1928; *Los Angeles Times*, 3 October 1928 (USC).
49. Mistinguett, *Mistinguett: Queen of the Paris Night* (London, 1954).
50. *The Sketch*, 4 June 1930.
51. Robert Wennersten, 'The Last of the Dollys', *Performing Arts* (May 1972).
52. Sophie Tucker, *Some of these Days* (London, 1948).
53. Basil Woon, *From Deauville to Monte Carlo* (New York, 1928).
54. *Vogue*, 1 June 1928; *Vogue UK*, 2 May 1928.
55. Unidentified, undated clipping (M&M).
56. *Tatler*, 30 May 1928.
57. *Variety*, 8 July 1928.
58. Jenny Dolly, 'Secrets of a Star'.

59. *Eve*, 8 August 1928.
60. *Chicago Tribune*, Paris edition, 25 August 1928.
61. Unidentified clippings dated 11 September and 18 December 1928 (M&M).
62. *Los Angeles Times*, 7 October 1928 (USC); unidentified clipping dated 18 December 1928 (M&M); *New York American*, 31 October 1928 (NYJAA).
63. *New York World*, 2 December 1928 (NYJAA).

Chapter 14

1. Jeanine Basinger, *Silent Stars* (New York, 1999).
2. Unidentified clipping dated 11 September 1928 (M&M).
3. Detail from Greta de Groat's Norma Talmadge website at http://www.stanford.edu/%7egdegroat/NT/home.htm. Norma eventually divorced Joe Schenck in 1934. The romance with Roland evaporated. Sometime in 1931 Norma was in the audience at the Palace Theatre in New York to see George Jessel and Eddie Cantor. Jessel persuaded her to come on the stage, beginning a love affair and eventual marriage in 1934, although they also divorced in 1939.
4. *Boston Traveller*, 17 March 1932 (HUL).

5. Unidentified press clipping from Chicago dated 27 June 1953.
6. Unidentified, undated clipping (JDC); *Sunday News*, 6 February 1955.
7. *Bystander*, 9 January 1929.
8. *Chicago Tribune*, Paris edition, 2 January 1929.
9. Unidentified clipping dated 5 January 1929 (USC).
10. *Daily News*, 7 March 1929 (M&M).
11. Unidentified clipping dated 7 April 1929 (USC).
12. *Chicago Tribune*, Paris edition, 9 April 1929.
13. *Ibid.*, 15 May 1929.
14. *Ibid.*,, 25 May 1929.
15. *Los Angeles Times*, June 1929 (USC).
16. *American Weekly* (1929) (SA).
17. *Bystander*, 29 May 1929, and unidentified clippings (M&M).
18. *The Sketch*, 29 May and 5 June 1929; *Tatler*, 5 June 1929.
19. Gordon Honeycombe, *Selfridges* (London, 1984); comments extracted from Reginald Pound, *Selfridge: A Biography* (London, 1960), although they are associated with the 1931 party.
20. *Bystander*, 5 June 1929.
21. *Eve*, Paris edition, 7 July 1929 (DSS/P).
22. *Tatler*, 10 July 1929; *Chicago Tribune*, Paris edition, 26 August 1929.

23. *Eve*, Paris edition, 7 July 1929; *Cyrano*, 20 October 1929 (DSS/P).

24. The Sketch, 31 July 1929.

25. *Chicago Tribune*, Paris edition, 10 August 1929.

26. Unidentified clipping dated 7 August 1929 (USC).

27. *Chicago Tribune*, Paris edition, 14 August 1929.

28. *Los Angeles Times*, 14 August 1929 (USC).

29. *Chicago Tribune*, Paris edition, 11 October 1929.

30. *Los Angeles Times*, 19 December 1929 (USC).

31. *Los Angeles Times*, 19 June 1930 (USC); picture caption dated 24 June 1930 (USC).

32. *Sunday News*, 15 June 1941 (JDC); *The Sketch*, 21 May 1930.

33. 'The Strange Telepathy between the Dolly Twins that Stopped a Divorce', interview, *San Francisco Sunday Chronicle* (July 1917) (HFS).

34. Jenny Dolly, 'Secrets of a Star', *Sunday Dispatch*, 19 August 1928 (M&M).

35. *The Sketch*, 21 May 1930.

36. *Chicago Tribune*, Paris edition, 29 February 1932.

37. Unidentified clipping dated 26 November 1933 (USC).

38. Unidentified clipping dated 9 August 1936 (USC).

39. *Chicago Tribune* (Paris edition), 29 February 1932.

40. *New York American*, 4 September 1935 (NYJAA).

41. Unidentified, undated clipping (M&M); *Los Angeles Examiner*, 13 June 1930 (USC); *The Sketch*, 8 June 1930; *Chicago Tribune*, Paris edition, 15 June 1930. David, Prince of Wales, made three more trips to Le Touquet, 1–8 August, 22–3 August and 11–18 September and spent some time in Paris. He may well have socialised with Jenny during these trips.

42. *Los Angeles Examiner*, 16 July 1930 (USC); unidentified, undated clipping (M&M).

43. *Los Angeles Examiner*, 7 August 1930 (USC).

44. *Variety*, 4 February 1970.

45. *Ibid.*, 13 August 1930; *Tatler* 30 July 1930.

46. *Variety*, 20 August 1930; *Chicago Tribune*, Paris edition, 21 August 1930.

47. *Variety*, 21 May 1930.

48. *Ibid.*, 12 November 1930; *Candide*, 6 November 1930 (DSS/P); *Paris Midi*, 1 November 1930 (DSS/P).

49. A.H. Williams, *No Name on the Door* (London, 1956).

50. *Ibid.*

51. *Chicago Tribune*, Paris edition, 26 May 1929.

52. *Variety*, 12 November 1930.

53. *Ibid.*

54. Williams, *No Name on the Door*.

55. *Variety*, 12 November 1930.
56. *Tatler*, 29 July 1931.
57. *Variety*, 12 November 1930.
58. Billy Milton, *Milton's Paradise Mislaid* (London, 1976).
59. Williams, *No Name on the Door*.
60. *Variety*, 12 November 1930.
61. *The Sketch*, 10 December 1930; *Bystander*, 17 December 1930.
62. Sophie Tucker, *Some of these Days* (London, 1948).
63. *Menton and Monte Carlo News*, 11 April 1931.
64. *Variety*, 9 June 1931.
65. *Menton and Monte Carlo News*, 7 March 1931 – staying at the Royalty Hotel.
66. *Variety*, 4 August 1931.
67. *Ibid.*, 9 June 1931.
68. *Tatler*, 2 September 1931.
69. *Ihid*, 19 August 1931.
70. *Chicago Tribune*, Paris edition, 1 and 22 September 1931.
71. *Ibid.*, 13 October 1931.
72. Williams, *No Name on the Door* – alas Williams, in describing the party and Jenny's cape and bracelets, omits to specify the exact date. But since he says it is the early 1930s, one must assume his description fits the 1931 party and not the one in 1929.
73. Reginald Pound, *Selfridge: A Biography* (London, 1960); Gordon Honeycombe, *Selfridges* (London, 1984); *Morning Post*, 28 October 1931.

74. *New York Mirror*, December 1931 (NYJAA).
75. *The Sketch*, 3 February 1932.
76. *Los Angeles Times*, 19 November 1931 (USC); *American Weekly* (1929) (SA); unidentified, undated clipping (M&M).
77. Jim McPherson, 'Movies Strictly from Hungary', *TV6*, 6 May 1990 (AMPAS); Glenn Shirley, *Hello Sucker! The Story of Texas Guinan* (Austin, Tex., 1989);
78. *Daily Express*, 28 February 1932 (M&M).
79. *Ibid.*
80. *Chicago Tribune*, Paris edition, 5 March 1932.
81. *Ibid.*, 9 March 1932.
82. *Paris Midi*, 27 May 1932 (DSS/P).
83. *Los Angeles Times*, 9 March 1932 (USC).
84. *New York Times*, 17 March 1932; *New York American*, 17 March 1932 (NYJAA).
85. *Boston Traveller*, 17 March 1932 (HUL); unidentified, undated clippings (M&M); *Chicago Tribune*, Paris edition, 9 March 1932.
86. *Los Angeles Times*, 20 March 1932 (USC).
87. *New York American*, 17 March 1932 (NYJAA).
88. Unidentified press clipping dated 1932 from Andrew Orr.
89. *Variety*, 14 June 1932.

90. *Tatler*, 16 August 1933.

91. *Los Angeles Times*, 15 August 1932 (USC).

Chapter 15

1. *Écoutes*, 7 January 1933 and other clippings (DSS/P).

2. Unidentified clipping dated 6 January 1933 (DSS/P).

3. *Tatler*, 29 July 1931.

4. Basil Woon, *The Paris that's not in the Guide Books* (New York, 1926).

5. The description of these events comes from 'France's Cruel Ingratitude to the Dolly Sisters', *American Weekly* (1934) (author's collection).

6. *Chicago Tribune*, Paris edition, 1 April 1932.

7. *Los Angeles Times*, 8 April 1932 (USC).

8. Unidentified press clipping dated April 1932 (M&M).

9. Unidentified press clipping dated June 1932 (M&M).

10. *Écoutes*, 4 March 1933 (DSS/BA/PAR); *Los Angeles Times*, 26 November 1933 (USC).

11. *Los Angeles Times*, 17 November 1933 (USC).

12. *Écoutes*, 4 March 1933 (DSS/P).

13. *Ibid.*

14. Unidentified clipping dated 6 June 1933 (M&M); *Paris Midi*, 4 June, 29 July and 30 October 1933 (DSS/P).

15. Internet Movie Database.

16. Repeated in numerous sources, including Marjorie Farnsworth, *The Ziegfeld Follies: A History in Text and Pictures* (London and New York, 1956).

17. Obituary in *Northrop News*, 25 May 1943, provided by Garry Pape, Curator of the Western Museum of Flight, Los Angeles.

18. Internet Movie Database.

19. Unidentified clipping dated 1945 (supplied by Eve Golden from NYPL).

20. Unidentified clipping dated 5 May 1934 (DSS/P).

21. *Variety*, 3 November 1931.

22. *Chicago Tribune*, Paris edition, 18 February 1932.

23. Information about the crash from *Chicago Tribune*, Paris edition, 12 March 1933; unidentified clipping dated June 1933 (M&M); *Los Angeles Times*, June 1933 (USC); *Écoutes*, 4 March 1933 (DSS/P).

24. *Écoutes*, 4 March 1933 (DSS/P).

25. *Paris Midi*, 14 March 1933 (DSS/P).

26. *Chicago Tribune*, Paris edition, 12 March 1933.

27. *Ibid.*, 13 March 1933.

28. *Variety*, 28 March 1933.

29. *Paris Midi*, 4 June 1933 (DSS/P); *New York Evening Journal*, 23 December 1933 (NYJAA).

30. *New York Evening Journal*, 23 December 1933 (NYJAA).

31. Unidentified clipping dated 1945; 'Now What Will Happen to Rosie Dolly', *American Weekly* (1941) (supplied by Eve Golden from NYPL).

32. *Écoutes*, 4 March 1933 (DSS/P).

33. After the accident Max Constant returned to America and continued his career as a pilot, taking part in numerous Bendix Trophy flight races in the late 1930s. He was also friendly with the MGM star Robert Taylor (1911–69), who was passionate about flying, and he became his flying instructor. With the outbreak of war he became a test pilot in Southern California and while working for the Northrop Aircraft Corporation and the US Army Corps flying the first N-9M he crashed and died on 19 May 1943 in the Mojave Desert near Muroc, California. (Information from an internet site featuring an auction of material from the collection of the actress Constance Moore, including photographs and papers belonging to Taylor; also from an obituary in *Northrop News*, 25 May 1943, provided by Garry Pape, Curator of the Western Museum of Flight, Los Angeles.)

34. *Los Angeles Times*, 6 June 1933 (USC).

35. Unidentified clipping dated June 1933 (M&M).

36. *Los Angeles Times*, 6 January 1941(USC).

37. *American Weekly* (1934); *New York American*, 18 June 1933 (NYJAA).

38. *New York Evening Journal*, 23 December 1933 (NYJAA).

39. *New York American*, 11 November 1933 (NYJAA).

40. *Los Angeles Times*, 2 June 1941 (USC); *New York Herald Tribune*, 17 June 1933 (JDC).

41. *Variety*, 20 November 1929.

42. *Tatler*, 16 August 1933.

43. *Los Angeles Times*, 1 August 1933 (USC).

44. *New York American*, 26 November 1933 (NYJAA).

45. *New York Evening Journal*, 16 November 1933 (NYJAA).

46. *The Sketch*, 15 November 1933.

47. Unidentified, undated clipping (SC).

48. Unidentified clipping dated November 1933 (M&M).

49. *Los Angeles Times*, 6 January 1941 (USC).

50. *Ibid.*, 26 November 1933 (USC).

51. Unidentified clipping dated December 1933 (SC).

52. Unidentified clipping dated November 1933 (M&M).

53. M. Esser, 'Les Cygnes', La Villa Des Dolly Sisters, Bibliothèque

Municiple Fontainebleau, quoting
Robert Soupault, *Pleins pouvoirs sur
la vie* (1969).

54. A.H Williams, *No Name on the Door*
(London, 1956).

55. The description of these events
comes from 'France's Cruel
Ingratitude to the Dolly Sisters',
American Weekly (1934) (author's
collection).

56. General clippings, the Dolly
Sisters (NYPL).

57. 'Jenny Dollys £32,000 gem',
unidentified, undated clipping
(M&M); unidentified clipping
dated 27 March 1931
(USC).

58. Unidentified clipping dated
27 April 1934 (USC); unidentified
clipping dated 1941 (WCFTR).

59. Unidentified clipping dated June
1934 (M&M).

60. *Los Angeles Times*, 5 August 1934
(USC).

61. 'France's Cruel Ingratitude to the
Dolly Sisters'.

62. *New York American*, 23 January
1934 (NYJAA).

63. *Los Angeles Times*, 16 May 1934
(USC).

64. Jim Heimann, *Out with the Stars*
(New York, 1985).

65. Unidentified clipping dated
16 May 1934 (USC).

66. *Los Angeles Times*, 1 March 1938
(USC); Bob Thomas, *Clown Prince

of Hollywood: The Antic Life and
Times of Jack L. Warner* (New York,
1990).

67. *New York American*, 3 March 1935
(NYJAA).

68. *Ibid.*, 10 April 1935 (NYJAA).

69. Gordon Selfridge eventually
lost control of Selfridges and
ended up living alone in a small
flat in Putney. He died in May
1947.

70. Unidentified, undated clipping
(JDC); *New York American*,
10 April 1935 (NYJAA).

71. Unidentified clipping dated
29 June 1935 from Scott Martin
in Chicago.

72. Unidentified clipping dated June
1935 (USC).

73. *Los Angeles Times*, 30 June 1935
(USC).

74. *New York American*, 4 September
1935 (NYJAA).

75. *Los Angeles Times*, 16 January 1936
(USC).

76. *Philadelphia Record*, 12 February
1936 (JDC).

77. Charles B. Cochran, *Cock-a-Doodle-
Do* (London, 1941).

78. Unidentified clipping dated
9 August 1936 (USC).

79. Robert Wennersten, 'The Last of
the Dollys', *Performing Arts* (May
1972).

80. Sophie Tucker, *Some of these Days*
(London, 1948).

Chapter 16

1. *Los Angeles Times*, 6 January and 3 June 1941 (USC).
2. *Ibid.*, 6 January 1941 (USC).
3. *Sunday News*, 15 June 1941 (JDC).
4. Jim Heimann, *Out with the Stars* (New York, 1985).
5. *Los Angeles Times*, 2 June 1941 (USC).
6. Obituary, *Daily Telegraph*, 1 June 1941.
7. Bernard Vinissky died in February 1968 (US Social Security Death Index on the Internet).
8. Information about Jenny's death and the theories of her motives from *Sunday News*, 15 June 1941 (JDC); *New York Times*, 2 June 1941; unidentified clippings (WCFTR); Sophie Tucker, *Some of these Days* (London, 1948); *Los Angeles Times*, 2 and 3 June 1941 (USC).
9. Unidentified clipping dated 3 July 1941 (JDC).

Chapter 17

1. Richard Lamparski, *Whatever Became of . . .* (New York, 1985); Robert Wennersten, 'The Last of the Dollys', *Performing Arts* (May 1972); Palm Springs Historical Society.
2. Cleveland Amory, *The Last Resorts* (New York, 1948).
3. Spitzer would have known the Dollies from their stage appearances in New York and later wrote one of the definitive books about the Palace Theatre, New York.
4. American Film Institute Catalogue/information in the Twentieth Century Fox Records of the legal department and Scripts Collection at UCLA Special Collections Library.
5. *Variety*, 26 September 1945.
6. Wennersten, 'The Last of the Dollys'.
7. *Variety*, 26 September 1945.
8. Jim McPherson, 'Movies Strictly from Hungary', *TV6*, 6 May 1990 (AMPAS).
9. American Film Institute Catalogue.
10. *Ibid.*; *Los Angeles Times*, 7 March 1947 (USC).
11. *Los Angeles Times*, 20 March 1947 (USC).
12. Unidentified clippings dated 20 and 21 March 1947 (AMPAS).
13. *Los Angeles Times*, 14 March 1947 (USC).
14. *Ibid.*, 20 March 1947 (USC).
15. *Los Angeles Examiner*, 29 March 1947 (AMPAS).
16. Unidentified clipping dated 2 April 1947 (AMPAS).
17. *Los Angeles Times*, 12 April 1947 (USC); *Le Matin*, 23 July 1947 (DSS/P).
18. Unidentified clipping dated 27 June 1953 (AMPAS); press

clipping from Chicago dated 27 June 1953 from Scott Martin.

19. *Variety*, 4 February 1970.

20. *Chicago Tribune*, 28 June 1953.

21. Unidentified clipping dated 17 March 1954 (RDC).

22. Wennersten, 'The Last of the Dollys'.

23. Information from George Allardice, clippings file at Palm Springs Library: Bruce Fessier, *PS Notebook*, 13 December 1986; Bruce Fessier, remembrance piece, *Desert Sun*, 30 September 2001; and obituary, *Desert Sun*, 24 August 2001. Allardice was born 20 March 1929 and died 17 August 2001 aged 72.

24. Unidentified clipping from Chicago headed 'The Netcher Story' from Scott Martin.

25. *Los Angeles Times*, 31 January 1956 (USC); *New York Times*, 29 January 1956.

26. Unidentified clipping dated 21 July 1959 (AMPAS). After a successful Broadway stage career, Fox had switched to the screen and had been under contract by Cosmopolitan Pictures, Warner Brothers and Twentieth Century Fox. He had latterly worked as a photo laboratory technician for Douglas Aircraft until his retirement due to illness in 1956.

27. *Variety*, 4 February 1970.

28. *Ibid.*

29. Manzi died in Los Angeles, September 1985 (US Social Security Death Index on the Internet). Klari became Mrs Mirabile and lived in New Jersey, but it has not been possible to trace further information. When Rosie died, she made various bequests to friends and to Manzi and her children in her will. The residue of her estate was left to Manzi. Klari was not mentioned. Clearly there had been some discord between Klari and Rosie.

30. Unidentified clipping dated 21 April 1962 (AMPAS); unidentified, undated clipping (RDC).

31. Wennersten, 'The Last of the Dollys'.

32. *The Times*, 3 February 1970; *Daily Telegraph*, 1 February 1970; unidentified clipping dated 2 February 1970 (HUL). When Rosie's will was read a year later, it was revealed that her assets had been greatly reduced because of her high living expenses, which included her home in Palm Springs and trips to Las Vegas. Most of her valuable jewellery collection was sold at prices below cost and established value. Her solicitor wrote that she was 'a strong willed

person, very well knowing her own mind' and in one clause Rosie stipulated 'there may be relatives, other than those specified in the will, with whom I have had no contact and feel no obligation to them'. Rosie left several substantial bequests to various people, but the balance of her estate, estimated to be worth in excess of $400,000, was given to Jenny's adopted daughter Manzi. Rosie did not leave anything to Klari.

Chapter 18

1. Andrea Stuart, *Showgirls* (London, 1996).

2. James Gardiner, *Who's a Pretty Boy Then?* (London, 1997).

3. *Los Angeles Times*, 1 January 1973 (AMPAS).

4. Press release from Lincoln Center Theatre Collection, New York. Written by Mady Christians with music by Bill Roscoe – pseudonyms for the playwright and composer, who wanted to remain anonymous.

BIBLIOGRAPHY

Books and Articles

Affron, Charles, *Lillian Gish: Her Legend, Her Life* (New York, 2001)

Allan, Tony, *The Glamour Years: Paris 1919–1920* (London, 1977)

Amory, Cleveland, *The Last Resorts* (New York, 1948)

—— *Who Killed Society?* (New York, 1960)

Anderson, John Murray, *Out without my Rubbers* (New York, 1954)

Astaire, Fred, *Steps in Time* (New York, 1959)

Bakish, David, *Jimmy Durante: His Showbusiness Career* (Jefferson, NC, 1995)

Baral, Robert, *Revue* (New York, 1962)

Basinger, Jeanine, *Silent Stars* (New York, 1999)

Berenson, Edward, *The Trail of Madame* Caillaux (Berkeley and Los Angeles, 1992)

Berliner, Louise, *Texas Guinan: Queen of the Nightclubs* (Austin, Tex., 1993)

Black, Alan, *Jenny Golder* (private printing, 2000)

Blume, Mary, *Côte d'Azur: Inventing the French Riviera* (London, 1992)

Bordman, Gerald, *The American Musical Theatre* (New York, 1978)

Brett, David, *The Mistinguett Legend* (London, 1990)

Bricktop, *Bricktop* (New York, 1983)

Brownlow, Kevin, *Hollywood: The Pioneers* (London, 1979)

Bryson, Bill, *Notes from a Small Island* (London, 1995)

Carter, Angela, *Wise Children* (London, 1992)

Carter, Randolph, *The World of Flo Ziegfeld* (New York, 1974)

Castle, Charles, *The Folies Bergère* (London, 1982)

Castle, Irene, *Castles in the Air* (New York, 1958)

Chaplin, Charles, *My Autobigraphy* (London, 1966)

Chisolm, Anne, and Davie, Michael, *Lord Beaverbrook: A Life* (London, 1993)

Cochran, Charles B., *The Secrets of a Showman* (London, 1929)

—— *Showman Looks On* (London, 1945)

—— *Cock-a-Doodle-Do* (London, 1941)

Collins, Jose, *The Maid of the Mountains* (London, 1932)

Cornyn, Stan, *A Selective Index to Theatre Magazine* (New York and London, 1964)

Courville, Albert de, *I Tell You* (London, 1927)

Damase, Jacques, *Les Folies du Music Hall* (Paris, 1960; London 1962, 1970)

Davis, Lee, *Scandals and Follies* (New York, 2000)

De Courcy, Anne, *The Viceroy's Daughters* (London, 2000)

Donaldson, Frances, *Edward VIII* (1974)

Driberg, Tom, *Beaverbrook* (London, 1956)

Durante, Jimmy, *Nightclubs* (New York, 1930)

Erenberg, Lewis A., *Steppin' Out: New York Nightlife and the Transformation of American Culture 1890–1930* (Chicago, 1981)

Etherington-Smith, Meredith, *Patou* (London, 1983)

Farnsworth, Marjorie, *The Ziegfeld Follies: A History in Text and Pictures* (London and New York, 1956)

Fielding, Xan, *The Money Spinner: Monte Carlo and its Fabled Casino* (Boston, 1977)

Fowler, Gene, *Schnozzola: The Story of Jimmy Durante Hammond* (New York, 1951)

Gardiner, James, *Gaby Deslys* (London, 1986)

—— *Who's a Pretty Boy Then?* (London, 1997)

Godfrey, Rupert, *Letters from a Prince* (London, 1998)

Golden, Eve, 'Little White Lies: The Elusive Life of Pearl White', *Classic Images* (July 1997)

Goldman, Herbert G., *Fanny Brice: The Original Funny Girl* (New York, 1992)

Graves, Charles, *The Cochran Story* (London, 1951)

Green, Stanley, *The Great Clowns of Broadway* (New York, 1984)

Hall, Carolyn, *The Twenties in Vogue* (London, 1983)

Hammond, Bryan, and O'Connor, Patrick, *Josephine Baker* (London, 1988)

Harding, James, *Cochran: A Biography* (London, 1988)

Heimann, Jim, *Out with the Stars* (New York, 1985)

Henderson, Mary C., *Theatre in America* (New York, 1986)

Higham, Charles, *Duchess of Windsor: The Secret Life* (New York, 1988)

Honeycombe, Gordon, *Selfridges* (London, 1984)

Hough, Richard, *Born Royal: The Lives and Loves of the Young Windsors* (London, 1988)

Howarth, Patrick, *When the Riviera Was Ours* (London, 1977)

Howell, Georgina, *In Vogue* (London, 1975)

Jeffers, H. Paul, *Diamond Jim Brady: The Prince of the Gilded Age* (New York, 2001)

Jenkins, Alan, *The Twenties* (London, 1974)

Kaln, Roger, *A Flame of Pure Fire* (New York, 1999)

Khan, Aga, *The Memoirs of Aga Khan* (London, 1954)

Kidd, Janet Aitken, *The Beaverbrook Girl* (London, 1987)

Kurth, Peter, *Isadora: A Sensational Life* (Boston, 2001)

Lamparski, Richard, *Whatever Became of . . .* (New York, 1985)

Leider, Emily W., *Dark Lover: The Life and Death of Rudolph Valentino* (London, 2003)

Leslie, Peter, *A Hard Act to Follow* (London, 1978)

McIver, Stuart B., *Yesterday's Palm Beach* (Miami, 1976)

Mackay, James, *The Man who Invented Himself: A Life of Sir Thomas Lipton* (Edinburgh, 1998)

McNamara, Brooks, *The Shuberts of Broadway* (New York, 1990)

Mander, Raymond, and Mitchenson, Joe, *Revue: A Story in Pictures* (London, 1971)

Margetson, Stella, *The Long Party* (Farnborough, 1974)

Maxtone Graham, J.A., *Eccentric Gamblers* (London, 1975)

Maxwell, Elsa, *RSVP: Elsa Maxwell's own Story* (Boston, 1954)

Milton, Billy, *Milton's Paradise Mislaid* (London, 1976)

Mistinguett, *Mistinguett: Queen of the Paris Night* (London, 1954)

Morell, Parker, *Diamond Jim: The Life and Times of James Buchanan Brady* (New York, 1934)

Morris, Michael, *Madame Valentino* (New York, 1991)

Noble, Peter, *Ivor Novello* (London, 1951)

Parker, John, *King of Fools* (New York, 1988)

Pessis, Jacques, and Crepineau, Jacques, *The Moulin Rouge* (London, 1989)

Pound, Reginald, *Selfridge: A Biography* (London, 1960)

Prasteau, Jean, *La Merveilleuse Adventure du Casino de Paris* (Paris, 1975)

Pratt, Theodore, *That Was Palm Beach* (St Petersburg, Fla., 1968)

Richman, Harry, *A Hell of a Life* (New York, 1966)

Ring, Jim, *Riviera, the Rise and Rise of the Côte d'Azur* (London, 2004)

Robert, Robert, *Paris Restaurant* (New York, n.d. (*c.* 1926))

Rosenblum, Constance, *Gold Digger: The Outrageous Life of Peggy Hopkins Joyce* (New York, 2000)

Samuels, Charles, and Samuels, Louise, *Once upon a Stage: The Merry World of Vaudeville* (New York, 1974)

Seroff, Victor, *The Real Isadora* (New York, 1971)

Shawn, Ted, *One Thousand and One Night Stands* (New York, 1960)

Shirley, Glenn, *Hello Sucker! The Story of Texas Guinan* (Austin, Tex., 1989)

Slide, Anthony, *The Encyclopedia of Vaudeville* (Washington, 1994)

Snyder, Robert W., *The Voice of the City: Vaudeville and Popular Culture in New York* (New York, 1989)

Spitzer, Marian, *The Palace* (New York, 1969)

Stuart, Andrea, *Showgirls* (London, 1996)

Swanson, Gloria, *Swanson on Swanson* (New York, 1980)

Talmadge, Margaret L., *The Talmadge Sisters* (London, 1924)

Taylor, A.J.P., *Beaverbrook* (London, 1972)

Terry, Walter, *Ted Shawn: Father of American Dance* (New York, 1976)

Thomas, Bob, *Clown Prince of Hollywood: The Antic Life and Times of Jack L. Warner* (New York, 1990)

Toll, Robert C., *On with the Show: The First Century of Show Business in America* (New York, 1976)

Tucker, Sophie, *Some of these Days* (London, 1948)

Tyrrell, Henry, 'The Delectable Dollys', *Cosmopolitan* (September 1912)

Ullman, S. George, *Valentino as I Knew Him* (New York, 1926)

Vanderbilt, Gloria, and Furness, Lady Thelma, *Double Exposure: A Twin Autobiography* (London, 1959)

Vernon, Doremy, *Tiller's Girls* (London, 1988)

Weltman, Manuel, and Lee, Raymond, *Pearl White: The Peerless Fearless Girl* (New York, 1969)

Wennersten, Robert, 'The Last of the Dollys', *Performing Arts* (May 1972)

Williams, A.H., *No Name on the Door* (London, 1956)

Wiser, William, *The Crazy Years: Paris in the Twenties* (London, 1983)

Woon, Basil, *The Paris that's not in the Guide Books* (New York, 1926)

—— *From Deauville to Monte Carlo* (New York, 1928)

Ziegfeld, Richard, and Ziegfeld, Paulette, *The Ziegfeld Touch* (New York, 1993)

Ziegler, Philip, *King Edward VIII* (London, 1990)

Zierold, Norman, *Sex Goddesses of the Silent Screen* (Chicago, 1973)

Magazines, Newspapers and Periodicals

The Bystander

Chicago Tribune (Paris Edition)

Daily Sketch

The Encore

The Era

Eve

Illustrated Sporting and Dramatic News

Menton and Monte Carlo News

Pictures and Picturegoer

The Sketch

The Sphere

The Stage

Tatler

Titbits

Variety

Vogue

The World

INDEX

Notes

1. Sub-entries are arranged in *chronological* order, where significant.
2. The following abbreviations are used: DS – Dolly Sisters; NY – New York.
3. Page numbers for chapters are **emboldened**.